Seven Days of Nectar

ANCIENT INDIAN TRADITION AND MYTHOLOGY

Mahāpurāṇas *Translated into English*
Gen. Ed. Dr. G.C. Tripathi
Founder Eds. Late J.L. Shastri and Late G.P. Bhatt

PUBLISHED VOLUMES

Vols. 1-4	ŚIVA PURĀṆA *Tr.* J.L. Shastri
Vols. 5-6	LIṄGA PURĀṆA *Tr.* J.L. Shastri
Vols. 7-11	BHĀGAVATA PURĀṆA *Tr.* G.V. Tagare
Vols. 12-14	GARUḌA PURĀṆA *Tr.* J.L. Shastri
Vols. 15-19	NĀRADA PURĀṆA *Tr.* G.V. Tagare
Vols. 20-21	KŪRMA PURĀṆA *Tr.* G.V. Tagare
Vols. 22-26	BRAHMĀṆḌA PURĀṆA *Tr.* G.V. Tagare
Vols. 27-30	AGNI PURĀṆA *Tr.* N. Gangadharan
Vols. 31-32	VARĀHA PURĀṆA *Tr.* S. Venkitasubramonia Iyer
Vols. 33-36	BRAHMA PURĀṆA *Tr.* J.L. Shastri
Vols. 37-38	VĀYU PURĀṆA *Tr.* G.V. Tagare
Vols. 39-48	PADMA PURĀṆA *Tr.* N.A. Deshpande
Vols. 49-71	SKANDA PURĀṆA *Ed.* G.P. Bhatt, *Tr. & Annot.* Shridhar Balooni & Pratosh Panda
Vols. 72-73	VĀMANA PURĀṆA *Tr. & Annot.* R.S. Shiva Ganesha Murthy
Vols. 74-76	GAṆEŚA PURĀṆA *Tr. & Annot.* Greg Bailey
Vols. 77-82	BRAHMAVAIVARTA PURĀṆA *Tr. & Annot.* G.P. Bhatt

Seven Days of Nectar

Contemporary Oral Performance of the Bhāgavatapurāṇa

McCOMAS TAYLOR

MOTILAL BANARSIDASS
PUBLISHERS PRIVATE LIMITED

OXFORD
UNIVERSITY PRESS

OXFORD
UNIVERSITY PRESS

Oxford University Press is a department of the University of Oxford. It furthers the University's objective of excellence in research, scholarship, and education by publishing worldwide. Oxford is a registered trademark of Oxford University Press in the UK and in certain other countries

Published in India by
Oxford University Press
YMCA Library Building, 1 Jai Singh Road, New Delhi 110001, India

ISBN : 978-81-208-4009-6

Reprinted 2017
Printed in India by Replika Press Pvt. Ltd.

For JMcDT

Pibata bhāgavataṁ rasam ālayaṁ
muhur aho rasikā bhuvi bhāvukāḥ

O discerning connoisseurs of the world,
every moment until your demise,
imbibe the nectar of the Bhāgavatapurāṇa.

BHĀGAVATAPURĀṆA 1.1.3

Contents

Preface

THIS BOOK LIES at the heart of three research areas nested one within another like the concentric rings of a mandala. At the outer ring is a broad question of power and knowledge: What makes texts powerful? How do written documents acquire the capacity to shape societies? What enables them to function as "true" for the particular community in which they circulate? How does power create knowledge, and how does knowledge then feed back into power? In the second ring of the mandala is a more specific focus on power and knowledge as they manifest in Sanskrit texts of Hindu traditions. This involves the search for the sources of authority in the texts themselves, especially the genre known as *purāṇas,* which contain the foundational mythology of most contemporary Hindu traditions. But texts consist of inert ciphers on a page or, in the case of premodern India, on palm leaves. They lie dormant until activated by a reader or a speaker. In a preliterate society, most people experience texts orally; they hear them spoken or sung in performance. This leads to the inner ring of the mandala. How are these texts used in oral performance? What makes these performances authentic and transformative?

One Sanskrit work in particular, the *Bhāgavatapurāṇa,* has a strong living tradition. This text of fourteen thousand verses dates from at least the tenth century of the current era and contains the most authoritative narratives concerning the deity Kṛṣṇa. Expert storytellers in northern India sing Sanskrit verses of the Bhāgavatapurāṇa and expound on them to audiences in Hindi. These seven-day events, known as *Bhāgavata-saptāha,* are well known to most Indians but are largely unknown to Western scholarship.

Not only is this tradition alive and well, but to all accounts, it is expanding rapidly. Every year, Bhāgavata-saptāhas are bigger, louder, and more extravagant than ever. This gives rise to the central questions of this book: What does this form of religious expression entail? And what factors are behind its growth and development? My basic contention is that

Bhāgavata-saptāhas are providing measurable social or existential benefits to participants. This books sets out to explore these oral performances and their outcomes from the point of view of each of the main groups of participants: the sponsors, the exponents, and the audiences.

I would like to pretend that this book is the outcome of a carefully planned linear process, but research is serendipitous, and I followed leads whenever and wherever they arose. The various elements came together as the result of good fortune more than good management. Accordingly, a grant offered by the POSCO TJ Park Foundation to investigate the impact of globalization and modernization on contemporary religious practice enabled me to undertake my first period of fieldwork as a participant-observer in India in October–November 2009. As a Sanskritist and a student of texts, I learned my ethnographic skills on the job at the four saptāhas I attended in full or in part during this visit. For the purposes of that project, I selected two contrasting events, one in the important pilgrimage town of Vrindavan, 150 kilometers south of Delhi, which I assumed would be more "globalized." The other, a "traditional" performance, was organized by my friend and colleague Yogendra Yadav in the small community of Naluna in the foothills of the Garhwali Himalayas, 200 kilometers northeast of the capital. Of course, things turned out to be more complicated, unpredictable, and interesting than I had anticipated. Much of the material in chapter 2 is drawn from data collected during this field trip.

My next stroke of luck came in April 2013, when I learned that a saptāha was to be held in my hometown of Canberra, Australia. This event was conducted in English by a highly accomplished exponent, Acharya Sri Satchitananda Sai, and an audio recording was made available. I was able to use my notes as a participant-observer and the recording to analyze two facets of performance in detail: first, the use of narratives of the Bhāgavatapurāṇa over the course of the seven days and, second, the way in which the exponent integrated the Sanskrit verses of the original text into his spoken discourse (chapters 5 and 6).

I had made some preliminary attempts to interview the exponents on the sidelines of the events I had attended, but I realized that this aspect of the research required a more focused effort. I returned to India in November 2013, when, thanks especially to Ilona Wilczewska Avadhuta, I was able to interview a number of exponents from a variety of backgrounds, including members of the hereditary priesthood and graduates from traditional schools known as *guru-kulas*. These semistructured interviews with exponents, conducted in a mixture of English, Hindi, and

Sanskrit, provided the background material for chapter 4. November is peak saptāha season, and I took the opportunity to drop in on half a dozen additional events while I was in Vrindavan.

One of the exponents I had interviewed in India, Sri Bhaktivedanta Siddhanti Maharaj, mentioned that he had been invited to give a saptāha in Brisbane, Australia, in June 2014. I was conscious of the fact that my data on audiences were still very weak, and if this project was to be about the reception of text, then understanding the audience experience would be essential. Accordingly, I joined the audience in Brisbane, where my fellow attendees were unfailingly generous with their time and patience. These interviews, conducted in English, combined with observations and interviews from previous events, formed the basis of chapter 7.

The final piece of the puzzle was the role of the sponsor. The saptāha in Queensland was organized by the Brisbane Bhakti Yoga Centre, and while my initial focus was on audience members, I was also able to interview several of the key organizers of this and earlier events about their roles and responses. This was supplemented with material from Yogendra Yadav about his experience as the organizer of the saptāha at Naluna, mentioned above. The experiences of these sponsors and organizers became the basis for chapter 3.

The answers to the fundamental questions about the nature of oral performance of the Bhāgavatapurāṇa are complex and varied. The experiences and outcomes for each of the various parties are as varied as the individuals themselves and in some cases appear to be contradictory. The breadth and depth of saptāha experience in all its diversity are explored in the two concluding chapters.

I have assigned each chapter a metaphor drawn from the ancient Vedic act of worship known as *yajña*, in which a priest makes a ritual offering of sacred substances into a consecrated fire. This system of metaphors is one way of expressing the relationship among the various elements of the book, while at the same time embedding each unit and the whole practice of saptāha within a set of ideas that resonates deeply in the Indic thought-world. I give a brief introduction to the significance of each metaphor in chapter 1.

This book is the result of a meandering voyage of discovery for me, one full of challenges and surprises, a journey that I am now delighted to share with others.

Mauni Amāvasyā, New Moon Day, January 2015
Meringo, Australia

Acknowledgments

FRIENDS AND COLLEAGUES at the Australian National University, especially Meera Ashar, Abhirav Bansal, Robert Cribb, Assa Doron, Peter Friedlander, Kirin Narayan, Barbara Nelson, John Powers, Ananth Rao, and Yogendra Yadav, have been a constant source of inspiration and guidance for this project. Other Australian colleagues, including Mark Allon, Greg Bailey, and Adam Bowles, have always expressed kind interest and support. Similarly, James Hegarty, Simon Brodbeck, and Louise Child at the University of Cardiff, where I enjoyed a sabbatical as William Jones Visiting Lecturer, provided invaluable feedback during the formative stages of this project, as did Kate Sullivan and colleagues at the South Asia Research Cluster, Wolfson College, Oxford.

I am especially grateful to the many wonderful exponents of this tradition who kindly shared their time, insights, and expertise, including Acharya Shri Satchitananda Sai (Melbourne), and the experts I interviewed in Vrindavan and Delhi in November 2013, including Acharya Shri Shrivatsa Goswami, Vaishnavacharya Shri Chandan Goswami, Vaishnavacharya Shri Abhishek Goswami, Goswami Dr. Achyut Lal Bhatt, Shri Bhaktivedanta Siddhanti Maharaj, Shri Bhaktivedanta Madhusudan Maharaj, Acharya Shri Chandradas-ji Maharaj "Radhikadas," Shri Krishna Chandra Shastri Thakur Ji, and the staff and students of Vedic Yatra Pathashala. Also in Vrindavan, Ilona Wilczewska Avadhuta, Robyn Beeche, Manjari Talent, and Kamala Wood were all most generous with their time and contacts and opened many doors for me. Special thanks to the director, Mahesh Narain Sharma, and staff of the Vrindavan Research Institute and to the staff of the Jai Singh Ghera Ashram. The sponsors, organizers, and audience members of the saptāhas held at Naluna, the Shri Vishnu Shiva Mandir in Canberra, and the Brisbane Bhakti Yoga Centre were consistently kind, patient, and welcoming.

I would especially like to thank the publisher's anonymous reviewers who suggested many improvements for this book.

At home, Janet Phillips held the fort during my many trips away, and Janet Taylor provided invaluable help in the field as my research manager and with her insightful comments and criticisms of the text.

Note on Transliteration

TRANSLITERATION OF INDIC terms is problematic, as many words may appear in Sanskrit, Hindi, or anglicized forms. For example, much of this book is about the deity known variously as Kṛṣṇa, Krishna, or Krishan. The site of his past-times is spelled Vṛndāvana, Vrindavan, Brindaban, Vrindaban, or Brindavan. The narratives of this tradition are preserved in a text known as the Bhāgavatapurāṇa, Bhagavatapurana, or Bhagwatpuran. For the sake of clarity, I have used a single form of each term based on the context in which it usually occurs. Words used primarily in the context of Sanskrit texts are given in standard scholarly form with correct diacritics. This includes the names of deities and some specialist terms. Words used usually in the context of modern spoken Hindi, such as proper names of individuals and institutions, are mostly given phonetically with minimal diacritics. I have followed the usual practice of indicating the long *ā* and the long *ī* in some Hindi words, especially those derived from Sanskrit. Place names are given in their usual anglicized forms. For words that are used in both textual and vernacular contexts, I have made an arbitrary decision to adopt one form or the other. Personal names, titles, and honorifics are generally given in the form in which they appear in the individuals' own websites or publications. Definitions of Sanskrit and Hindi terms are given in the glossary at the back of this book.

Seven Days of Nectar

I

Introduction—Kṣetropadhāna

AN OCEAN OF humanity stretches as far as the eye can see, sheltering from the blistering Bombay sun in the shade of a cavernous tent. For many hours each day, for seven days on end, the audience of twenty thousand or more sits in rapt attention. Above a stage at the front of the tent is a painted backdrop of a sylvan scene with cowherd boys and big-eyed cattle. Seated at the center of the stage on a raised dais is an immaculately groomed speaker. He holds the vast crowd in thrall; devotees drink in his stories, which are said to be the nectar of immortality. They center on the deity Viṣṇu and his most significant *avatāra*, the beloved cow-herding god Kṛṣṇa. The speaker expertly weaves verses from the great Sanskrit classic, the *Bhāgavatapurāṇa*, with his own commentary on the text and devotional songs in Hindi. For many in the audience, these week-long events, known as *Bhāgavata-saptāhas*, are deeply moving; for some, they are life-changing. What makes them so? What attracts, retains, and transforms those who attend? What spiritual thirsts and social needs do these performances satisfy? Why do Bhāgavata-saptāha events seem to be growing in size, complexity, and number by the year? How does this trend fit into a broader sociopolitical picture of globalization, secularization, emergent middle-class religiosity, and a rejuvenated sense of Indian nationalism? These are the questions explored in this book.

The organizing metaphor for the chapters that follow is the ancient Vedic ritual of sacrifice in which a priest offers an oblation of sacred substances into a fire to nourish the deities. The preliminary task for this ritual is the preparation of the sacrificial ground, a process called "measuring out the field for the fire" (*agni-kṣetropadhāna*). In this introductory chapter, I measure out the field for this inquiry, setting the boundaries and laying the groundwork. I begin by introducing the genre of mythological texts known as the *purāṇas*. This is followed by a brief description of the Bhāgavatapurāṇa itself, which is the main source of narratives for these week-long performances. Next, I introduce the concept of the seven-day performance with a description of an idealized saptāha, probably dating from the early eighteenth century. This is followed by an outline of contemporary practice and an overview of scholarly writing on the subject. I then describe how the Bhāgavata-saptāha fits in with other forms of oral performance of sacred texts in India. The chapter concludes with a rationale for the work as a whole, an outline of the theoretical framework, and an overview of the contents of the following chapters.

What Is a Purāṇa?

At the heart of these week-long events, known colloquially as *saptāhas*, is the Sanskrit text of the Bhāgavatapurāṇa. The basic meaning of the word *purāṇa* is "old." The texts that constitute this genre contain the foundational cosmology, mythology, and theology of many contemporary Hindu beliefs and practices. According to tradition, there are eighteen great purāṇas, the *mahāpurāṇas*, and the same number of lesser texts known as *upapurāṇas*, although there is some argument over which texts belong in which category. There are also hundreds, possibly thousands, of local purāṇas, known as *sthalapurāṇas*. These may be in Sanskrit but are often written in vernacular languages, and they preserve narratives associated with specific places of pilgrimage and communities.

For traditionally minded Hindus, the question of the authorship and age of the purāṇas is clear-cut. According to custom, they were created by the gods themselves or by divine sages in far-off mythical times. The contemporary academic consensus is that most of the mahāpurāṇas approached their current form between the fourth and the fourteenth centuries CE. This estimate is vague because some purāṇas evolved over many centuries as material was added by generations of authors and editors. To paraphrase Wendy Doniger (2009, 264), they are like premodern Indic Wikipedias, which were improved and expanded by many hands. It has been suggested that purāṇas "seem to welcome additions with open bindings" (Coburn 1984, 453). Traditional palm-leaf manuscripts deteriorate rapidly—the most voracious consumer of

Sanskrit texts is often "his majesty the white ant" (Lutgendorf 1991, 57)—and new copies must be made every few generations. Each time a manuscript was copied, it was a simple matter for the scribe to add to the text according to his own tastes or those of his patron. As is the case with many other scriptural traditions worldwide, the human authors of the purāṇas remain unknown.

The mahāpurāṇas are usually regarded as the most authoritative sources of narratives within their respective traditions. Most Hindus are familiar with major purāṇic themes: how the gods churned the nectar of immortality from the Ocean of Milk, how Śiva broke the descent of the river Ganga with his matted locks, and how Kṛṣṇa danced with the cowherding girls, the *gopīs*, of Vrindavan. To be a Hindu is to have internalized these purāṇic narratives. Traditionally, children first heard these stories on their grandparents' laps, saw them illustrated on temple walls, and learned about them from dance, song, and oral performance. In modern times, generations of Indian children experience purāṇic narratives in comics, in movies, on television, and now also in the form of online videos and mobile apps. Ironically, being in Sanskrit, the original purāṇic texts are not directly accessible to most people, as few know enough of the classical language to read them in the original. For this reason, the narratives are constantly reinterpreted, recreated, and performed orally in vernacular languages.

The idea that purāṇic discourse is originally and fundamentally oral and only secondarily written is a very old one. According to the Bhāgavatapurāṇa, the gods first narrated the text to the sage Nārada, the famous intermediary between the divine and human realms. He retold it to the sage Vyāsa, who told it to his own son Śuka. Śuka narrated it to the king Parīkṣit, and so on. As such, the texts as we encounter them are written accounts of (legendary) oral performances. Little is said about the textual nature of these narratives in the corpus itself. Western scholarship has tended to treat the purāṇas primarily as written texts. This is partly a result of the cultural practice of privileging the written over the spoken and partly because scholars in the West originally had access only to written text, not the oral performance tradition. I will return to this point in more detail later.

The Bhāgavatapurāṇa

Within the vast genre of purāṇas, the Bhāgavatapurāṇa is of key interest for us, as it contains the narratives on which these seven-day events are based. *Bhāgavata* means "of, or relating to, the Lord," and *purāṇa*, as we have seen, means "old." Thus, the title of the text may be taken to mean "Ancient Narratives of the Lord." In the tradition that created it, the "Lord," or *Bhagavān*, usually indicates both Viṣṇu and Kṛṣṇa, who are regarded as one and the same. Some devotees maintain that Kṛṣṇa is a form, or avatāra, of Viṣṇu, while others hold that Kṛṣṇa is the primary deity and that Viṣṇu is the secondary form. Many also believe that both deities are forms of a single ultimate divine entity.

According to tradition, which is widely accepted by saptāha audiences, the Bhāgavatapurāṇa was created five thousand years ago at the beginning of the Kali-yuga, the current "Age of Decadence," by the sage Vyāsa at his hermitage, Badarikā ("Place of the Jujube"), in the Himalayas. The contemporary scholarly consensus is that the text was created between the sixth and ninth centuries of the current era in South India. The concrete evidence for this position is rather thin. The trope of intense personal devotion to the Divine, known as *bhakti*, first appeared in the songs of Tamil poet-saints known as the Alvars between the sixth and ninth centuries in South India. As the Bhāgavatapurāṇa is deeply suffused with this emotion, it is argued that the text cannot predate these poets. And because the Alvars were active in the south, it is often assumed that it is also where the text was composed.

The concept of bhakti is central to the Bhāgavatapurāṇa. The word is derived from the Sanskrit root *bhaj*, which includes the meanings of "sharing" and "partaking." Thus, a devotee "shares in" or "partakes of" the Divine, through intense, direct, personal devotion. This differentiates it from yoga, meditation, ritual, meritorious action, and the various other paths to liberation promoted by different traditions. According to the Bhāgavatapurāṇa, it is through bhakti—praising, singing, dancing, and rejoicing in the name of the Lord—that a devotee attains the state of union with the Divine.

In addition to bhakti, the basic theology of the Bhāgavatapurāṇa as interpreted by many contemporary saptāha exponents is the "nondualist" or Advaita Vedānta position that "All this is One."[1] That is, all of creation, including the *ātman*, or "soul," of the individual, is not different from the Divine. The Supreme Deity, the Absolute, Brahman, Viṣṇu, and Nārāyaṇa are mutually identical and are not differentiated from Kṛṣṇa. All these forms of the Divine are referred to interchangeably as Bhagavān, "the Lord." The entire universe and indeed one's own self are none other than this. The basic intent of the Bhāgavatapurāṇa as expressed in saptāha performances is to enable audiences to realize this truth. With this realization, a devotee achieves a sense of unity with the Divine, which is sometimes also described as liberation, or *mokṣa*, the ultimate goal in many Hindu traditions.

In contemporary saptāha performances, the emotion of bhakti and the Advaita theology are couched within a philosophical framework known as Sāṁkhya. According to this world view, the universe consists of *puruṣa* ("spirit") and *prakṛti* ("matter"), and all matter consists of three *guṇas*, or elements: *sattva* ("purity"), *rajas* ("energy"), and *tamas* ("inertia"). As such, the Bhāgavatapurāṇa expresses a union of devotional bhakti with the Advaita Vedānta position within a Sāṁkhya world view.

Some scholars have pointed to the stylistic and narrative unity of the Bhāgavatapurāṇa as evidence of a single authorial hand (Rohlman 2005; Gupta and Valpey 2013, xi). This also suggests that the Bhāgavatapurāṇa may not have undergone the long process of evolution that some of the other purāṇas experienced. Irrespective of when and where the Bhāgavatapurāṇa was composed, it was first accorded canonical status in the sixteenth century by the founders of the Gauḍīya Vaiṣṇava traditions emanating from Bengal. Since that time, it has enjoyed uninterrupted and growing popularity, as demonstrated by the large number of manuscripts of the text found all over India, the number of commentaries dedicated to it, and the number of modern printed editions (Rocher 1986, 138), not to mention contemporary oral performance.

The underlying structure of the Bhāgavatapurāṇa is a chronological history of the universe from its earliest creation to the "present," that is, the death of the central character, the king Parīkṣit. It contains narratives of the greatest avatāras and devotees (*bhaktas*) of Viṣṇu-Kṛṣṇa, with an emphasis on their songs of praise for the Lord. The individual narratives, and the Bhāgavatapurāṇa as a whole, serve to illustrate the salvific power of meditating on the Lord, reciting his holy name, and realizing the true nature of the self and the universe.

Many of the narratives found in the Bhāgavatapurāṇa also exist in earlier collections, including the Mahābhārata, the Harivaṁśa, and the Viṣṇupurāṇa. In the Bhāgavatapurāṇa, they are adapted to the text's own discursive purposes; most have been retooled in such a way as to express the most fulsome praise of Viṣṇu and deep emotional devotion to Kṛṣṇa at every opportunity, with the continual refrain of "All this is One." In some cases, the narratives have been inverted for literary effect, such that a troublesome demon of an earlier version is revealed to be the most sincere devotee in the later text.

The Bhāgavatapurāṇa is divided into twelve sections, or books, called *skandhas*. Each skandha has between ten and thirty chapters, with the exception of the famous tenth skandha, which deals with the life of Kṛṣṇa in ninety chapters. This skandha alone accounts for nearly one-quarter of the entire work. Each chapter has an average of about fifty verses, and the whole Bhāgavatapurāṇa is traditionally said to have eighteen thousand verses, an auspicious number, but the actual total is closer to fourteen thousand. The narratives of the Bhāgavatapurāṇa and the ways in which they are deployed in saptāha performances are described in chapter 5.

Editions, Translations, and Scholarship

The Bhāgavatapurāṇa exists in myriad potted versions, translations, transcreations, recreations, and retellings. It is available in bookshops and pilgrimage centers, at railway stations and street corners all over India, and of course, anyone can now download Bhāgavatapurāṇa apps for mobile devices. As one of the most important texts among Hindu traditions, the Bhāgavatapurāṇa has also spawned a vast body of scholarly literature from the perspectives of history, linguistics, theology, cosmology, and mythology.

The most commonly used Sanskrit text of the Bhāgavatapurāṇa is published by Gita Press of Gorakhpur, India. This publisher has brought out new editions of the text every decade or so since the early 1970s, with an aggregate print run of four hundred thousand copies, an eloquent statement of the text's enduring popularity.[2] Gita Press has also issued bilingual editions of the text in Sanskrit and the major Indian regional languages, plus English. The main drawback of the bilingual Sanskrit-English edition is that the translation is flowery and verbose and contains a large amount of parenthetical material (Goswami 2005).

Several versions of the entire Sanskrit text of the Bhāgavatapurāṇa are available online. The Maharishi University of Management has a clear, largely error-free version.[3] The International Society for Krishna Consciousness (ISKCON) maintains the online Bhaktivedanta VedaBase, which contains an accurate text with a searchable word-by-word translation and a fairly accurate prose translation.[4] There is also an interpretation ("purport") of each verse by the founding guru of ISKCON, A. C. Bhaktivedanta Swami Prabhupada.[5]

A complete English translation of the Bhāgavatapurāṇa was undertaken by Ganesh Vasudeo Tagare in five volumes (Tagare 1976–1978). The English of this version is rather antiquated, but the final volume has a useful index. At present, there is no complete contemporary English translation of the text. Edwin Bryant has published an excellent modern translation of the tenth skandha and part of the eleventh, which deal with the most popular sections of the text, the life of Kṛṣṇa (Bryant 2003). Ravi M. Gupta and Kenneth R. Valpey, of the Bhagavata Purana Research Project based at the Oxford Centre for Hindu Studies, are soon to publish an abridged translation of the text.[6]

The best guide to pre-1985 Bhāgavatapurāṇa scholarship is Rocher (1986), while more recent scholarship has been summarized by Gupta and Valpey in their edited volume, *The Bhāgavata Purāṇa: Sacred Text and Living Tradition* (2013). This also contains twelve original and refreshing thematic essays and is an excellent contemporary introduction to the text.

For generations, Western scholarship labored under the influence of an early British Orientalist, Horace Hayman Wilson (1786–1860). In his assessment, the purāṇic corpus consisted of second-rate, disorganized grab bags. An important corrective to this view is found in an article by Elizabeth Rohlman (2005), "Textual Authority, Accretion, and Suspicion." Rohlman reminds us that some purāṇas, including the Bhāgavatapurāṇa, display a stylistic, thematic, and philosophical unity, a feature that has never been in doubt for Indian audiences.

The Archetypal Saptāha

A Bhāgavata-saptāha is a week-long oral performance based on narratives of the Bhāgavatapurāṇa. As *saptāha* means "seven days" or "week," a Bhāgavata-saptāha may be understood as a *week* dedicated to the *Bhāgavata*-purāṇa. In its simplest form, these events are undertaken to fulfill a sacred vow, or *vrata*, to read the entire text over a seven-day period. This is usually carried out by one or more Brahmin males, who read the text silently or in a low murmur. This meritorious act is said to benefit the reader or the individual who sponsors the reading. Besides this form of private reading, known as *pārāyaṇa*, an expert storyteller, usually a scholar (whom I call the exponent), may relate narratives from the Bhāgavatapurāṇa to an audience over a seven-day period. These oral renderings invariably include some Sanskrit verses from the text and are supplemented with material from other well-known scriptures, from oral tradition, and from daily life. As few in the audience are able to understand Sanskrit, the explanation and added narration are provided in the local vernacular language. Among the Indian diaspora and in cosmopolitan cities such as Mumbai, exponents often speak in English.

Indian tradition holds that the first saptāha took place many thousands of years ago, but the earliest concrete evidence of the practice is found in a text called the *Śrīmad-bhāgavata-māhātmya*, "The Greatness of the Glorious Bhāgavatapurāṇa." This appears as an appendix to the Padmapurāṇa and is also included as a preface in popular modern copies of the Bhāgavatapurāṇa, such as the Gita Press edition (Goswami 2005). As the oldest manuscripts of the Māhātmya date from the first half of the eighteenth century (Hawley 2009, 95), we can say with confidence that the practice is at least two to three centuries old but may possibly be much older. The Māhātmya contains a set of detailed instructions for how a saptāha is to be conducted (Bhāgavatapurāṇa [BhP] 0.6.1–103), which I will call the archetype. In the following paragraphs, I summarize these directions, as many of the features and practices it mentions are still followed today.

The Māhātmya advises the prospective sponsor to consult an astrologer to determine an auspicious time and date for the event. The hot season in North India (June and July), the rains (July to October), and the cooler months (November and December) are most favorable. The sponsor should be prepared to spend as much on the saptāha as he would on a wedding. News of the event should be sent out in all directions, and everybody is to be made welcome. Invitees may include those who "stand remote" from the stories and praise of the Lord, such as "women, śūdras, and the rest," *śūdras* being the fourth and "lowest" community in idealized Brahminical society (BhP 0.6.1–6). This is an interesting point, as many Hindu scriptures, especially the Vedas, were restricted to males of the "higher" three communities. The inclusion of women and others suggests a broader social basis for purāṇic religion and a break with the earlier, more orthodox traditions. It also suggests that saptāhas may have been conducted in the local language, as few except for an educated elite understood Sanskrit. The instructions suggest the following wording for the invitations:

> A week-long assembly of the pious, a very rare event, is forthcoming, and there, an exposition of unprecedented charm will take place. You who are eager to imbibe the nectar of the glorious Bhāgavata, having love foremost, come quickly! If you have no time, then come for just a day. Come in any case, as even a moment here is very difficult to obtain. (BhP 0.6.8–9)[7]

Ideal venues for a saptāha are said to include places of pilgrimage, forest groves, and private residences. The site is to be tidied, swept, freshly plastered, and decorated. Household items and other distractions are to be cleared away, matting should be placed on the ground for seating, and awnings should be spread overhead to provide shelter from the elements. The whole area should be decorated with banana palms, fresh leaves, flowers, fruits, and bunting. At the front of the venue, there should be an elevated seat for the exponent and for other Brahmins and renunciants.

As for the all-important question of engaging a speaker, the instructions call for a devout Vaiṣṇava Brahmin who must be capable of expounding on the Vedas and other scriptures. He must also be skilled in providing suitable explanations and be free from worldly attachments. Those who chase after women or entertain heretical ideas are to be avoided, "even if they are well educated." The exponent should also have a seconder who can help him resolve any difficulties with the text (BhP 0.6.20–22).

Before the saptāha begins, the exponent should worship Gaṇeśa to ensure that all obstacles are removed. He should then honor Viṣṇu, Kṛṣṇa, and the text of the Bhāgavatapurāṇa with incense and lights. Five additional Brahmins should chant the twelve-syllable mantra of Kṛṣṇa ("oṃ namo bhagavate vāsudevāya") continuously for the whole week. Beginning at sunrise, the exponent is supposed to speak "in a suitably moderated tone" for three and a half watches (*praharas*), the equivalent of ten or eleven hours. During the one-hour break at midday, devotees should sing praise to Viṣṇu. Attendees are advised to eat only one small meal a day in order to reduce the need for toilet breaks (BhP 0.6.24–40).

The sponsor and others may undergo a form of initiation (*dīkṣā*) to listen to the saptāha in its entirety. In theory, they should remain celibate for the week, sleep on the floor, eat off platters of leaves, and abstain from all negative thoughts and deeds. Attendees are advised to fast for the full week, or at least to restrict themselves to a pure diet of milk, ghee, fruit, vegetables, and a single type of grain, while excluding legumes, honey, oil, heavy foods, and leftovers. Sensibly, the instructions note that fasting should not detract from one's ability to listen to the exposition. During the event, one should not denigrate the Vedas, Vaiṣṇavas, or Brahmins. Menstruating women, members of "lower" castes, non-Indians (*mlecchas*), and non-Hindus are to be avoided (BhP 0.6.45–49). Some of these restrictions are still followed with varying degrees of fidelity in contemporary practice. In larger urban settings, their application is very liberal, but at smaller rural events, such as those documented by Desai (2013, 110–111), traditional restrictions may be followed more closely.

At the end of the seven days, everyone attending the event should worship the exponent "with great devotion." Blessed food (*prasād*), leaves of the sacred basil plant (*tulsi*), and garlands of flowers are distributed to attendees. Praises to Viṣṇu and Kṛṣṇa should be sung to the accompaniment of drums and cymbals. There should be cries of Jaya! and Namaḥ! ("Victory!" "Homage!"), and a conch shell should be sounded. Money and food are then distributed to the officiating Brahmins and mendicants. Oblations should be offered into the fire as atonement for any shortcomings in the event. Finally, the sponsor is supposed to present the Brahmins with sweet rice pudding, a gift of gold, and a cow. If he can afford it, the sponsor should also give the exponent a golden book stand in the shape of a lion, with a fresh copy of the Bhāgavatapurāṇa "written in beautiful letters," along with money, clothes, jewelry, sandal paste, and so on. By following all these injunctions carefully, the instructions assure us, a person will obtain "the ultimate reward"—liberation—the final escape from cyclical existence (BhP 0.6.56–68).

What do we know of actual saptāha performance in premodern times? The procedures summarized above give a sense of what a saptāha might have been like, but how common were they in practice? To what extent did actual performances resemble the event suggested by the Māhātyma? Potential sources of documentary evidence of premodern performances include colonial-era records such as F. S. Growse's (1880) *Mathura: A District Memoir* and D. L. Drake-Brockman's (1984 [1911]) *Mathura: A Gazetteer*. These two works contain detailed descriptions of local religious practices, including the Banjatra (or forest pilgrimage through Vraja), the festivities relating to Holi, the performance of Raslīlā, and descriptions of the gosains (goswamis) of Vrindavan. Surprisingly, however, I found no mention of the oral performance of the Bhāgavatapurāṇa among these detailed records. This does not prove that such performances did not take place, but the paucity of evidence does suggest that they were not as prominent a feature of the religious landscape as they are now.

Desai's (2013) research in Andhra Pradesh also suggests a possible model for premodern saptāha performances. She describes two relatively low-tech, low-cost events in different villages that were attended by small audiences of up to thirty-five people each day. One of these events was the ninetieth consecutive annual saptāha held in that particular village. As we will see, these simple village saptāhas resemble more closely the performances described in the Māhātmya than they do the elaborate large-scale contemporary events in North India. One could easily imagine small village-based events such as these, largely independent of the trappings and impacts of modernity, as the forerunners of the contemporary saptāha.

We might also seek evidence for the popularity of premodern saptāhas in the manuscript tradition. We know that this text was popular and widely distributed, as large numbers of manuscripts have been found all over India (Rocher 1986, 138). The prevalence of manuscripts at least suggests (but does not confirm) the possibility of a widespread tradition of oral performance.

The Contemporary Saptāha

Contemporary saptāha events are usually advertised on posters, on roadside billboards, in the media, by word of mouth, and today, of course, on Facebook and Twitter. Admission is free, and the performances are open to the public, as they are usually financed by an individual, a family, a community, or a temple organization. Attendees may also make a donation at the venue. As all these forms of oral performance are based on religious narratives, saptāhas are ritualized, sacred events and are distinct from common, popular entertainments.

Contemporary saptāhas vary greatly in scale, style, and content. In its simplest form, the saptāha is a week-long recounting of the narratives by a speaker among a group of friends in a private residence, a temple, or a community hall. At the other end of the spectrum are major gala events held in sports arenas or under acres of canvas. These may feature internationally recognized speakers and musicians and may incorporate dance, drama, and the distribution of prasād among tens of thousands of the faithful.

As is the case with other public religious events, community and religious leaders, politicians, and other important local personalities may sometimes make an appearance. This is a way of publicly expressing the individual's piety and status, and it also enhances the status of the event and its sponsors.

In step with the growth of other forms of religious expression and consumption in India, Bhāgavata-saptāhas have also grown in scale, number, and popularity in recent decades. As recently as the mid-1980s, Lutgendorf (1991, 115–116, 195) believed that Bhāgavata-kathā (the oral performance of narratives based on the Bhāgavatapurāṇa) "appears to be in decline" and "is comparatively rarely heard," but throughout North India, and especially in the region known as Vraja, the heartland of contemporary Bhāgavatapurāṇa performance, the situation is very different. The towns of Mathura and Vrindavan, 150 kilometers south of Delhi, are the traditional sites of Kṛṣṇa's birth and youthful escapades. In the peak months of October and November, dozens of week-long performances may be running simultaneously in these places. Bhāgavata-saptāhas have spread well beyond this region and now take place across the country, especially in the north. Well-known exponents tour India at the invitation of devotees, giving back-to-back performances over a period of months or sometimes years. Indian communities all over the world also sponsor Bhāgavata-saptāhas. One exponent I interviewed in Delhi had just returned from giving saptāhas in South Africa and was en route to Russia between two visits to Australia.

The modern saptāha is a continuously evolving phenomenon. A recent development is "saptāha tourism"; one enterprising travel agent in Vrindavan advertised a luxury cruise through Southeast Asia with a saptāha performance on board (Taylor 2012b, 84).[8] Other travel agents are now offering sightseeing trips to Europe, including Spain, Italy, Switzerland, and France, with a saptāha component. For example, one itinerary included the following: "Morning listen to Srimadbhagawat Katha. Later you have the option to visit the Leaning Tower of Pisa."[9]

Writings on Saptāhas

Little has been written about these performances, and there are several reasons for this. First, Sanskrit scholars focus on texts, and few, if any, have asked how these texts are used in contemporary situations. Second, few scholars who are interested in religious practice, primarily anthropologists, are particularly interested in Sanskrit. More than half a century ago, Dumont and Pocock (1957, 7, 9) commented on the need to integrate the knowledge of texts with the social sciences: "In our opinion, the first condition for a sound development of a Sociology of India is found in the establishment of the proper relation between it and classical Indology." This requires "the sociologist to be acquainted not merely with the living language but also with Indian literature and with classical Indology in general." Milton Singer (1972, 39–40) also articulated this fundamental position in the 1970s:

> Because they are not usually Sanskritists and cannot often obtain the collaboration of Sanskritists, anthropologists must perforce bypass the textual corpus and content themselves with noting the references to it that turn up in their interviews and observations. . . .

> The problem is equally formidable on the other side: The knowledgeable scholar of the philosophical and religious literature will appear casual in his references to the social and cultural context of the literature by comparison with his thorough and systematic analysis of the texts themselves. The literary scholar who is willing and able to incorporate interviews and observations of the living religion into his work is as rare as is the anthropologist who employs textual studies.

There are notable exceptions. Tambiah (1970) explored the textual elements of the Theravadan Buddhist tradition as incorporated into contemporary village religion in northeastern Thailand. Hiltebeitel's (1988) *The Cult of Draupadī* looks at the oral performance of regional versions of the Mahābhārata in South. His *Rethinking India's Oral and Classical Epics* (Hiltebeitel 1999) examined both Mahābhārata and Rāmāyaṇa narratives among Rajput, Muslim, and Dalit communities. Obeyesekere (1984), in his study of postharvest rituals in Sri Lanka, analyzed oral performance of various texts related to the goddess Pattini. Lutgendorf's (1991) magisterial *The Life of a Text* explores the role and performance of the sixteenth-century vernacular classic, Rāmcaritmānas. Despite these important leads, there has been only limited success in bridging the gap between anthropology and Sanskrit texts or in exploring the relationship between these texts and the contexts in which they are used. As recently as 2010, Sihlé (2010, 35) wrote:

> Anthropologists of complex, literate religious traditions have rarely succeeded at properly integrating local corpora of written religious texts (canonical scriptures, ritual manuals, etc.) into their ethnographically based analyses.... There would thus seem to be some inherent lack of fit between written religious texts as objects of study and (at least traditional) understandings of anthropological practices and concerns.

In addition to the difficulty that researchers have in crossing disciplinary boundaries, another reason for the lack of writing on saptāha events is that they are an emerging form of religious practice. Prominent Sanskrit scholars such as V. N. Rao (2007, 103–104) wrote of oral purāṇic performances in the past tense, as if they were a historical tradition with no current equivalent: "The Purāṇas were read/performed in temples and other religious locations. A class of *paurāṇika* performers made it their profession to perform these texts, and they were patronized by kings, local chiefs, elders of society, and temple authorities." Rao's (2007, 114) opinion that *paurāṇikas,* expert exponents of the purāṇas, are "absent" and have "disappeared" is still widely shared among international scholars.

In my earlier writing on saptāha practice, I set out to compare the traditional instructions with contemporary practice (Taylor 2012b). I investigated the role of the Sanskrit text of the Bhāgavatapurāṇa in saptāha events (Taylor 2012a). The inclusion of Sanskrit verses in all Bhāgavata oral performances raised this question: Why sing in a language no one can understand? In an article titled "How to Do Things with Sanskrit," I explored this question in terms of speech act theory (Taylor 2015). I argued that the Sanskrit verses have what J. L. Austin (1980 [1962]) called "perlocutionary" power and perform a social function in lieu of any semantic meaning. One saptāha I attended in the hamlet of Naluna in Uttarakhand, North India, was unique, as it was conducted under the auspices of the local village deity, or *grām-devtā*. Both the deity and the text of the Bhāgavatapurāṇa were important loci of authority and focal points of ritual action. I adopted the analogy of hospitality to explain the ways in which power was shared and negotiated between these two powerful entities: the deity as host and the text as guest (Taylor 2011).[10]

The only other published work on saptāha practice of which I am aware is an excellent article by Ilona Wilczewska (2013, 202), who, in her own words, "decided to physically immerse myself in the Bhāgavata Purāṇa's world in order to know how it comes to life in people's minds and bodies." In addition to recording interviews with audiences, exponents and sponsors in Jaipur and Vrindavan, Wilczewska had the unique opportunity to attend a training college for prospective Bhāgavata exponents and reports in brief on her experiences there.

Sangeeta Desai's Ph.D. thesis written at the University of Wisconsin–Madison documents saptāhas conducted in Andhra Pradesh between 2006 and 2007. In her performance-centered exploration of saptāha traditions, the author sets out to answer two questions: "How do participants of *Bhāgavata* performances make meaning from the *Bhāgavata Purāṇa*? In particular, how do participants inform and shape their own contemporary visions of Hinduism through these performances of the *Bhāgavata Purāṇa*?" (Desai 2013, 2). By exploring the "metacommunicative" processes, that is, the communication that surrounds and colors the reception of saptāha discourse, she compared two case studies, one from a rural area and the other in the major urban center of Hyderabad. Desai argues convincingly that "participants use the *Bhāgavata* to reconstitute the very Hinduism they seek to follow" (Desai 2013, 54).

Other Oral Performance Traditions

Where does this book fit within the literature on other forms of sacred oral performance? There is a vast amount of scholarship on ritual studies, ritual speech, religious language, the anthropology of religion, and performance studies that bears on this project. In this section, I restrict myself to some of the more salient works on sacred oral performance in South Asia that have direct relevance to the Bhāgavata-saptāha.

There is a long tradition of what Lutgendorf (1991, 164) termed "the oral mediation of sacred text" in South Asia. All the great texts of the Sanskrit archive were first and foremost oral performances. As V. N. Rao (2007, 114) wrote, "What is recorded on palm leaf, and later on paper, is not the entire text, it is only part of it. It acquires its fullness in performance, at which time it is appropriated by the *pauraṇika*, who is trained in reading the Purāṇas and interpreting them." The Vedas themselves were primarily oral. The earliest reflective texts known as Upaniṣads are said to be oral teachings given to disciples who "sat up close" to their gurus. The Mahābhārata was told by Ugraśravas, who heard it from Vaiśaṁpāyana, who heard it from his teacher Vyāsa. The Rāmāyaṇa was passed orally from Brahmā to Vālmīki, then from Vālmīki to the twins Lava and Kuśa, who sang it to their father, Rāma. All the purāṇas are couched in the dialogic form of narratives related by a speaker to a listener.

In addition to these legendary lines of oral transmission, there is evidence of historical performance of oral texts such as the Mahābhārata. In the Pallava era in South India (second to ninth centuries CE), local rulers provided patronage to particular religious establishments or practices by dedicating income from certain villages for their support. These arrangements, known as *grāmadeya* ("village gifts"), were recorded on plates of copper which have come down to us. One such set, the Taṇḍantōṭṭam Plates, dated 789 CE, show that a reader of the Mahābhārata was a regular recipient of such financial support (Mahalingam 1988, 303, line 198).

The obvious place to start a survey of contemporary oral performance of sacred texts is Philip Lutgendorf's (1991) *The Life of a Text: Performing the* Rāmcaritmānas *of Tulsidas* (1991). The Rāmcaritmānas is the most popular, widely read, and performed version of the Rāma epic. It was composed by the poet-saint Tulsidas (1532?–1623?) in a vernacular language known as Avadhi, a precursor of modern Hindi. Lutgendorf explores three genres of performance. The first is the simple recitation of the text, sometimes even in the absence of an audience. This may be carried out in an unbroken reading (*akhaṇḍ pāṭh*) over twenty-four hours by individuals or families or over nine days (often a public performance such as the Gyan Vapi event in Banaras). A thirty-day program of reading is also common, usually conducted in private by individuals as part of daily devotional activities. The second performance genre is the exposition of the text by a performer for an audience (*kathā* or *pravacana*), which is similar in structure to the performance of Bhāgavatapurāṇa in contemporary saptāha events. Third is the full-scale dramatic enactment of the Rāma legend, Rāmlīlā. This has its equivalent in the Raslīlā, the dramatic performances of the life of Kṛṣṇa which draw on narratives from the Bhāgavatapurāṇa (Hein 1972; Case 2000). Although the Mānas is a more recent vernacular text, Lutgendorf's work is highly relevant to the study of Bhāgavata-saptāha for two reasons: first, Rāmcaritmānas is the only other premodern Hindu text with a significant living tradition and a mass following. Second, Lutgendorf is one of the few scholars who have explored an Indic textual tradition from the perspectives offered by performance theory.

A form of oral performance closely related to the Bhāgavata-saptāha is known as Bhāgavata-kathā, and indeed there is some overlap between the two. The word *kathā* means "story" or "narration," and in popular use, it refers particularly to the telling of religious narratives. *Bhāgavata-kathā* simply means "Stories about the Lord" or, alternatively, "Stories from the Bhāgavatapurāṇa." This term is sometimes used interchangeably with *Bhāgavata-saptāha*. However, a Bhāgavata-kathā event does not usually run for a fixed period, nor does it bear the earnest ritual connotations of the saptāha. Bhāgavata-kathās are usually much smaller and simpler affairs than Bhāgavata-saptāhas and often take the form of a one-off lecture or a series of talks by a qualified individual. A Bhāgavata-saptāha may be understood as a seven-day series of Bhāgavata-kathās.

It is useful to distinguish Bhāgavata-saptāha from three other oral performance traditions. The first is *purāṇa-pravacana*, which might be translated as "purāṇic narration." Like a Bhāgavata-kathā, a pravacana is not performed in the context of a sacred vow, nor is it as highly ritualized as a typical Bhāgavata-saptāha. It may be conducted over any length of time, from an hour or two to a series of sessions over many months. Significantly, while the Bhāgavata-saptāha and the Bhāgavata-kathā always focus on the Bhāgavatapurāṇa, the purāṇa-pravacana draws on a wider range of source material, including stories from any of the purāṇas, the Rāmāyaṇa and the Mahābhārata, and other vernacular traditions.

A tradition of oral performance in South India and Maharashtra is known as *Hari-kathā* ("stories about Hari," another epithet for Viṣṇu) and *Kathā-kāla-kṣepa* ("spending time in storytelling"). The term *Hari-kathā* is more commonly used in Karnataka, and *Kathā-kāla-kṣepa* is more frequently heard in Tamil-speaking regions. In common with purāṇa-pravacana, these two art forms feature a professional performer or a talented amateur who takes as his or her subject an episode from the epics, the Bhāgavatapurāṇa, or another popular source. The performer sings verses from the original text, with or without musical accompaniment, and then interprets and expands on them in the vernacular. In the past, the performers were Brahmin men, but women and members of other communities are also now seen and heard (Ananth Rao 2011). While the subject matter is invariably pious or devotional at root, the distinguishing features are musicality and aesthetics, which are perhaps more highly valued than in the other traditions (Damle 1960; Sundaram 2001).

Other classical texts besides the Bhāgavatapurāṇa are sometimes the subjects of similar oral performances. Lutgendorf mentions a nine-day reading of the Devī-bhāgavata, the purāṇa dedicated to the Great Goddess, and there are scattered references to this event known as *navāha-yajña* ("nine-day sacrifice") in the Indian media, but I am not aware of any scholarly writing on the subject. Pintchman (2005, 20) makes a passing reference to the public reading of the "Kartik Mahatmya" in Benares. Coburn (1991, 160), Erndl (1993, 28–30), and McDermott (2011, 29, 33) all make brief references to ritual recitation of the Devī-māhātmya. In Uttarkashi, I once saw an old poster advertising a Śivapurāṇa-saptāha but was unable to pursue that tantalizing lead. There is a substantial literature on the oral performance of the vernacular epics with an emphasis on the varied relationship between oral performance and written text in South and Southeast Asia (Burkhalter Flueckiger and Sears 1991).

Another important study of the oral performance of religious narrative is Kirin Narayan's (1989) *Storytellers, Saints, and Scoundrels: Folk Narrative in Hindu Religious Teaching*. This is an account, which manages to be both affectionate and scholarly, of a *sādhu*, or holy man, whom the author calls Swamiji, in the city of Nasik, Maharashtra. Every morning and afternoon, disciples, devotees, and members of the public would visit Swamiji's simple apartment and, seated on the floor, would listen to him speak as he drew on a vast repertoire of folk narratives. The book has two main concerns: first is the fluid nature of the narrative, which is reflected in the narrator's skill in selecting and molding a given oral text to the needs of a given audience; second is the subjective nature of reception, with each listener creating his or her own meaning from Swamiji's stories in response to his or her own needs or situation.

All of the examples of oral performances of sacred texts just mentioned are drawn from Hindu traditions. It is worth adding that, not surprisingly, there are examples of similar traditions of oral performance in other Indic religious cultures. For example, Cort (1993, 203) describes the practice among Jaina sādhus of delivering sermons on one or another of the Jaina purāṇas in which sections are read in Sanskrit or Prakrit. These are followed by a translation or summary and a commentary in the vernacular.

Theoretical Approach: From "Stuff" to "Performance"

There are at least three good reasons for writing this book. First, these performances are now a major and burgeoning form of Hindu religious practice and expression, attracting large numbers of devotees in India and abroad. Especially since the economic reforms of the 1990s, members of the emerging Indian middle class have chosen to invest a growing portion of their newly acquired wealth in religious activities, including pilgrimages, temples, teachers, and events such as this (Nanda 2011). Any Internet search on the Sanskrit terms *Bhāgavata, saptāha, kathā,* or their vernacular equivalents yields hundreds of thousands of hits. Similar searches of databases of scholarly writing yield very few results. This alone should be enough to excite the researcher's interest: the Bhāgavata-saptāha, a conspicuous and growing form of contemporary religious practice, has largely escaped scholarly attention.

The second major reason for writing about saptāhas is that the Bhāgavatapurāṇa is the only major member of the genre, and indeed one of the few Sanskrit works of any description, that supports a living tradition. For the past two millennia, Sanskrit narratives have held a central place in the Indic cultural universe, but few are seen or heard in public today. Vālmīki's Rāmāyaṇa has largely been superseded in public by Tulsidas's vernacular Rāmcaritmānas. The Sanskrit text of the Mahābhārata is rarely seen or heard in public. The other purāṇas are seldom, if ever, encountered in their original language, with this single exception. The oral performances of the Bhāgavata are the living, thriving tips of a textual tradition whose roots go back more than a thousand years.

The third reason for writing this book is that it brings novel theoretical perspectives to the study of premodern Indian texts. The predominant approach to Sanskrit texts, as practiced by most classical Indologists, has been to concentrate on the production of text. When classical Indology evolved as a distinct discipline in the nineteenth century, early scholars had access to texts but not to their contexts, as travel to India was expensive, risky, and widely regarded as unnecessary. Many early Western Indologists grew up on a diet of European classics, and their approach to Indic texts was based on the European model, with its particular emphasis on textual criticism, textual history, and textual archaeology. Their major concern was with the way in which a given text developed over time as editors and authors added layer upon layer to a preexisting work. Scholars undertook the excavation of textual strata and the excision of "interpolations" and "contamination" from successive periods, with a view to laying bare the original "Ur-text" that underlay the accretions of subsequent centuries. This is still the approach favored by many Sanskrit scholars today.

In the following section, I outline the theoretical approach that I have adopted for this investigation. My interest is not in the history of the development of the text or how it reached its current form but in its reception. That is to say, I seek to understand how texts are read, performed, and understood; how they create discourse and shape societies; how audiences make meanings from them. In doing so, I draw on critical theory (Nietzsche, Foucault, and Pollock), reader response and reception theory (Iser and Jauss), and especially the theory of performance (Schechner, Bauman, and Hall).

Texts are important, powerful, and authoritative to the extent that they create discourse. The master texts of the Sanskrit archive, especially the epics and purāṇas, have been great pillars of orthodoxy and orthopraxis, but they have achieved this through their reception, not their production. Scholars who have investigated the phenomenology of text within the archive—that is, the ways in which text is experienced and perceived—include James Hegarty (2012), Brian Black (2007), Simon Brodbeck (2007), and Christopher Austin (2014). These studies deal with the Mahābhārata and its "appendix," the Harivaṁśa, and with the premodern reception of text. Like Abhimanyu, the hopelessly outnumbered lone warrior of that epic, I am championing not only textual reception over production but also contemporary reception over historical reception.

The first point to be made about reception relates to the nature of the "book" in the Sanskritic thought-world.[11] Some Sanskrit scholarship treats a text as a book in itself, which individuals might take into their hands and read sequentially from one end to the other, much as we would read Jane Austen or J. K. Rowling. I will argue that Sanskrit narrative texts do not usually function as books in the sense that we understand. They are, I suggest, sources of narratives, fonts of stories, which are selected and related orally to an audience. Sanskrit texts were not written to be read like novels, yet this is the way some textual scholars have regarded, analyzed, and represented them. As Coburn (1984, 438) remarked, the "writtenness" of scripture may mask the fact that holy words have primarily entered human lives not through the eye but through the ear.

Sanskrit texts require oral exposition to bring them to life. Coburn (1984, 444) relates a traditional tale of an aged guru, who, lacking a student worthy of inheriting his teachings, threw his manuscripts into a river. The implication is that a text without a teacher to enliven it through spoken discourse, and without an audience capable of receiving the oral transmission, has no value: "Written documents, unvivified by personal relationship, are lifeless." The legendary sage Nārada is quoted as saying, "That which is learned from dependence on a book and that which is not learned in the presence of one's guru does not shine in the midst of an assembly, like a person conceived by a woman with a paramour."[12] That is to say, there is something faintly illegitimate about book learning without the backing of the personal authority of a teacher.

What can we say about the reception of texts in the past? There were few, if any, accounts of how audiences responded to texts in premodern India. In fact, we know very little about how the texts were actually used or performed. In the absence of historical evidence for how audiences created meaning and how the texts created discourse in the past, I suggest that current practice might be used, until a better model becomes available, as an analog for, or a guide to, premodern practice.

Historically, folklorists and ethnographers used to collect "oral texts"—folk tales, songs, spells, and myths. This "oral literature" was duly recorded and transcribed, translated, edited, and sometimes "improved." To quote Bauman (1986, 2), "oral literature has been conceived of as stuff—collectively shaped, traditional stuff that could wander around the map, fill up collections and archives, reflect culture, and so on." In the process of collection and categorization of this "stuff," the original performative context was lost. A song sung during a specific festival or a spell made on a given occasion by a specialist was stripped of its particularity and its context and rendered as printed words on a page in the language of the collector.

Folklorists and ethnographers such as Dell Hymes and Dennis Tedlock, working with native North American narratives in the 1960s, were among the first to emphasize the importance of the performative aspects of oral texts. They began to investigate the emic view, that is, the insider's view, of oral narratives, how and why they were performed, and how they were appreciated and understood. From the marriage of folklore studies and anthropology arose what is now known as performance theory. This approach to oral texts yields a more complete, better-rounded, fuller understanding of the narrative than the etic view, the outsider's view, produced by earlier approaches.

To distinguish oral performance from "everyday" nonperformative speech, Bauman (1984 [1977], 11) offers this definition:

> Fundamentally, performance as a mode of spoken verbal communication consists in the assumption of responsibility to an audience for a display of communicative competence. This competence rests on the knowledge and ability to speak in socially appropriate ways. Performance involves on the part of the performer an assumption of accountability to an audience for the way in which communication is carried out, above and beyond its referential content. From the point of view of the audience, the act of expression on the part of the performer is thus marked as subject to evaluation for the way it is done, for the relative skill and effectiveness of the performer's display of competence.

That is to say, a performance is an event in which the audience expects the performer to have something to say and to say it well. The performer, on the other hand, may expect the audience to cheer or jeer, as the case may be. As Schechner (1993, 1) puts it, performance is "Behaviour heightened, if ever so slightly, and publicly displayed." Schechner (1993, 20) also spoke of the "four great spheres of performance—entertainment, healing, education, and ritualizing"—which are constantly in play with each other. This is also a useful framework for understanding Bhāgavatasaptāha, as all four of these "spheres" are important elements of the performance.

The word *theory* is derived from the Greek *thea*, which means "view."[13] A theory is therefore fundamentally a way of seeing. Performance theory supplies us with novel and productive ways of viewing oral literature. Among these is the important notion of artfulness or the poetics of oral performance. Changes of register and inflection, speech patterns, rhyme, and even pauses all contribute to the aesthetic impact of oral literature and are part of its situatedness. An oral performance, as opposed to everyday speech, is elevated and enriched by its artful elements, which are expected and appraised by the audience. Along with the shift from etic to emic approaches to oral literature comes the acceptance that artfulness is locally defined and experienced. Artfulness lies not in the eye (or ear) of the fieldworker but in the perception of the local audience.

Performance theory emphasizes the centrality and importance of the context in which the performance is held. The context serves to attune an audience's expectations; it activates a certain set of criteria for the way in which a performance is experienced and evaluated. Goffman (1974) and Bauman (1984 [1977]) refer to this as "keying," that is, the process by which an audience is "keyed in" to receive and experience the performance in a particular way. These keys are specific to particular settings, and in the case of the saptāha, we will see many of these attributes at work: the cultural setting, the appearance and bearing of the exponent, and so on. As Bauman (1986, 3) put it:

> Oral performance, like all human activity, is situated, its form, meaning, and functions rooted in culturally defined scenes or events—bounded segments of the flow of behaviour and experience that constitute meaningful contexts for action, interpretation, and evaluation. In the ethnography of oral performance, the performance event has assumed a place beside the text as a fundamental unit of description and analysis, providing the most concretely empirical framework for the comprehension of oral literature as social action by directing attention to the actual conduct of artistic verbal performance in social life.

Another important concept that arises from this theory is the emergent nature of oral performance (Bauman 1984 [1977], 37). No two oral performances are identical, as they are contingent on many variables: the inclinations of the performer, the responsiveness of the audience, the ambience, and so on. Even the local weather or the news of the day may affect the shape and content of a given performance. We see this in successive saptāha performances by the same exponent. For example, as one participant said of two successive saptāhas given by one speaker, "Swamiji's framework is the same, but the actual words change." Skillful speakers weave contemporary events and issues into their narratives as a means of engaging their audiences and tying the classical discourses to contemporary situations. One exponent I heard in Brisbane told his audience about a legendary saptāha given by the sage Nārada. The people who had come to hear Nārada were locked out of the hall, but, undaunted, they sang and danced outside the venue until someone came with the key. Everyone in the Brisbane audience laughed, as this was precisely what had happened to them earlier that evening.

Performance theory also reminds us that the Sanskrit texts, which have always been the central concern of classical Indology, are perhaps only byproducts, or the handmaidens, of oral performance. We tend to think of the saptāha as being a performance of the text, but as we have seen, the "original" text was only the record of an oral performance, even if it was a mythological one.

In adopting Bauman's (1984 [1977], 4) performative approach to oral texts, I am making a shift from text-as-material to text-as-communication. From this perspective, the oral performance of the Bhāgavatapurāṇa is best understood as a complex event that involves the interaction of the performer, the audience, and the text in a given setting.

This Book and the Metaphor of Yajña

The organizing principle of this book is based on the form of worship known as *yajña*. In this ancient ritual, a priest offers sacred substances, such as clarified butter, milk, grains, herbs, and a plant extract known as *soma*, into a consecrated fire in order to nourish the deities. This ritual has its origins in the second millennium before the current era and is practiced in Hindu, Buddhist, and Jaina communities to mark various stage-of-life events and to ensure health, wealth, and prosperity. Yajña is perhaps the paradigmatic form of worship in the Indic world and is enjoying a revival and reinvention in contemporary practice. Other forms of ritual are modeled on it, and some, like the Bhāgavata-saptāha, may be understood in terms that it suggests. While the Vedic ritual and the Bhāgavata-saptāha differ in practical terms, including their goals, conduct, and emotional atmosphere, the act of worship provides a metaphor for each of the various elements of a saptāha, for their interrelationship, and for the chapters of this book: preliminaries, performance, sponsor, exponent, text, verses, audience, and outcomes.

The metaphor of this introductory chapter was *kṣetropadhāna*, "laying out the field," as it prepared the groundwork for the rest of the book. The performance of a Bhāgavata-saptāha is regarded as a form of worship and is often referred to as a *jñāna-yajña*, or "knowledge-sacrifice." It is seen as a ritual act in which spiritual knowledge in the form of narratives about the Divine are offered up for the pleasure of the deity, the benefit of the listeners, and the general good of the world. In chapter 2, I illustrate the richness and diversity of contemporary saptāha practices with three contrasting case studies drawn from the dozen or so performances that I have attended in full or in part. The first is from Vrindavan, in which the musicality of the performance was central, Kṛṣṇa's consort Rādhā played a leading role, and the atmosphere often bordered on the ecstatic. The second case study is from the small rural community of Naluna in the Himalayan foothills of North India, where the function of the local village deity was central. The third saptāha—sophisticated, sedate, and cerebral but also with moments of great intensity—was held in suburban Canberra, Australia, for a largely middle-class diasporic audience.

Chapter 3 explores the saptāha from the perspective of the sponsor. Traditionally, in the context of the Vedic ritual, the sponsor, or *yajamāna*, is "the one who causes worship to be carried out." The same term (*yajmān* in Hindi) is used for the sponsor of the contemporary saptāha. Who chooses to sponsor a saptāha? What is their motivation? What do sponsors experience? What are the outcomes for them in terms of religious and social capital?

The Vedic act of worship is presided over by an officiating priest known as the *hotṛ*, "the offerer," who carries out the act of oblation into the fire. The hotṛ also provides a metaphor for the exponent, the key performer who presides over the saptāha. Chapter 4 explores the world of the exponent, looking at varied backgrounds and lineages. Exponents speak of their motivation for entering the practice, their training, their understanding of the saptāha, and their aspirations and concerns.

The metaphor for chapter 5 is *Veda*. From the earliest times, the invocations made at a fire sacrifice were compiled and preserved in oral anthologies known as the Vedas. Just as these are collections of sacred songs, so, too, the Bhāgavatapurāṇa is a collection of divine narratives. Indeed, like a number of other master texts in the Sanskrit archive, the Bhāgavatapurāṇa is sometimes reverentially referred to as the Fifth Veda. In chapter 5, I describe how an exponent uses the text in performance and apportions the twelve skandhas of the Bhāgavatapurāṇa over the seven days. The aim of this chapter is to provide a sense of the oral text that an audience experiences during a saptāha. Most of these embedded narratives are already well known to attendees. For many in the audience, pleasure is derived not from hearing something novel but from hearing something familiar.

In the paradigmatic act of worship, the priest eulogizes and supplicates the deities with sacred songs known as *mantras*. Much power is attributed to these utterances, and their correct intonation is deemed critical to the success of the ritual. The mantra is the powerful oral text essential for the success of the *yajña*. Similarly, many participants hold that the Sanskrit verses drawn from the Bhāgavatapurāṇa are essential for a successful and authentic saptāha. Audience members and exponents alike remark on the power, sanctity, and affective quality of the Sanskrit verses, even if they cannot understand them semantically. Chapter 6, for which I have chosen the metaphor of *mantra*, explores the way in which a skilled exponent selects verses from the root text and weaves them into the fabric of his oral presentation. I also include here a discussion of the effect of the Sanskrit verses on the discourse and on its reception by the audience.

The people who inhabited Vedic society were known collectively as *viś*, a word that originally connoted a settlement or a dwelling but came by extension to mean "community" and "the people." Chapter 7, with *viś* as

FIGURE I.1. The text of the Bhāgavatapurāṇa wrapped in brocade and gold tape at the Mumbai saptāha.
Source: Vipul Music Co.

its metaphor, focuses on the community aspects of saptāha performances, looking specifically at the event from the perspective of the audience. In this chapter, I explore the motivations and expectations of audience members. What attracts them to these events? What outcomes do they hope for? To what extent are the restrictions on diet and conduct still observed? Most important, I look at the ways in which audience members experience and understand Bhāgavata-saptāhas.

If the yajña is performed correctly, Agni, the god of fire, conveys the nourishing substances to the other deities, who in return maintain the cosmic order by bestowing rain, sun, progeny, cattle, and victories in due proportions on the worshiper. These auspicious circumstances and desired outcomes arising from a successful yajña are known as its fruit or results (*phala*). In chapter 8, I draw together the various threads introduced earlier in a discussion of the Bhāgavata-saptāha's outcomes. This will provide some answers to the questions posed in the opening vignette: What attracts and retains countless thousands of devotees to saptāha events? What unmet needs does the saptāha appear to fill? Why do these events seem to be growing in number, scale, and appeal year by year? From the perspectives of the sponsor, the exponent, and the audience, what makes the saptāha meaningful, authentic, and transformative? Edward Luce (2008) wrote of India's modernization taking place "in spite of the gods." This book is not so much an exploration of the success of the gods "in spite of modernity," but it takes the view that emergent religious practices, such as the contemporary saptāha, are themselves an aspect of modernity. I explore some internal, external, and global factors, including the sociopolitical context of rising middle-class religiosity, resurgent Hindu activism, and the wider context of Indian nationalism. All these are contributing to the development of the practice.

In the final act of the yajña, known as the *pūrṇāhuti*, the "complete oblation," the officiating priest pours one last ladleful into the fire. In the concluding chapter, my final offering, I reflect on the popularity of the Bhāgavatapurāṇa vis-à-vis other texts, I compare Bhāgavata-saptāhas with other oral performance traditions, I speculate on the future of this form of religious expression, and, finally, I share my personal experience of the transformative potential of these performances.

2

The Saptāha—Yajña

NOW THAT THE field for the ritual has been measured and prepared, it is time for the yajña itself, the act of worship in which the priest makes his offering to the deities. In Bhāgavata-saptāha performances, as exponents often remind their audiences, the offering consists of "spiritual knowledge" (*jñāna*), specifically in the form of narratives of the Divine. Like the Vedic offerings, this spiritual knowledge is offered up for the benefit of the deities, the sponsor, the audience, and the world at large.

In this chapter, I attempt to convey the look and feel of these "knowledge sacrifices," contrasting the different settings and the manner in which they were conducted. Of the dozen or so saptāha performances I have attended in full or in part, I have selected three to illustrate their great diversity, two from India and one from Australia.[1] Each of the three has a contrasting emotional atmosphere, a different approach to the text, and a distinctive theological thrust. This chapter provides, in effect, the context of the saptāha. The actual content of these events, the narratives from the Bhāgavatapurāṇa, are presented in chapter 5.

The first saptāha I will describe was held in October and November 2009, in the Shri Radha Sneh Bihari Ashram in Vrindavan. The exponent, Shri Mridul Kṛishna Shastri, is a famous and highly successful performer descended from a long and illustrious line of musicians. Much of his performance consisted of song, both Sanskrit verses from the Bhāgavatapurāṇa and songs of praise, known as *bhajans*, in Hindi. There was a great deal of communal singing and dancing on the part of the four hundred or so members of the audience, and as the tempo of the music accelerated, the atmosphere often bordered on ecstatic. Theologically, the discourse of this performance, like most I have attended, was rooted in the

Gauḍīya Vaiṣṇava tradition and was dominated by glorification of Rādhā, Kṛṣṇa's favorite consort among the gopīs.

The second event was held in November 2009 in the hamlet of Naluna on the banks of the Ganga River in the Garhwal foothills of the Himalayas. This was a much smaller, more intimate affair conducted in the setting of a rural community. As a personal guest of the sponsor, I was able to observe the proceedings closely and take part in the planning, preparation, and conduct of the event from start to finish. Unique features of this saptāha included the central role played by the village deity, or *grām-devtā*, and the fire offerings, the *havan*, which are always an integral part of saptāha performances in this district. As with the saptāha in Vrindavan, the theological focus of this event was also on Rādhā.

Radically different from these two performances was the third case study, a saptāha given by Acharya Shri Satchitananda Sai in Canberra, Australia, in April 2013. This event, conducted in English, was earnest, intense, sophisticated, and cerebral. The attendees ranged from students to families, mainly middle-class Indians living in Australia, some of whom were devotees of the Indian guru Sathya Sai Baba. The theological import of this event was strongly colored by the Advaita Vedānta nondualist philosophical position that "All this is One." At the same time, this saptāha was deeply suffused with bhakti, the intense personal sentiment of devotion to the Divine in the form of Viṣṇu-Kṛṣṇa. In the following sections, I attempt to bring to life the contrasting sights, sounds, and even scents of each of the events. These phenomena constitute the "meta-communicative" environment of the performances, which help condition the audiences' response and reception (Desai 2013, 9).

Mridul Krishna's Saptāha, Vrindavan

As soon as I stepped out of the three-wheeled taxi on arriving in Vrindavan, I knew that I would have no trouble locating a saptāha.[2] All around were large multicolored banners and posters advertising twenty different saptāha events, past, present, and future. According to one of them, an event was to run from 2:00–7:00 p.m. October 30 to November 6, 2009, at the Shri Radha Sneha Bihari Ashram. The exponent was Shri Mridul Krishna Shastri Ji Maharaj, a Vrindavan native and a direct descendant of Swami Haridas, a famous sixteenth-century poet-saint and composer. Mridul Krishna was born into an eminent musical family, and his performances are renowned for their musicality, especially for the devotional singing.

FIGURE 2.1. Poster advertising a saptāha by well-known exponent Shri Mridrul Krishna Shastri, Vrindavan, 2009.

The ashram was a handsome white four-story building in the heart of old Vrindavan, hemmed in by shops, ramshackle two- and three-story buildings, and wayside shrines under spreading banyan trees. A ceremonial arch of cloth stretched over a timber frame stood across the alley beside the ashram, and the street was filled with amplified devotional music. The lanes around the ashram were spotlessly clean and roofed over with white cotton awnings. Green synthetic carpet covered the ground, and comfortable folding chairs lined both sides of the street. Gathered around the entrance to the ashram were stalls selling garlands of red roses and marigolds and cheap plastic bangles. A few people were hovering around the entrance. It was a little before 2 p.m.

FIGURE 2.2. The approach to the Shri Radha Sneh Bihari Ashram, Bihari-pura, Vrindavan.

Stepping into the ashram was like entering another realm, a brilliantly lit Bollywood fantasy, part disco ballroom, part Hindu temple. Festooned with fairy lights, it was also lit by six vast chandeliers and twenty carbon-arc floodlights. Throbbing devotional music filled the hall through four huge speakers. High up on either side were balconies where musicians in white and orange kurtas were tuning up, and sound, light, and video technicians bustled about. The balustrades along the balconies were adorned with bunches of sparkling orange fabric and with posters of the young cow-herd Kṛṣṇa and his lover Rādhā, the gopī princess. Wreaths of plastic flowers hung on the pillars and arches. The space below the balconies formed long galleries, at the front of which were large flat-screen TVs, where the audience on each side could watch the proceedings.

The focal point was the stage at the front of the hall, standing one and a half meters above the hall floor. Painted canvas backdrops depicted an idealized temple scene, with arches and domes in bold primary colors, draped in garlands of marigolds. In the center of the stage was a double-paneled silver door behind which stood the main shrine with images of Kṛṣṇa and Rādhā. Two golden peacocks studded with "jewels" arched over the central door. On either side were life-size painted images of ascetics in saffron robes. Figures of two female attendants appeared to be waiting for the doors of the inner sanctum to swing open. The artwork was in a naive style, with the various flat canvas surfaces set at different depths giving the whole backdrop a three-dimensional appearance. The right-hand half of the stage was filled with a vacant peacock throne. On the left was a pot containing a *tulsi* plant, the species of basil sacred to Viṣṇu.

The front third of the hall was separated by white wooden fencing and was reserved for invited guests. By this time, about thirty VIPs, mostly women, were seated on the floor in front of the barrier. The older and middle-aged women wore gorgeous saris and gold jewelry, while the younger women and girls were in salwar-kamiz or Western-style clothes. The back of the hall was open to the public. Here numbers were growing slowly as people drifted in and sat down without ceremony on thin cotton mattresses, men on the right and women on the left, in about equal numbers. Old folks occupied folding chairs around the perimeter of the hall.

Live musicians eventually took over from the recorded music. The hall was filled with the booming of drums and the *ching-ching* of hand cymbals, with flute, harmonium, violin, and vocals. The devotional music was rhythmic, hypnotic. In the audience, heads and bodies swayed; some clapped in time, while others followed the words to the sacred songs in booklets in their laps.

By 3:10 p.m., the hall was nearly full. There were about four hundred people in the back area and about one hundred VIPs. In the public section, the men were mostly well dressed and appeared to be predominantly lower-middle-class, such as small-business people, shopkeepers, office clerks, and teachers. With the exception of one young man who was dressed in a grubby white kurta, dhoti, and colored scarf such as the rickshaw drivers wear, few appeared to be manual laborers or farming people. There was a scattering of shaven-headed renunciants in saffron robes and several sādhus in white. Half the men in the hall sported the single lock of hair of Kṛṣṇa devotees.

Four male ceremonial assistants (*pūjārīs*), in white kurtas and dhotis, each with a red scarf, bustled about on the stage. The music grew quieter, and one of the pūjārīs, a middle-aged man who acted as master of ceremonies, announced the arrival of the exponent, Mridul Krishna. We all stood as he entered the stage from the right. Mridul Krishna appeared to be about fifty years old, wearing a gleaming cream cloak over a pure white dhoti. A handsome man, he was immaculately groomed and slightly heavy, with a round face, black mustache, and carefully coiffured hair. He

FIGURE 2.3. Shri Mridul Krishna Shastri in performance. The text of the Bhāgavatapurāṇa is wrapped in fabric and heaped with marigolds on the lectern in front of the exponent.

bowed to the copy of the Bhāgavatapurāṇa that lay in front of the throne, half hidden beneath garlands of roses and crowned with a coconut. He then bowed before the silver doors at the center of the stage.

The sponsor of the saptāha, Ishvar Prasad Goyal, a merchant from Vrindavan, was a tall, thick-set man of sixty-five or seventy, with a powerful, prosperous air. He entered the stage, accompanied by his wife and family, and bowed to the exponent. In pairs, the party performed *āratī* to the speaker, a ritual offering with lights, incense, and flowers on a silver platter. The exponent then led a series of salutations to a number of deities, to which the audience responded with cries of "Victory!" while throwing their hands in the air.

Mridul Krishna sat in meditation for a moment, then began a song of praise to the guru in Sanskrit to the accompaniment of a violin: "The guru is Brahmā. The guru is Viṣṇu . . ." He continued to sing in Hindi and sometimes in Sanskrit, accompanied by violin, flute, or harmonium. This was followed by a bhajan in Hindi, "Beloved Rādhā, Glorious Rādhā," and as the music swelled, he added, "Beloved Śyāma, Śyāma, Śyāma," in homage to the "dark" image of Kṛṣṇa as the youthful cow-herd. The backing vocalists and the whole audience responded. A slight, birdlike woman with a sun-darkened face and a red and gold sari, her head veiled, stood and gyrated in time with the music, her eyes closed, smiling to herself and clapping her hands above her head.

After a time, as the beat accelerated, the atmosphere began to grow electric, and more and more people in the hall were infected by the rhythm. A few other members of the crowd began to dance and sing along, hands held aloft, including a beaming middle-aged man, his expression blissful. Several women leaped to their feet and danced facing the stage, hands in the air, swinging from side to side in time with the music. All the time, above all the other sounds, the flute, the favorite instrument of Kṛṣṇa, could be heard. The dancing was sensuous and abandoned, yet each woman seemed to be dancing in her own world, as if in the forests of Vraja itself.

The rhythm accelerated again, and now most of the crowd was on its feet. Two girls in the VIP section spun each other around in circles. The performance sped to a climax, and the atmosphere became ecstatic again. Too fast for clapping along, too fast for singing along, the exponent maintained his call of "Jay! Rādhe Rādhe Rādhe!" as the melody climbed up the scale in semitones. The tempo grew ever faster, climaxed, then exploded into silence. A slow release followed, as the tension drained away, and the audience joined hands in añjali as if in prayer.

As calm returned, everyone resumed his or her seat on the floor. It was now 4:00 p.m., and the exponent began the story of how Kṛṣṇa lifted Mount Govardhan with one finger to provide shelter from a storm for the people of Vraja. He spoke in clear, highly Sanskritic, "pure" (*shuddh*) Hindi, with a minimum of English loan words, as befitting the "traditional" religious atmosphere of the event. He included just the occasional verse of Sanskrit, while a violin played softly in the background as accompaniment. In the quiet hall, the audience listened attentively. Whenever Mridul Krishna sensed the audience's attention drifting, he punctuated his discourse with a call-and-response: "Bhagavān ki . . ." ("To the Lord . . ."), to which the audience would respond with "Jay!" ("Victory!") while throwing their hands in the air.

To the accompaniment of a flute, the exponent went on to speak about the love of the gopīs for Kṛṣṇa. Sometimes when he spoke with rising passion to make a point, the audience would clap a little in appreciation. In general, the exponent was extemporizing. He certainly never referred to the Sanskrit text on the front of the throne, which remained firmly wrapped in its crimson and gold cover,[3] but he did glance down from time to time at a notebook lying discreetly in his lap.

Mridul Krishna spoke on, his eyes closed. The music began to swell again; flute, bells, and harmonium played while the drums throbbed incessantly. The audience began to clap. Ten women in the central area leaped up to dance, swaying from side to side while singing along. The hall was packed, and the temperature was rising. At one point, two young men wove through the hall dousing the audience with rose-scented water from spray bottles. The birdlike village woman danced with eyes closed, smiling to herself. The exponent led a call of "Śrī Rādhe!" and the audience roared back.[4] Young girls danced energetically at the front of the VIP area. Older women swayed and clapped, arms aloft, palms forward as if for *darshan*. The music eventually built to a climax and suddenly fell silent again.

The exponent resumed his discourse without missing a beat. He repeated a famous verse from the Gītā ("Whenever obstacles to dharma appear . . . ," Bhagavadgītā 4.7), and those in the crowd who knew the words joined in. Again, he spoke of Kṛṣṇa and the gopīs in Vrindavan. By this point, he had performed for two hours without a break, yet he remained as composed as when he began.

By 5:30 p.m., the audience was reinvigorated with another round or two of "Śrī Rādhe!" as Mridul Krishna spoke of the centrality of love (*prem*) and gave the example of Hanumān's love for Rāma. This pattern of measured spoken discourse interspersed with call-and-response, leading up to periods of energetic dancing lasting up to twenty minutes, was repeated throughout the afternoon and early evening.

At 7:35 p.m., a young female actor wearing a brown sari, a red dupatta, and a tall gold crown appeared on the stage. This was Rukmiṇī, Kṛṣṇa's bride-to-be, accompanied by two attendants in pink and blue saris. The three danced somewhat awkwardly on one side of the stage as the exponent sang and the audience clapped. Suddenly, an actor playing Kṛṣṇa appeared from the right and "pursued" Rukmiṇī around the stage, eventually "capturing" her. The master of ceremonies entered, placed garlands around the couple's necks, and chanted benedictions in Sanskrit. The pair exchanged garlands as in a wedding ceremony and were showered with flowers. At this point, the sponsor and his family also reappeared onstage and presented gifts of clothes and trays of sweets to "Kṛṣṇa" and "Rukmiṇī" and performed āratī to them and to the exponent. Calls of "Jay ho!" filled the hall. The MC led a rendition of the well-known Sanskrit prayer "Tvam eva . . . ," while assistants helped the exponent arrange his possessions. Members of the audience performed half- or full-body prostrations facing the stage, before drifting toward the door. It was now 8:00 p.m., and piped sacred music replaced the live musicians as the crowd began to thin. The patron's family gave gifts to the exponent, who blessed them in return by placing his hand on their heads. He eventually rose from his throne, bowed once more to the bundled-up purāṇa, and disappeared into the inner sanctum behind the silver doors. A curtain closed behind him.

The floodlights were dimmed while prasād (blessed food), in this instance in the form of sweet deep-fried pellets of yellow batter, was distributed to the public. The hall emptied out as the piped music blared on. Finally, the sound cut out, the lights went down, and I ventured back out into the dark alleyway.

Saptāha at Naluna, Garhwal

The abiding impression of the hamlet of Naluna is the roar of the Ganga. Day and night, the rushing river is a constant presence. Less than eighty kilometers from its source, the Ganga at this stage of its journey has been likened to a young girl: pure, vivacious, and unsullied. In this region, steep hills spring up one thousand meters on both sides of the river, sometimes bare and rocky, sometimes dotted with forests, villages, and terraced fields. Yogendra Yadav, a friend and colleague from the Australian National University and part-time resident of Naluna, first raised the possibility of

FIGURE 2.4. The hamlet of Naluna on the Ganga, Garhwal district, Uttarakhand.

FIGURE 2.5. The garden at Naluna, showing the temporary tent for the saptāha on the left and the thatched pavilion for the fire sacrifice on the right.

holding a saptāha on his estate in March 2009.[5] Yogendra's property, set in two acres of gardens, consists of half a dozen bungalows on a narrow strip of land squeezed between the mountains and the river. An iron gate at the bottom of the garden opens directly onto the rocky bed of the river itself.

Naluna is about twenty kilometers upstream from Uttarkashi, a market town in Garhwal. Uttarkashi is about one day's drive from the railway station at Haridwar, which is itself about half a day by train from New Delhi. Three villages, Senj, Syawa, and Kumalti, lie within a rugged one to two hours' walk uphill from the road at Naluna. Each village is home to three hundred or four hundred people, mainly subsistence farmers growing wheat, dhal, sesame, and potatoes. Among themselves, the villagers speak Garhwali, but with outsiders, they communicate in Hindi.[6]

During winter, the nights at Naluna are freezing, and an icy wind blows down the river. The sun only creeps over the mountain ridge at about 9:30 a.m. By mid-morning, it is pleasantly warm, but as soon as the sun disappears below the hills again at 4:00 p.m., the temperature plummets.

By the time we arrived in early November 2009, a great amount of preparation had already been done. As early as April, the staff at Naluna had consulted the local village deity, the *grām-devtā*, who had given permission for the saptāha to proceed and had determined auspicious dates for the event: November 19 through 25. As Yogendra put it, "Whatever happens in the area of Senj, they have to ask the devtā."

The Senj Devtā

After the roar of the river, the yodeling shriek of the meter-long bugle that accompanies the devtā everywhere is the second-most-abiding impression of Naluna. The devtā, known as Kandar, inhabits a shrine in the village of Senj but communicates with devotees through a *ḍolī*, or palanquin. This consists of a hollow wooden cube about five hundred millimeters on each side, which is carried on two poles five meters long. The whole structure is covered with brilliant red drapes and brocades. The central box is ornamented with a silver girdle and capped with a peaked silver crown. The ḍolī is borne on the shoulders of two men from the village and is similar to palanquins used to carry brides during weddings in the Garhwal area (Sax 1990, 491).

FIGURE 2.6. The Senj devtā's palanquin, or *ḍolī*, carried by two men from the village.

FIGURE 2.7. The devtā's musicians, Lakshmi Lal, Dinesh, and Mayadas Minan.

While the ḍolī itself is empty, the devtā gives it *prāṇ* ("life" or "breath"), which causes it to rock from side to side and bob up and down. It is usually accompanied by three musicians from the village; two men beat large silver drums (*ḍhol*), and the other produces a piercing skirl on the horn (Alter 2008, 58, 69). Anyone may put questions to the devtā, and in response, the devtā induces movements in the ḍolī. Individuals may interpret the devtā's responses themselves, or they may consult one of the three or four senior men from the community who are able to interpret the ḍolī's movements for them.

In addition to the dates, the devtā also determined the site of the pavilion built to contain the ceremonial fire. This was a handsome structure about six meters square, with pillars on each side, a thatched roof, and a central pit where the sanctified fire was kindled and maintained throughout the saptāha. The fire ceremony and the conduct of much of the saptāha were under the direct supervision of Jagatram Uniyal, the senior Brahmin from Senj, a stocky, dour man in his sixties.

The other important structure was the tent in which the saptāha itself would be held. About ten meters square, it was erected on the concrete parking area at the top of the garden. Half a dozen chandeliers were suspended from the rafters, and lengths of green synthetic carpet were rolled out on the ground. At the front of the tent, a low stage with a throne was set up. To the left was a space for musicians and honored guests, and on the right was a bank of amplifiers and a tangle of wiring. Four old speakers were lashed to the tent poles. Two vintage bullhorns were mounted on the roof to broadcast the saptāha up and down the valley.

In the days leading up to the event, the garden was filled with activity. Women from the village delivered great loads of firewood. Local schoolgirls spent the day threading marigolds to make garlands. Bunting, garlands, and lights were hung all around the site. For several days, supplies from Rishikesh and Uttarkashi were delivered by truck or taxi to be stockpiled in a godown: five-gallon tins of ghee; sacks of rice, semolina, beans, flour, sugar, potatoes, and cauliflower; and thousands of paper plates and disposable cups. In addition to the main kitchen, four temporary kitchens were set up in the garden.

Twelve Brahmins were required for the fire ceremony; extra staff had been hired to help with the cooking, in addition to the half dozen workers usually on-site. Fifteen house guests and the devtā's musicians all had to be accommodated. A small guest house across the road had been fully booked, and additional bundles of bedding were borrowed from a pilgrims' hostel down the road.

The tempo increased measurably with the arrival of the Senj devtā on the evening of November 16. It is considered a great honor to host the devtā; this was his first visit to Naluna, where he would remain for the whole week. His approach through the darkness was heralded by the thump of his two drums and the shriek of his bugle. There was a commotion at the front gate as first the musicians and then the devtā burst into the light. Yogendra and the head Brahmin greeted the ḍolī with garlands and a platter of offerings. The blare of a conch shell and the clanging house bell added to the cacophony. After a moment, the devtā headed back into the darkness toward the fire pavilion, where he would spend the night.

The Saptāha Commences

Many years previously, Yogendra's paternal grandfather had died while serving in the Indian army, but his final funerary rites had never been performed. One of the goals of the saptāha was therefore the "salvation and homage" of the sponsor's ancestor. Yogendra had assembled four items that belonged to his grandfather: part of his military uniform, a small

FIGURE 2.8. The exponent, Shri Bhadri Prasad Nautiyal (center) arrives at Naluna. A senior man from the community carries the text of the Bhāgatapurāṇa on his head.

vessel, a wooden bowl, and a copper kettle. These were all carefully placed in the fire pavilion.

At 11:30 a.m. on the first day of the saptāha, there was a sudden burst of activity. The devtā's drums had started, and people streamed toward the front gate. A white truck pulled up, and an older man got out and placed a thick, oblong red bundle on his head—the text of the Bhāgavatapurāṇa. Surrounded by the drums and horns, the exponent also appeared, wearing a white sweater, pink kurta, and cream dhoti. Around age forty, Sri Bhadri Prasad Nautiyal Ji Shastri was neatly groomed, with the single long lock of a Kṛṣṇa devotee and a confident, friendly disposition. The devtā bowed long and low to the text of the Bhāgavatapurāṇa. After the exponent was greeted, honored, and garlanded, the devtā led the procession into the tent.

Over the next four hours, two important rituals were completed: the *kalaśa-sthāpana* ("setting up the pitchers") and the *saṃkalpa* ("statement of intent"). The devtā led a procession of nine young girls, each representing one of the nine planets, all neatly dressed in school uniform, down to the Ganga. Each girl filled a small brass pitcher with water, and after a brief pūjā, the procession returned toward the tent. Seated on the floor, the head Brahmin, the exponent, Yogendra, and his family undertook a long ritual in which the pitchers were transformed into miniature auspicious universes, into which specific deities were invoked.

The Yadavs are not considered to be one of the three higher *varṇas* (castes) and are therefore not normally able to take part in the fire ceremony. In the second ritual, Yogendra and his elderly father were given temporary "twice-born" status to allow them to do so. Yogendra also took a vow (saṃkalpa) to complete all seven days of the saptāha. At the conclusion of the ceremony, a grand procession advanced from the tent to the fire pavilion, led by the devtā and Yogendra's father carrying the Bhāgavatapurāṇa on his head. Family and guests carried the nine pitchers, all accompanied by blasts on the conch, the ringing of bells, and devotional music. The whole procession then walked around the pavilion, where the sacred pitchers were installed.

By 4:30 p.m., after months of planning and weeks of preparation, the first kathā session finally began. Before a sparse audience of twenty people, the exponent took his place on the throne in the tent, with the Bhāgavatapurāṇa wrapped in red fabric on a low altar in front of him. Three young Brahmin musicians sat on the left: a vocalist/harmonium player, a mridanga player, and a flautist. The devtā rested on a bench on the right. While the musicians sang bhajans, Bhadri Prasad unwrapped the text and rapidly cast his eyes over the first few pages. At the conclusion of the bhajans, the devtā was brought before the throne, and the head Brahmin led Yogendra and his wife in a brief pūjā. All the while, the energetic drumming of the devtā mixed with the Brahmins' chanting. To an outsider, the juxtaposition could hardly have been more striking: the wild mountain music of the village deity and the sweet melodiousness of the bhajans, harmonium, and flute. Yet the cultures of the mountains and the plains are regarded by the local people to meld into a single syncretic whole.

Bhadri Prasad completed his silent reading by 5:00 p.m. and, accompanied by the flute and the harmonium, began a slow song of praise in Sanskrit, "Keśava mādhava, o deva madhusūdana." His first spoken words were "Victory to Viṣṇu! Victory to the Glorious Great Bhāgavatapurāṇa! Victory to the glorious deity, Kandar!" He then delivered a discourse on the power and significance of listening to the Bhāgavatapurāṇa. He spoke clearly, confidently, with conviction and passion. The pattern of his performance, with flute or harmonium improvising softly in the background, the rise and fall of his intonation, and his overall manner and presentation were all strongly reminiscent of those of Mridul Krishna in Vrindavan. The two exponents were clearly of the same "school" of saptāha performance.

By 5:30 p.m., it was already cold and gloomy, and most of the villagers had set out for home. Few risked the one-to-two-hour trek uphill in the dark; leopards, bears, and ghosts are said to make the path dangerous at night. The exponent went on to recount familiar narratives from the Māhātmya (see chapter 5). After about an hour, the session ended with a round of "Victory" calls. The dozen or so people in the audience, primarily Yogendra's family, staff, and guests, approached the throne and joined in the āratī led by a young Brahmin. The devtā's drums and horn rang out, and we again experienced that strange but haunting blend of mountain and plains culture. The exponent wrapped the Bhāgavatapurāṇa in two layers of cloth, while prasād, in this case sweet semolina halva, was distributed. We ended with a final round of "Victory" calls at 6:45 p.m. Bhadri Prasad packed up his effects and retired to the guest house across the road for the evening.

The Middle Days

For the staff at Naluna, the following days of the saptāha began before 4 a.m., when the exponent expected his hot water for bathing. Seated on his throne in the tent, long before dawn, he would read one or two skandhas

FIGURE 2.9. Shri Bhadri Prasad Nautiyal (far right), exponent at Naluna. A sādhu (holy man) and the musicians (at left).

(books) of the Bhāgavatapurāṇa each day, finishing by about 11 a.m., with the aim of reading the entire text during the course of the week.

Rituals were conducted in the fire pavilion every morning, starting at dawn and finishing just before midday. The head Brahmin, assisted by eight to ten others and accompanied by various members of Yogendra's family, sat on the floor around the fire in the central pit. The yajña consisted of offering sacred substances into the fire to the accompaniment of continuous recitation of Sanskrit mantras.

At 11:30 a.m. on the second day of the saptāha, there was a burst of drumming, accompanied by shrieks from the bugle and the incessant clang of the house bell. This marked the arrival of the second devtā, the "brother" of the first. This devtā, whose home village was Kumalti, had a palanquin identical to that of the Senj devtā. Amid the drumming and bugling, the Kumalti devtā bowed long and deep to the throne, after which Yogendra welcomed him with a brief ritual. The two devtās then bowed deeply and circled each other with "heads" down, their silver spikes almost touching. The Kumalti devtā bowed long and low to the drummers, before heading down the hill toward the fire pavilion.

At 1:30 p.m. when the second kathā session was due to commence, the tent was empty, except for the harmonium and mridanga players and one or two expectant onlookers. Bhadri Prasad appeared ten minutes later, bowed to the throne, and saluted the Bhāgavatapurāṇa. He began with tributes, sung in Sanskrit, to Vyāsa and Gaṇeśa and followed with a round of "Victory" calls and bhajans in Hindi. Village folk began to drift in, placing offerings of small bags of grain, flowers, fruit, or ten-rupee notes at the front of the stage. The audience, smaller at first, gradually swelled to seventy or eighty as the week progressed. Women and children presented a rainbow of colors in their Garhwali skirts, blouses, sweaters, and scarves. A few younger women wore plains-style salwar-kamiz. The village men, who sat apart from the women, wore Western clothes or Nehru jackets in shades of beige, gray, and brown. The only group under-represented was boys and young men, who probably had preferred to attend two weddings in nearby villages. Every day, one or two sādhus would drift in and take a seat next to the musicians.

Clapping and singing became much more enthusiastic as the crowd grew. Between songs, the audience sat still for hour after hour in rapt attention. The sessions began to develop a palpable sense of occasion. I tried to imagine the perspective of a villager who lived in a smoky, windowless hut two hours' trek from the road. The white tent with its pink valances, Chinoiserie backdrop, chandeliers, and booming sound system, not to mention the free meals, must all have seemed exotic, otherworldly, and the peak of sophistication.

During the middle days of the saptāha, the exponent progressed through the narratives of the Bhāgavatapurāṇa, sometimes lingering over a single episode, other times skipping rapidly over entire sections. Each session included only three or four verses of Sanskrit, some of which were from sources other than the Bhāgavatapurāṇa, such as the Bhagavadgītā. Like Mridul Krishna, this exponent spoke in pure, shuddh Hindi, with only the occasional English loan word, fitting for a solemn, "traditional" religious event.

Interspersed with the discourse was some contemporary sermonizing in a socially conservative vein. At various points, Bhadri Prasad spoke of the power of remembering the name of God, the importance of respecting Brahmins, and the necessity of adhering to the traditional duties of one's varṇa (caste). He lamented the fact that people in India were "losing their culture" and were, for example, wearing jeans instead of traditional garments such as the dhoti.

By 4:00 p.m. each day, we reached the final round of "Victory" calls. The devtā's drums and horn led Yogendra and his family to the throne, where they performed āratī. Everyone threw flower petals in the direction of the throne and performed a "circumambulation" by turning around on the spot with hands held in an añjali gesture. After the prasād had been distributed, the villagers, cheerfully chatting among themselves, drifted toward the gate, where small paper plates of halva were distributed. The tent was empty except for the boom of piped music and the rose petals and marigolds scattered on the green carpet.

I asked several people what had attracted them to the event. One man in his twenties said that he came to hear the "stories about God"; another said "to get good knowledge." A woman of about the same age said that listening to the kathā "causes you to think about God." Another person cynically added that a good outing, a break from manual labor and a chance to escape from his mother-in-law were further attractions. The saptāha, he added on a more serious note, was also an opportunity for local people to experience and demonstrate their faith.

During these middle days, I also had the opportunity to ask the exponent about himself. Bhadri Prasad had been born in Senj. Speaking in Hindi, he told me that his father had sent him to "university" in Vrindavan to specialize in purāṇic recital, because "he wanted the Sanskrit tradition to continue." During his five years of training, he studied two to three verses of the Bhāgavatapurāṇa per day: "Just as a bee takes nectar from a flower, we took the honey of the Bhāgavatapurāṇa just a little at a time and returned often." He graduated with a *shastri* (master's) degree in 1994. This was the seventh saptāha he had conducted since graduating. He now lived in the nearby village of Gangori.

The Final Day

On the last day of the saptāha at Naluna, the kitchens were busy as usual starting at around 4:30 a.m. The devtā was "woken" with drums and the horn at 5:40, and devotional music was blasting over the PA an hour later. The final kathā session was scheduled for nine o'clock. There was some unexplained delay, but no one seemed perturbed. At 10:15, a pretty half-grown white calf with garlands and ribbons around its neck was led down the drive to be presented to Bhadri Prasad as part of his fee. The bhajans began, and the exponent started his opening Sanskrit chants while the devtā's drums reverberated in the background.

Between the bhajans and the "Victory" cries, Yogendra ascended the stage and placed a gold ring on the exponent's finger. The final session

FIGURE 2.10. The devtā on the banks of the Ganga.

FIGURE 2.11. A crowd gathers around the front gate of Naluna.

was similar to those of the preceding days, concluding at around 1:20 p.m., when the two devtās arrived in the tent. Both were rocking "excitedly" in front of the throne. The air was thick with drums, horns, bells, and incense. A large crowd had gathered, and the atmosphere grew frenzied. A young woman fell into a trance, writhed across the floor, and attempted to wrest the āratī salver from the hands of the officiating priest, before falling back anonymously into the crowd.

The two devtās then led a procession to the Ganga, where the exponent sat in contemplation on a rock by the river while bells and conches rang out and the drums and bugle were sounded. Both devtās bowed so deeply to the Ganga that their silver spikes touched the water. As the head Brahmin conducted a brief pūjā at the water's edge, I was amazed at the dazzling colors, the primal sounds, the beauty of the river and the mountains, and the mystique and power of the devtās.

Back at the tent, in the presence of both devtās, the head Brahmin conducted a closing ceremony in which everyone was thanked, and the coconuts, which had crowned the pitchers in the fire pavilion, were distributed. At this point, a second person, this time a middle-aged man, become possessed, and, hissing and panting, he surged forward to pour a handful of rice into Yogendra's palm. Meanwhile, tarpaulins had been spread out in the garden, and plates and cups had been set out for prasād, the final meal of blessed food. About seventy men took their places, while the staff moved up and down the lines, doling out rice, dhal, and curried vegetables. A popular devotional song, "Śrī Rādhe Rādhe," blared out over the PA as we ate together in the sun. Almost as one, the men finished their meal and stood up. Their places were taken immediately by the women and girls, and plates, cups, and food were dealt out a second time. Once the women had eaten, three more places were set, and three more meals were served, this time for the devtā's musicians. Being members of the Dalit ("Untouchable") community, they ate last and separately.

By 4:00 p.m., the sun was already setting, and many of the attendees headed for home, eating halva from paper cups as they went. Both devtās were preparing to leave, their "skirts" tucked up for the return journey. The Kumalti devtā received a last round of honors and a new red and gold scarf from Yogendra and his wife. At last, after a final bout of bobbing, bowing, and "affectionate" touching of spikes, the Senj devtā escorted his "younger brother" out of the gate. The Kumalti devtā was lifted onto the roof of a battered truck and disappeared up the road.

Back in the tent, Yogendra presented the Brahmins with white envelopes containing their fees for the week. Then, carrying the text of the Bhāgavatapurāṇa on his own head, led by the drums and bugle, Yogendra and the devtā escorted Bhadri Prasad up the drive and onto the road. The Bhāgavatapurāṇa, the exponent, his assistants, and all their luggage were loaded into a second truck, which headed off downhill. Finally, at 4:50 p.m., the drums and bugle led the Senj devtā and his entourage up the drive one last time. They turned onto to the road and headed for home. We watched the procession until the devtā, on the shoulders of his bearers, disappeared around a bend in the road.

In the days that followed, the sound system was hurried off to its next venue, and the tent was dismantled. All the borrowed bedding, pots, and pans were returned to their owners. The decorative lights came down, and the leftover sacks of flour and tins of ghee were given away. Naluna slowly returned to normal, and once we were gone, the only sound in the garden would be the never-ending roar of the river again. It is difficult to imagine a sharper contrast between the wild mountain setting of Naluna and suburban Canberra, the site of my third and final case study.

Sri Vishnu Shiva Mandir, Canberra

It was already dark when I drove into the parking lot of the Sri Vishnu Shiva Mandir, a community temple in Canberra, Australia, for the first session of the saptāha in April 2013. I was feeling nervous, a little excited, and lucky to be getting in at all, as I had only heard about the event on the grapevine a few days before. This was an excellent opportunity to attend a saptāha in my own hometown and was a chance to experience a saptāha in a diasporic setting conducted in English. This was in contrast to the other events I had attended, all of which had been in India and in Hindi.

Light from the temple porch streamed out. The forecourt was crowded with tidily aligned pairs of shoes and sandals, just as the little notice had requested: "Please place your shoes neatly." A large bowl of fresh fruit stood as an offering before an image of Gaṇeśa in the vestibule, where I signed the attendance register. The gray brick interior of the hall had been transformed into a breathtaking sacred space. Gorgeous bolts of orange and purple silk were suspended from the ceiling all around the perimeter walls. Against the back wall hung a huge glossy backdrop depicting Viṣṇu holding a conch, discus, lotus, and mace, set amid an idealized pastoral scene. All around the mandir, the regular shrines and images had been freshly garlanded. The air was sweet with incense, and the sounds of a distant flute and sylvan birdsong were playing softly over the PA system. With sights, scents, and sounds, the senses were being prepared for a virtual excursion to the forests of Vraja. Physically, we were in Canberra; mentally, the audience was being primed for mythical Vrindavan.

I found a place among the forty or so devotees already occupying the rows of stackable plastic chairs toward the rear of the hall. A dozen people in their teens and twenties sat on rugs on the floor toward the front, males on one side, females on the other. Everyone was beautifully dressed, the older women in saris, the younger women in salwar-kamiz, the young men in brilliantly colored kurtas, decked out as they would be for a wedding.

On a carpeted platform in the center of the hall was a golden throne draped in brocades, with a low table in front of it. Here sat the exponent, Acharya Shri Satchitananda Sai, smiling warmly to devotees as they settled in. He was in his late thirties, corpulent and kindly, with thick black hair tied back in a short topknot and a dark beard lightly frosted with silver, dressed in a traditional white wrap with orange trim.

As an audio technician fine-tuned the sound system, a devotee tended to bunches of flowers on the low table, and a young assistant took up his

FIGURE 2.12. Acharya Shri Satchitananda Sai during the saptāha in Canberra, 2013.

position behind the throne, the exponent propped up his iPad on the table in front of him. An expectant silence descended over the gathering. A young female singer started a round of bhajans, accompanied by harmonium and tabla, while a boy no more than ten years old kept time conscientiously with a pair of hand cymbals. The congregation knew all the bhajans and sang along while clapping energetically.

Once we had settled back into silence and after some housekeeping announcements, the MC, a leading figure of the *mandir* (temple) management team, welcomed us and introduced the exponent. This was Shri Satchitananda Sai's fourth saptāha in Australia, following earlier events in Melbourne and Sydney. The MC wished us all happiness and hoped that the end of the saptāha "journey" would see us ready "to take the next step into life."

After the introductory speeches, the exponent rose and performed a brief pūjā before an image of Gaṇeśa, and to Rādhā, Kṛṣṇa, and Viṣṇu, to ensure that the event would run smoothly. Bearing a small copy of the Bhāgavatapurāṇa in his hands, Satchitananda Sai, accompanied by the temple's resident priest, performed a circumambulation of the various shrines. Settled again on the throne, with a garlanded image of Kṛṣṇa on the low table in front of him, he tweaked the controls of his electronic drone and then began his discourse.

The First Session: Māhātmya

The introductory session that first evening dealt, as usual, with the Māhātmya, the prefatory text that describes the "greatness" of the Bhāgavatapurāṇa. This consists of several narratives that illustrate the salvific power of hearing the saptāha. Satchitananda Sai's delivery was rapid, witty, warm, and charismatic. Satchitananda Sai also gave his own introduction to the Bhāgavatapurāṇa:

> Śrīmad-bhāgavata is the greatest treasure that was ever given to mankind. The Bhāgavata itself will say it in several places, and in the Bhāgavata-māhātmya we will also be talking about it, how it is a rare, inestimable gift that has been given to mankind. This is a seven-day yajña. When we think of a yajña, we might immediately conjure a vision in our minds of sitting around a sacred fire offering various things into it. That is only one type of yajña, called *dravya-yajña*. There are several other types of yajña that are spoken about, and the Śrīmad-bhāgavata is called the *jñāna-yajña*—a sacrifice like every other yajña, but this is an offering of wisdom. The Śrīmad-bhāgavata-saptāha jñāna-yajña is the greatest Kṛṣṇa-pūjā that one can do. It is the greatest *Kṛṣṇopāsana* ["Kṛṣṇa worship"] that one can perform. Various types of worship are spoken about in our scriptures, but this, Kṛṣṇa himself says, is the greatest worship for him. What we are going to be doing over the next seven days is guaranteed to change your life if you listen to it with your heart. (Satchitananda Sai 2013, disc 1, track 1)[7]

This passage gives a taste of the discourse as it was spoken. I have left detailed analysis for a later chapter, but even at this early stage, it is instructive to draw attention to several strategies mobilized by the speaker here. First is the status accorded to the text, which he described as "the greatest treasure ever given to mankind." Speakers frequently reiterate the point that the text is powerful, transformative, and authoritative in its own right. Second is the use of the text itself as evidence: the Bhāgavatapurāṇa is the greatest treasure, as the text itself says. One of the primary functions of the Bhāgavatapurāṇa in saptāha performances is to provide scriptural evidence or justifications for points made during the spoken discourse. The third point of interest is the explicit linking of the contemporary saptāha with the yajña, the Vedic fire sacrifice described in chapter 1. By drawing this parallel, the speaker claimed equal status for the saptāha and the yajña, traditionally held to be the most profound and powerful ritual, thereby conveying the sanctity of the next seven days. The final point is the transformative nature of the saptāha itself. From the very outset, Satchitananda Sai, and indeed most exponents I have heard, sought to instill in the minds of audience members the belief that the saptāha will change their lives in some beneficial way.

For an hour or so, Satchitananda Sai continued to expound on the narratives from the Māhātmya, to which I return in detail in chapter 5. After the first session ended, I had Satchitananda Sai's portentous "solemn promise" stuck in my head: "At some time during the next seven days, each one of you will be touched to the core of your being."

Mornings

Arriving at the mandir a little before 9:30 the next morning, I found an atmosphere of brisk efficiency. Attendants and devotees hovered about the throne and the altar, adjusting microphones, attending to the flowers, plumping cushions. At 9:30 a.m. sharp, Satchitananda Sai entered with an open case in his hands, followed by four or five young attendants. From the case, he drew out an image of Kṛṣṇa, which he reverently installed on the altar and affectionately garlanded. He shared warm smiles with his attendants and with members of the audience, while one attendant set up his iPad on the altar. As the exponent was seated only a few meters from the nearest members of the audience, direct personal communication was possible, in great contrast to the more impersonal atmosphere of many of the larger saptāha events I had attended. This more intimate setting allowed the exponent to laugh and joke, weep and empathize with people seated in the hall.

The morning session, like all later ones, opened with three rounds of *Oṁ namo nārāyaṇāya*, "Homage to Nārāyaṇa" (one of the forms of Viṣṇu-Kṛṣṇa) and invocations and prayers to gurus and deities. This was followed by the first three verses of the Bhāgavatapurāṇa, sung very softly by Satchitananda Sai. He then led a number of bhajans, during which the audience clapped in time and sang along. These served to create a sense of *communitas*, a shared experience of togetherness, sanctity, and expectation. After a moment of silent meditation, the exponent roused the audience with the call *Sarvatra Govinda-nāma-saṅkīrtanam* "Praise the name of Govinda everywhere!" The audience responded with a hearty "Govinda, Govinda!"[8]

The narratives from the Bhāgavatapurāṇa were, as expected, the central organizing feature of the seven days' discourse, and Sanskrit verses from the root text, as many as thirty in a session, served to anchor the spoken discourse in the authority and rhythm of the written text. Occasionally referring to his iPad, Satchitananda Sai also glanced from time to time at a fat exercise book in his lap. While he chanted the Sanskrit verses, he also occasionally sang snatches of devotional songs in Tamil in a sweeter, melodious register. The main points from Satchitananda Sai's discourse in the first session are summarized as follows. They include many of the central doctrinal themes that recurred during later sessions.

According to the speaker, Kṛṣṇa appears in the world at times such as these when dharma ("tradition") is in decline. He has taken an avatāra as the Bhāgavatapurāṇa to protect Mokṣa-dharma, Bhāgavata-dharma, and Bhakti-dharma, the last of which is the supreme dharma. Kṛṣṇa himself "entered the ocean of the Bhāgavata"; the text is actually Kṛṣṇa in the form of speech, the "verbal, oral, aural form of the Lord." It is the embodiment of the Lord in the Kali-yuga and is the most expedient means of attaining the Divine in this decadent age. As such, the Bhāgavata has power. Simply by listening to it, "Bhāgavan is entering you through your ears." "Every word of the Śrīmad-bhāgavata is Bhāgavan." Reciting or listening to the Bhāgavata results in emancipation, or *mukti*. It was revealed by the Lord to establish bhakti (devotion), jñāna (spiritual knowledge), and vairāgya (detachment). In reciting and hearing the Bhāgavata, these qualities will flourish, and Vaikuṇṭha—the highest goal in life, the abode of the Lord, the state of pure bliss and happiness—will come into the palm of one's hand. Vaikuṇṭha is "the *ānanda*, the transcendental bliss, that comes naturally while listening to stories of the Lord." In listening with devotion to the Bhāgavata-saptāha, one's life and attitude toward the world will be transformed. One will not relate to God in the same way but will see him in an entirely different light. "Bhāgavan will be more intimate to you than yourself." "No other sādhana is easier, more efficacious, or quicker, because the self is already you. You are already the Divine Absolute, Brahman. You yourself are Vaikuṇṭha. Your real nature is Vaikuṇṭha: pure peace, pure bliss, pure love."

Some of the themes mentioned above in relation to the Māhātmya are reiterated here. First is the empowerment of the text, this time by stressing its identity with Kṛṣṇa. Second, the exponent also stresses the transformational nature of the discourse, saying that by attending closely, an individual will be "changed forever." Third, there is an infusion of Advaita philosophy which recognizes the unity of the individual and the Divine.

In addition to the narratives and the core theology, Satchitananda Sai laced his exposition every day with catchy homespun wisdom. For example, "If you don't want to do something, you'll find a million excuses. If you do want to do something, you only need one excuse." There were multiple references from a wide range of sources including Jesus, Abraham Lincoln, Saint Francis of Assisi, Guru Nanak, and the Jewish tradition. He skillfully maintained the audience's attention by laughing, joking, and teasing and by throwing in the occasional rhetorical prompt "Do you follow?" While there was plenty of humor, the general atmosphere was at the same time earnest and attentive, with none of the musical interludes or abandoned dancing and shouting of the saptāha in Vrindavan.

Satchitananda Sai could also evoke strong emotional responses and was at times choked with tears himself. There were moments of great intensity; at one point, he lifted the image of Kṛṣṇa from the table and, cradling it in his arms, led the audience in an intense *kirtan* (song of praise), "Kṛṣṇāya vāsudevāya hare nārāyaṇāya," which I described in my notes as "ecstatic and discordant." One female devotee, overcome with emotion, sobbed aloud, "Kṛṣṇa!" So engrossed was one young man in a particular narrative that at one point, seeming to forget where he was, he called out unselfconsciously, "What happened next?"

The morning session each day ended at eleven. During the thirty-minute break, lines quickly formed in the canteen next to the hall. Tea and coffee were served in paper cups, and volunteers doled out cookies, cake, and halva on paper plates. Attendees carried their morning tea out into the courtyard to find warming patches of autumn sun, where they stood chatting in groups of three or four. Satchitananda Sai moved regally among the participants with an attendant or two, greeting devotees as he went.

During saptāha events, the exponent "becomes" the sage Vyāsa. Satchitananda Sai had also said, "For the next seven days, I am Kṛṣṇa and Śrīman Nārāyaṇa himself." Wrapped in a certain aura, exponents may seem formal, distant, and difficult to approach during saptāha events, and mundane chitchat is generally discouraged. Satchitananda Sai had earlier instructed the audience simply "to imbibe the nectar" of the Bhāgavatapurāṇa, and he warned against asking "silly questions." I felt that most of my research questions, being largely practical and non-spiritual, relating as they did to the nuts-and-bolts aspects of the saptāha, would fall into this category. I was slightly embarrassed to be introduced to Satchitananda Sai as the "Sanskrit professor from the university," but he was unfailingly warm, and with perfect manners and disarming humility, he apologized for the fact that he had "never learned Sanskrit properly."

While Satchitananda Sai might have been unreceptive to "silly questions," these daily tea breaks, both morning and afternoon, provided excellent opportunities for interacting with fellow attendees, who were always happy to share their opinions, insights, and experiences. Most were devotees of the late Indian guru Sathya Sai Baba, and belonged to various Sai groups all over Australia. The Sri Vishnu Shiva Mandir, which was hosting the saptāha, usually caters to the local Tamil community, and most of the attendees, like Satchitananda Sai himself, were Tamil speakers. An average of about seventy-five people attended each day, more on the public holidays, fewer on workdays. Men and women were represented in about equal numbers, and there were many older people and retirees, but there were also plenty of younger people, including students and professionals in their twenties. Most had come because of Satchitananda Sai's reputation, either having attended his previous saptāhas or having heard of him from others.

Satchitananda Sai had grown up in Sai Baba's ashram in Andhra Pradesh, where he had become a "direct disciple" of the guru, and thus enjoyed special status among the devotees at the saptāha. With an MA in computer programming and in the middle of a successful career as an IT business analyst, he told me in an email, he had "received a call from the Divine to take up this mission." He has lived in Australia since 2006 and has now established an ashram in suburban Melbourne, the Jnana Vedanta Institute. Satchitananda Sai has grown in stature in the Sai community. As one member said, "He was like our son; now he is our guru." He was the object of great affection among many attendees, who could see in him the imprint of their late guru, who had died not long before. A devotee said, "He is very like Sai Baba. He speaks very like Sai Baba." An Anglo-Australian in his forties who had also been a devotee of the elder Sai commented that "Sai Baba speaks through Guru-ji. His way of speaking and gesticulation reminds me of Sai Baba." A Sri Lankan in her fifties put it this way: "Acharya's teachings are Swami's teachings. He teaches what he learned from Swami."

Each day, the second session started promptly at 11:30 a.m. Once the attendees were all seated, Satchitananda Sai, leading his small entourage, returned to the throne. The sessions proceeded as described earlier, and although the exponent remarked humorously on the first day that "Brahmā alone exists. This is the truth. Śrīmad-bhāgavata is finished," there was plenty of further material. Breaking for lunch at one o'clock, Satchitananda Sai and his attendants would return the image of Kṛṣṇa to its carrying case before leaving the hall in procession.

Afternoons and Evenings

Lunch was different every day but was usually a variation on dhal, vegetable curry, roti, papadams, and halva. The chef, a young man from the local Indian community, efficiently managed teams of volunteers in the kitchen. Everyone was encouraged to take part in devotional service known as *sevā*, and a roster had been drawn up on butcher's paper for morning tea, afternoon tea, and lunch. I joined a group of women chopping cauliflower, carrots, and pumpkins for the next day's menu. While many attendees went home for an afternoon rest, sevā afforded a good opportunity to chat with those who stayed behind. I had many conversations with other attendees who were reading, dozing, or chatting in the mandir, during which they spoke about their motivations, experiences, and general reactions to the saptāha.

One older Indian man who had moved to Australia some years ago commented on Satchitananda Sai's "godly appearance" and magnetic personality: "If he laughs, you would like to laugh." This man confided that he had had "big problems" in his meditation in the last two months, but as a result of listening to the saptāha, "My doubts got cleared." An Anglo-Australian woman in her forties commented, "I am listening to the stories like a child listening to bedtime stories. I am not listening with this [tapping her head], but I want to listen with this [placing her hand on her heart]. I am waiting for something to split this open." Another Anglo-Australian, a man in his late sixties who had only joined a Sai group recently, said, "I don't understand much. I let it flow over me. Every now and then, something jumps out." One day, I was washing dishes in the kitchen with an Australian-born Indian IT professional in his early twenties. He told me, "The saptāha is amazing. The best experience of my life. As the *āchārya* said in the Māhātmya, it is a wonderful transformative experience. How you get close to Bhagavān is through bhakti." Another man, in his thirties, reported that he had come to the saptāha "to hear the name of the Lord and to get away from all the rubbish," contemptuously waving one hand in the direction of the outside world.[9]

At 4:30 p.m. sharp, Satchitananda Sai returned from lunch with his entourage. He reinstalled the image of Kṛṣṇa on the altar. After another round of opening prayers and a hearty response of "Govinda!" from the audience, he resumed his exposition on the familiar pattern: verses from the Bhāgavata intoned in Sanskrit to initiate a new direction in the narrative, to prove a point, or to carry the narrative forward. Unfailingly humorous, Satchitananda Sai prodded the audience with rhetorical questions and teased them with frequent digressions about modern life: PowerPoint, Outlook, Bluetooth, Google Maps, and hands-free technologies all received mentions. After a tea break from 6:00 to 6:30 p.m., the final session concluded at 8:00 p.m. each evening. Such was the pattern for all seven days. Satchitananda Sai appeared to be tireless, in spite of trying to fight off a head cold, and his energy never flagged.

Two Events

For a number of days, the mandir's resident priest and one or two assistants had been working discreetly on two small construction projects on the sidelines of the saptāha. In one, a child's outdoor swing set was artfully transformed into a divine cradle wreathed with leaves and garlands. During the evening session of the fifth day, the whole assembly took part in a nativity play—part tableau, part pūjā—in which an image of the infant Kṛṣṇa was lovingly laid in the cradle on the converted swing and worshiped in turn by every person present. Satchitananda Sai's four-year-old daughter, dressed gorgeously as Kṛṣṇa's elder brother Balarāma and supervised by her mother, was the first to rock the cradle. Women from the audience then offered milk, butter, and curds to the baby, and all devotees waited in line to worship the infant, some with a simple añjali gesture, others with a full-body prostration, before devoutly rocking the cradle with their own hands.[10]

The second project that had been occupying the priest and his helpers was a throne and canopy for a wedding. The last book of the Bhāgavatapurāṇa, the twelfth skandha, ends with the destruction of Kṛṣṇa's clan, the Yādavas, and his own death. To avoid ending with such tragedy and to bring the event to a suitably joyous, auspicious conclusion, the last day, as is often the case with saptāhas, ended with a flashback to the tenth

FIGURE 2.13. The marriage of Kṛṣṇa and Rukmiṇī at the Canberra saptāha.

skandha: Kṛṣṇa's wedding to Rukmiṇī. Each attendee had received a beautifully printed wedding invitation, and we had been requested to wear our finest clothes for the occasion. During the final session on the last day, the hall had been reconfigured for the wedding. The exponent's throne had been dismantled, and the audience seating had been rearranged to face the brilliant nuptial throne at the other end of the hall. Outside the main entrance of the mandir, a great throng, which had now swollen to several hundred, all in their most gorgeous wedding clothes, lined up on both sides of the entrance. Images of Kṛṣṇa and Rukmiṇī, borne on a palanquin by half a dozen young men from the community, were welcomed with music, kirtans, and joyous noise. A coconut was ritually cracked open as devotees stretched forward to touch the images. Kṛṣṇa and his bride-to-be were carried into the mandir and placed on the throne, and the community's regular priest intoned appropriate nuptial mantras. The couple "exchanged" garlands, and the ritual was completed. In the space at the feet of the images, the final events of the saptāha took place: offerings of song and dance and speeches of thanks from various people. Attendees shared a final banquet of blessed food, prasād, before dispersing. The last words I wrote in my field journal on leaving were "Feeling of peace, *saṁpūrṇatā* ['fullness'], sanctity."[11]

Three Saptāhas Compared

The outstanding features of the typical day of Mridul Krishna's saptāha in Vrindavan were the emotional intensity of the experience; the hypnotic rhythms and sensual overload of sights, sounds, and scents; the high level of musicality of the performance and the centrality of song in both Sanskrit and Hindi; and especially the moments of ecstatic transport during which many in the audience, people of all ages, both men and women, appeared to be infected by the mood of intense devotion.

The unique features of the Naluna saptāha included the role of the devtā as a significant locus of authority, the central importance of the fire ceremony that accompanied the kathā each day, and, finally, the relatively low-tech, rural village setting. As the personal guest of the sponsor, I was privy to the preliminary arrangements and was able to take part in various ritual aspects of the event from start to finish.

The Canberra saptāha was special for a number of reasons. First, the physical text of the Bhāgavatapurāṇa did not play a particularly prominent role. On the first day, a small edition of the text was carried on a circumambulation of the mandir. In most saptāhas, the text is an important symbol and ritual focal point. Second, there was no single yajmān, or chief sponsor. One or two leading members of the mandir management committee had undertaken the primary organization, with the support of many volunteers. Nor was there a single sponsor responsible for giving the *dakṣiṇā*, or sacrificial fee; rather, attendees were invited to make donations for the exponent on the final day. Third, no formal saṁkalpa had been made to complete the reading in seven days, but it is likely that some individual attendees had made their own saṁkalpas for the week. Fourth, there was a pervasive Advaita orientation: time and again, Satchitananda Sai made that point that "All this is One," "You are Brahman," "You are the self," and so on. Finally, Satchitananda Sai was the most worldly, sophisticated exponent I heard, equally fluent in English, Tamil, and Sanskrit, equally at home in the globalized present and in the Bhāgavata imaginary universe.

No two saptāhas, even those conducted by the same exponent, are identical, yet all share some features. There is no such thing as a typical saptāha, although the event at Naluna was said to be "identical" to others held previously in the valley. Mridul Krishna's performance in Vrindavan was similar in style and content to many of his other performances, which are available on DVD and online. The Canberra saptāha was certainly similar to a performance I attended later in Sydney given by the same exponent. Mridul Krishna gives saptāha performances all over the world, and Satchitananda Sai could just as well have given his Canberra saptāha in Bangalore. That is to say, there is no "diasporic" saptāha or *desi* (authentic Indian) saptāha, because exponents and audiences flow so easily around the world, blurring the distinction between the two.

I have used these three case studies to illustrate the depth and breadth of the practice and to give a sense of the diversity within the tradition and also to illustrate their shared features. These include especially the centrality of the exponent and the structuring role of the Bhāgavata narrative, but before we turn to these subjects, I look at the saptāha from the point of view of the sponsor.

3

The Sponsor—Yajamāna

THE METAPHOR FOR this chapter is *yajamāna,* the sponsor or "instituter" of the Vedic act of worship. It is the yajamāna who finances the yajña and reaps the rewards of its successful conduct. The Hindi equivalent of this word, *yajmān,* is still used for the primary sponsor and beneficiary of a saptāha today. Contemporary performances may be held in the name of a single sponsor, but they are often arranged by a committee or a group of organizers (*āyojak*). This chapter explores the saptāha from their perspective. What sorts of individuals decide to initiate a saptāha? What are their motivations? What preparations do they make? What do they experience during a saptāha? What restrictions, if any, do they observe? What are the outcomes for them?

Before we begin this discussion, four terms need to be clarified. First, there are two important and sometimes overlapping roles, those of yajmān (sponsor) and āyojak (organizer). The role of sponsor, as the primary "hearer" of the discourse and beneficiary of the event, is ritual and ceremonial, whereas organizers undertake all the practical arrangements. In some saptāha events, there is a nominated sponsor and a separate organizer or organizing committee. In others, an individual or group may fulfill both roles, for example, a husband and wife may be both the sponsors and the organizers.

Second, contemporary saptāhas fall into two broad categories: *sakāma,* those "with a desire," and *niṣkāma,* those "without a desire." In saptāhas "with a desire," the sponsor has a specific outcome in mind, such as remembering a deceased family member (as in the Naluna saptāha) or removing a particular obstacle. These events are usually sponsored and organized by an individual or a family group. The sponsors may make a specific ritual undertaking (*saṁkalpa*); for example, they might vow to adhere to a set of observances (*niyama*), such as a restricted diet, sleeping only on the floor, and refraining from negative thoughts and emotions. They formally express their determination to complete all seven days of the event without hindrance so that their desire might be achieved.

More common in contemporary practice are niṣkāma saptāhas, those "without a desire." These are usually organized by a temple committee or community group, rather than an individual sponsor or family. The Canberra saptāha described in chapter 2 was a niṣkāma event, as was the saptāha organized by the Brisbane Bhakti Yoga Centre (chapter 7). The reason often stated for holding a saptāha of this kind is the simple desire to impart religious instruction to the broader community, or "to please the Lord," as one organizer put it. In niṣkāma events, specific desired outcomes are not normally expressed by the sponsors or organizers, and few, if any, participants follow any particular restrictions of the sort described later. In niṣkāma events, no single individual usually takes the ritual role of yajmān or primary "hearer," but members of the organizing committee, individuals, or family groups may take turns fulfilling some of the yajmān's functions, such as garlanding the exponent and performing āratī at the beginning and end of each day's discourse.

Typology

The difficulty of organizing a saptāha obviously depends on its scale. A group of friends may simply congregate in a private home to listen to a prerecorded saptāha over seven days. At the other end of the scale, a saptāha in a stadium with tens of thousands of attendees is a major logistical undertaking, requiring a small army of professional event organizers. Between these two extremes is the typical event with an audience numbering in the hundreds. Even a modest saptāha of this size will require many hands to manage all the diverse tasks. These include booking the exponent and the musicians, hiring and decorating the venue, arranging the sound and video systems, producing and distributing invitations, publicity and promotion, organizing the seating and catering, and arranging gifts and remuneration for the speaker and other performers.

Desai (2013, 77, 59–60, 70–71) found that local saptāhas in Andhra Pradesh were sponsored by a temple committee, members of the community, or a single wealthy patron. One such local event was sponsored by a former resident of the village, a Brahmin widower now living in New Jersey. The larger urban events were organized by corporate and/or religious groups, such as the Akhila Bharatiya Vaishya Maha Sammelan, "a national, multi-caste *Vaiṣṇava* organization that specializes in promoting spiritual discourses, public education and other charitable acts." Wilczewska (2013, 215) stated that sponsors are usually couples or senior male members of wealthy middle- and upper-class families. These findings accord well with my own, which I introduce later.

Saptāhas in Vrindavan, Mathura, and elsewhere are usually advertised along the main streets and pilgrimage routes. In the past, simple posters were hung on walls in public places, and local newspapers carried ads. In 2009, the most common form of advertisement in the Vrindavan area was a full-color A1- or A2-size poster. Four years later, saptāha advertising had undergone a revolution. By 2013, the standard form was a giant laser-printed billboard, five meters wide and two meters high. Scores of these were displayed on towering steel frames up and down the main streets of Vrindavan. The brightly colored panels usually feature a head-and-shoulders portrait of the exponent and an image of the deity. Along with the essential details of time, date, and place, they also advertise the names of the saptāha organizers and often add the name of the ritual sponsor.

Saptāhas are often sponsored by family groups. Billboards in Vrindavan in 2013 listed family sponsors, such as "Javaharlal and Mohini Gupta and the whole Gupta family, Chandigarh" and "Sri Rajarama and Bharat Bhushan Garg, Haryana." In addition to family groups, charitable trusts and religious associations also appear as saptāha organizers; these included, for example, the Chimay Mission, Kanpur, and the Sri Braj Vaibhav Seva Charitable Trust, Vrindavan. The Canberra saptāha was organized by a local temple management committee. Similarly, the saptāha in Brisbane (chapter 7) was organized by a community group, the Brisbane Bhakti Yoga Centre, drawing principally on the energies of the four or five most active families in the society.

Sponsoring a saptāha is not only a way for individuals, families, and communities to demonstrate their piety and to accrue religious and social capital. Organizers may also seek to promote their businesses by sponsoring a saptāha and listing their company name next to their own. For example, one billboard in Vrindavan listed "Mahavir Prasad Mittal, Delhi Electric Company" as an organizer. This billboard was also one of very few that incorporated text in English. Most advertising seeks to create a more "traditional" impression by using Hindi alone, befitting a pious, religious context.

The sponsor normally plays an active ritual role as the "primary hearer," but sometimes a saptāha may be dedicated in the name of a particular person,

FIGURE 3.1. Billboard advertising a saptāha by Shri Chandradas-ji Maharaj "Radhikadas" of Vrindavan. The event was held in honor of the infant Radhakand, pictured on the left.

even though that individual does not take an active part. One such example was the infant yajmān of a saptāha presided over by Shri Chandradas-ji Maharaj "Radhikadas" of Vrindavan. This event was held at his ashram just before we visited in November 2013. The yajmān was a six-month-old baby boy named Radhakand. Obviously, the child would not be able to perform any of the ritual functions of the office in the normal sense, but he was the central figure of the saptāha, which was held in his honor and for his benefit.

Radhakand, whose image appeared on the billboard that advertised the saptāha, was the son of two of the exponent's devotees. His mother had played DVDs of Radhikadas's saptāha performances during her pregnancy so that the baby in the womb was exposed to the sacred sound. As a result, according to Rādhikādas, the baby was exceptionally beautiful and *adbhūt* (extraordinary), as he put it. He explained that Radhakand's ātman (soul) was auspicious (*puṇya*) and added, "This child is very divine, so every sādhu and *sant* [holy man] loves Radhakand. In the Bhāgavata-kathā, this child always laughed."

As we can see, there is considerable variety in the backgrounds of organizers and sponsors. I also learned of one saptāha that ran perfectly well without either. Bhaktivedanta Madhusudan Maharaj, whom I interviewed in Vrindavan, spoke of one such occasion. Without any prior advertising or organization, he simply seated himself in a temple in Nepal and began expounding on the Bhāgavata. News of the event spread by word of mouth, and the audience eventually swelled to several hundred.

Some forms of Hindu religious expression and practice are restricted to Brahmins and other members of the "higher" varṇas. Is there any relationship between varṇa and sponsorship of saptāha events? Desai (2013, 283) found that all four of the Telugu saptāhas that she investigated in Andhra Pradesh were sponsored by Smārta Brahmins. Among the family names of sponsors recorded in Vrindavan, Sharma and Bharadvaj are certainly Brahmin families, while Gupta and Garg are usually vaiśya, the third of the three "higher" varṇas. One billboard named "the whole Seksaria family" as saptāha sponsors. This is a famous Agarwal Marwari clan, also vaiśya, who have been leading industrialists for more than a century.[1] The sponsor of the Naluna saptāha is nominally a member of the Yadav community, traditionally a nonelite agriculturalist group, usually associated with the fourth and "lowest" varṇa. He was able to sponsor a saptāha, but as we have seen, he was required to undergo a ritual elevation to "twice-born" status for the week. A billboard in Vrindavan listed Sri Prabhat Kumar Jain of Karnal as organizer. This individual's family name indicates that he is a member of the Jain community. We can see from these examples, in contrast with Desai's experiences in Andhra Pradesh, that sponsorship of saptāhas is undertaken by families from a variety of community backgrounds.

An individual's ability to pay seems to be more important than membership in a particular community, because running a saptāha is expensive. As Wilczewska (2013, 214–215) notes, most sponsors are members of wealthy middle- or upper-class families. It appears that sponsorship is open to any individuals, irrespective of community, providing they have the social or religious inclination and, perhaps more important, the ability to pay. To put it bluntly, class trumps caste.

Motivations

There are two traditional reasons for holding a saptāha: for the benefit of the living and for the benefit of the deceased. The first motivation is reflected in the main narrative of the Bhāgavatapurāṇa; just as King Parīkṣit obtained mokṣa (liberation) having heard the story of the Bhāgavata during the last seven days of his earthly life, those who listen attentively to a saptāha "will obtain the ultimate reward." When they die, they will achieve liberation from the cycle of birth and rebirth and will advance to a heavenly abode. Heaven in this context is usually understood to be Viṣṇu's realm of Vaikuṇṭha or a realm known as Goloka, which is associated with Kṛṣṇa. The second reason for holding a saptāha is an extension of the first: not just a living individual but also the spirit of a deceased person who hears a saptāha may be released from suffering. This concept is probably a later development, as it is reflected in the comparatively recent narratives of the Māhātmya. In the relevant episode, the virtuous Gokarṇa convenes a saptāha to pacify the ghost of his dead brother, the wicked Dhundhukārī. This latter idea is behind the more traditional sakāma saptāhas. A pious individual or family will organize an event so that the ātman (soul) of a deceased relative will find final rest. This, for example, was the primary motive behind the saptāha at Naluna, which was held for the benefit of the yajmān's long-deceased grandfather. Wilczewska (2013, 215) gives the example of a family who had sponsored a saptāha because they were being troubled by the ghost of a deceased family member. As happened with the spirit of the wicked Dhundhukārī, that saptāha successfully brought the ghostly harassment to an end. As for the relative proportion of sakāma and niṣkāma events, Siddhanti Maharaj, an exponent I interviewed in Delhi, estimated that ten percent of the saptāhas he had given were sponsored by individuals specifically for the salvation of deceased ancestors or relatives.

Rather than seeking a specific outcome from a saptāha, contemporary events are more often held as a result of an individual's or a community's wish to perform a pious act and to accrue religious merit. Madhusudan Maharaj, an exponent from Vrindavan, said that his sponsors were usually his own devotees who liked to hear the stories: "The reason they sponsor is so that every person can be happy. . . . Bhāgavata is the soul's food. Without that, there is no life." Another reason, related to this, was repeated by several organizers of the saptāha in Brisbane. The primary audience of the Bhāgavata narratives was not the devotees who gathered to listen but Lord Kṛṣṇa himself. It was said that he was present in person at every saptāha and "relished" the opportunity to listen to his own narratives.

Organizing a saptāha is an important stage-of-life rite for many sponsors, by which one may make known one's piety, position in society, and arrival at a higher state of religiosity. Such was the case, for example, with Yogendra Yadav, the sponsor of the saptāha at Naluna. As Ilona Wilczewska mentioned in a conversation in Vrindavan, "in India, business and the spiritual are all part of life; they are not separate. If you are successful in business, then you repay your karmic debt by investing in your spiritual life. Successful business families sponsor prestigious exponents; the business gains prestige, and the exponent gains prestige."

Abhishek Goswami, another exponent in Vrindavan, mentioned a family that had sponsored a saptāha recently, having wished to do so for twenty-eight years. At the time of marriage, the young bride had said to her husband that she wanted to have a Bhāgavata in her new home. According to Abhishek, having seen saptāhas in her childhood home, the young woman wanted to continue that legacy in her new situation. Accordingly, her husband had promised that they would sponsor such an event one day. Time passed, and she continued to nurture this desire. Recently, Abhishek gave a saptāha in the couple's neighborhood in Delhi. They heard him speak and asked him to give a saptāha for them, too. Abhishek said, "One fine day, I get a call: 'We are all set, and we want you to come and do a Bhāgavata.' "

It is part of the wider discourse surrounding Bhāgavata-saptāha that these events are like the fabled "wish-granting tree" and will provide everything that an individual might desire. In addition to the otherworldly benefits described above, it is believed that Bhāgavata-saptāhas are equally potent in providing worldly outcomes. To deny this would be tantamount to denying the power and efficacy of the practice itself. However, it is also very bad form to admit to actively seeking such worldly rewards. As Siddhanti Maharaj said:

> There are different purposes. Someone wants to do it for the benefit of their forefathers who are departed. For their own devotion, they want to hear for seven days. They want to get spiritualized for seven days: their mind, their body, everything, their hearing and serving. There are a few people who want material benefit from Bhāgavata-saptāha. They might want their business to go in a more prosperous way. Till now, I have not come across this kind of yajmān. But I have heard about them.

While it seems that no one will admit to seeking material rewards for himself or herself, or even knowing someone who might do so, it is important within the tradition to confirm that such rewards exist or are theoretically possible, as this reaffirms the potency of the practice.

The Role of Sponsors

Perhaps the most important decision of the sponsor is choosing a suitable exponent. In the first instance, it is possible to "cold-call" a speaker, as mobile numbers and email addresses are prominently displayed on roadside billboards, websites, and Facebook pages. Local networks can also be used. In organizing the saptāha at Naluna, Yogendra Yadav made inquiries though the local Brahmin network to identify and engage a suitable speaker. Audience members at one of Siddhanti Maharaj's saptāhas were so impressed when they heard him speak that they engaged him for their own event. Sponsors and speakers are often linked though shared membership in religious organizations. For example, the Brisbane Bhakti Yoga Centre has engaged several speakers who are members of their parent body in India, the International Pure Bhakti Yoga Society, whose teachers are listed on the society's website. If a guru is in the habit of giving saptāhas, it is natural for his devotees to invite him to perform one on their behalf. Shrivatsa Goswami of Vrindavan mentioned that the sponsors of most of the saptāhas he had given were either his own disciples or those of his father. Similarly, Radhikadas's most recent saptāha had been sponsored by one of his own disciples. This also appears to be the case with a saptāha advertised in Govardhan where the organizers were simply listed as *samasta bhakta-gaṇa*, "the entire community of devotees" of that particular guru exponent.

In many practical senses, the responsibilities of the contemporary sponsor or organizer are little different from those of the premodern organizer as described in chapter 1. An astrologer is still sometimes consulted to determine an auspicious commencement date, although in the case of the Naluna saptāha, it was the village deity who made this determination. Saptāha performances may be held at any time of the year, but it is still the case in India that the cooler months after the rains are the most popular season, with a peak in October and November. More often, however, particularly among the diaspora, the date of a saptāha will be determined by the exponent's availability and travel plans, rather than by the stars and planets.

The organizers are responsible for publicizing the event. Billboards are seen throughout North India and have largely replaced old-fashioned handbills and newspaper ads. Organizing committees overseas advertise saptāhas through community- and temple-based email lists, newsletters, and websites.

The organizers are also responsible for booking the venue. Many established groups have their own spaces, such as a temple hall or annex, or a space in a community hall will be used. It is common in India for a tent to be set up on fallow land or on the local Rāmlīlā ground. The venue for every saptāha I have attended, large or small, was beautifully decorated. Such decoration is ultimately the responsibility of the organizer, some relying on their own labor and that of their community, others outsourcing the task to a commercial operator. At Naluna, we made our own bunting and flags by gluing triangles of colored paper to lengths of string and bamboo sticks. Along with young girls from the village, we spent a happy afternoon making garlands of marigolds from the garden. In Canberra, the temple priest worked tirelessly with a small team of volunteers for many days to decorate the hall and to construct the swing and the bridal bower. At the other end of the spectrum are the gala events for which the organizers hire professional companies, sometimes the same companies that handle venues for glitzy wedding receptions. Organizers may also be responsible for catering. This varies from modest home-cooked meals contributed by friends and families to expensive commercially produced prasād in festive cardboard boxes distributed to thousands of people.

Turning from the practical responsibilities of the organizer to the ritual role of the yajmān, this also varies. At the start of the first day, the yajmān (usually a male), along with his wife, might accompany the exponent to the venue. In one saptāha given by Mridul Krishna in Bombay, the sponsor carried the text of the Bhāgavatapurāṇa on his head, while his wife carried a kalaśa, a metal pitcher filled with auspicious substances. The couple walked in procession to the venue followed by the exponent in a horse-drawn silver chariot, five elephants, and more than two thousand village women also bearing kalaśas on their heads.

At the venue, the sponsor and his wife might then take part in a number of preliminary rituals. These include a pūjā to Ganeśa to remove obstacles, the taking of vows, and the statement of intent (saṁkalpa) to complete the seven days. As mentioned above, the sponsor of the saptāha at Naluna was not of the "twice-born" varṇas and was required to undertake a ritual that gave him temporary Brahmin status for the duration of the saptāha. He was then expected to observe the rules of purity that normally pertain to members of those communities. In addition, he was required to bathe every morning, to remain celibate, and "not to do anything that a pious person would not do." Smoking and drinking are usually forbidden for a sponsor. Yogendra Yadav reduced his intake: "I don't think I was smoking as much during saptāha, just when it was really necessary, and I was not doing it so openly as well. I was being mindful about this."

Shulakshna Narayan and her family were the organizers of a saptāha at her home in suburban Brisbane in 2005 (chapter 7). As this was the first saptāha that she and her husband had initiated, their guru, who officiated at the event, instituted a formal saṁkalpa and required that Shulakshna and her family adhere to a set of restrictions, which she described as follows:

> With the Bhāgavata-saptāha at my place, we had saṁkalpa, and Guru-ji offered all the prayers and made the saṁkalpa that within this seven-day period, there should not be any destruction from anywhere or anything: "So please, Lord, take care of these things, and we take vows so that everything goes according to your wishes." And [the guru] did those [prayers], and at the last day, we did the ending ceremony. So the niyama [restrictions] were there, especially for the people in our home. Our own people—myself, my husband, my kids, my mother-in-law—were there at that time, so it was wonderful.
>
> The saṁkalpa was: "Because we are starting the Bhāgavata from today, we are saying, 'Please, Lord, we are doing the saṁkalpa, saying that if anyone comes to my place, nothing should happen to them, if they fall or are killed or anything. If someone is cooking, the gas shouldn't explode, or if someone is chopping, any sort of destruction—so please take care of that." We do the saṁkalpa, saying, "Whatever we do, big or small, for these seven days, it's all on you. You take care of everything. We are doing it, but you are the one who is giving us guidance."

The guru imposed a number of restrictions to be observed during the seven days. The family was required to forgo salt, except for one small taste in the afternoon. The family had to sleep on the floor. New clothes like those that would be needed for a wedding had to be purchased. The family was forbidden to eat from a pot that anyone else had touched, and once food had been cooked and dedicated, their own portion was taken out first and set aside to avoid any direct or indirect contact with menstruating women. As Shulakshna put it delicately, "If there are ladies present there, you don't know how they are."

Once these preliminary rituals have been completed and the exponent has taken his seat, the sponsor and his family will usually present him with garlands and perform āratī before him and the text of the Bhāgavatapurāṇa. This may be repeated at the start and conclusion of each day's discourse. As primary listener, the sponsor, with his family and his invited guests, is typically seated in the front row of the venue facing the exponent for each of the seven days. In some larger events, the entire front section of the venue may be cordoned off for members of the sponsor's party and for other honored guests, as was the case in the saptāha described in chapter 2.

At the end of the week, the sponsor's final responsibility, and obviously one that is both important and delicate, is the distribution of payments and gifts. According to the instructions given in the Māhātmya, the sponsor should be prepared to spend as much on a saptāha as would be spent on a wedding. A modest saptāha in Vrindavan today might cost $10,000 to $15,000. In 2009, the rate for a top-ranking exponent was twenty-five to fifty lakh rupees ($50,000 to $100,000) (Wilczewska 2013, 216). For one exceptionally extravagant event, the exponent was rumored to have received ten crores of rupees ($2 million) plus a helicopter. The total cost of the saptāha at Naluna was a relatively modest $4000, with about $1000 spent on each of the following: the Brahmins' fees, the tent and sound system, the construction of the pavilion for the fire sacrifice, and food and other supplies. Every person who attended the kathā at Naluna left a small donation for the exponent on the altar at the front of the venue—cash, a piece of fruit, or a little packet of home-grown grain. All these contributed to his dakṣiṇā, or traditional fee.

Personal Narratives

Naluna Sponsor

Yogendra Yadav had been aware of saptāhas but had never actively participated in one. As a schoolboy in rural India and later as a university student in Aligarh, he had been a casual visitor to saptāhas and had participated "just as somebody passing by," without paying any particular attention to the Bhāgavata and the discourses. For the young student, saptāhas were simply a social occasion when friends met and ate together. Between his university days in Aligarh and the event at Naluna, saptāhas had not been important in his life largely because he had been living overseas for much of the time.

Preparations for the saptāha in Naluna began many months before the event. The first task was to find the right exponent. Yogendra was in regular contact with one local pandit whom he had previously engaged to conduct several minor rituals. In consultation with this Brahmin, Yogendra proposed Bhadri Prasad, who was well qualified to give a saptāha as the holder of a shāstrī (master's) degree. It was agreed that Yogendra's regular pandit would take charge of the ritual side of the event and would supervise the fire sacrifice as "master of the pavilion," or *maṇḍapācārya*. There was an element of mission creep in the preparations: at first, it was planned that there would be seven Brahmins, but in the end, thirteen were engaged, twelve to conduct the fire sacrifice plus one cook-pandit. Brahmins are traditionally permitted to eat only food prepared by a member of their own community. Rituals such as saptāhas are an important source of income for Brahmins, and maximizing the number employed for these events increases the flow of wealth into that community.

According to Yogendra, with the exception of the tent and the audio system, which had to be booked well in advance, most of the other arrangements just fell into place in time. Everybody knew what had to be done, and with the help of a number of local retainers and volunteers, friends, and neighbors, Yogendra drew up a list of requirements, including ritual substances for the fire sacrifice and food and gifts for the Brahmins. Among the many other tasks was advertising the saptāha locally; handbills were distributed throughout the neighborhood, and banners displaying details of the event were erected over the road next to the venue.

Yogendra describes himself as a pious man, adding with reference to the saptāha, "I like to do the ceremonies, and I love these ceremonies." He was attracted to the idea of holding a saptāha but was at first reluctant to act as yajmān himself. He suggested to the local Brahmins that one of his elderly retainers or his own son and daughter-in-law would be more suitable candidates. The Brahmins prevailed, and Yogendra agreed to take on the role himself, along with his wife, Prakash. He said: "When I look back, I think I did become the yajmān. First I thought I'd just do it, but then I really became involved with my heart and soul. It fell upon me, and I'm very happy that it happened and turned out that way." Explaining this transition in his attitude from reluctant yajmān to wholehearted participant, he added:

> When the flag ceremony was taking place early in the [first] morning—it was about 4 a.m.—the *Hanumān-dhvaja* [Hanumān's banner] had to be erected before the beginning of the official saptāha, and Hanumān being the protector, and this was also a live tree, and as I was planting it with the help of other people, I really felt very spiritually emotional from that point onward. My parents were there, and I knew that saptāha is done for forefathers or for the

> peace of the ancestors, and I was thinking, "Oh, good, my parents are living, and this wonderful thing is happening in their lives, and I don't have to do anything when they are not around [laughs]." So those sorts of thoughts were going on, and I was really happy—I had goosebumps I was so happy.

During the preliminary rituals that followed the raising of Hanumān's banner, the presiding Brahmin instructed Yogendra on his conduct during the week. It was during these rituals that Yogendra took on the *janeu*, the sacred thread worn by members of the "higher" varṇas, which gave him temporary "twice-born" status for the duration of the saptāha.

Yogendra spoke of a sense of deepening commitment and involvement as the week progressed: "The first day, something struck me. 'Oh, God, I am doing saptāha, and I'm in it.' Day by day, I got more and more involved in it." As the central figure in a large and complex ritual, and as the host of several hundred guests, he was conscious of having to balance many conflicting demands, especially meeting his ritual responsibilities during the fire sacrifice for several hours each morning, his required presence during the kathā every afternoon, and the hospitality expected for a never-ending stream of well-wishers, friends, neighbors, and local celebrities:

> I woke up with the thought, "What will I do today? What should be the best way to let this day pass? Whom will I meet? I'm so busy. How will I meet my friends who are coming to visit me?" But then I thought, "No, they will understand that I'm busy."

During the winter, early mornings in Naluna are very cold, the temperature barely above zero. Every day except the first and last days of the saptāha, Yogendra substituted a ritual bath known as *pañca-snāna*, "the washing of five limbs" (arms, legs, and head) for the full-body ablution. Yogendra was keen that his elderly father take part in the fire sacrifice, along with Yogendra's wife. Speaking of the ritual, Yogendra said, "I never experienced such a thing before.... Every action was so holy, pious. That whole temperament was different. It was long, but it was beyond my belief that I could sit so long." The fire sacrifice was followed by the midday meal, after which Yogendra rested or met with visitors.

> In the afternoon was the kathā, which I did listen to very carefully. It was good, but most of all, what I liked was the fact that people were

> really feeling about saptāha—all those villagers who came—and I would see these women coming, bringing grain. Whatever little offerings they had, they brought. I was just thinking how pure their minds were. All of them who came there were very nice and very religious people, which really made it very fulfilling for me. I was always, of course, listening to kathā, but at the same time, my eyes were watching these things.... Their devotion—how should I put it—not compelled me, lured me, and made me a devout person as well. Their belief, the purity of their minds, was something that really grasped my heart and mind, and that was powerful, I thought. Some women came, which was two hours' walk easily, and going uphill back to their village would be two and a half hours. Of course, they would still have fun, but still it was a lot of work coming down from there and going back.

There are two points of interest here. The first is the centrality and importance of the family in the saptāha, as in so much else in Indian life. The sponsor's family involvement in this event spanned five generations. The first generation included Yogendra's own grandfather, whose remembrance was the nominal motivation for the saptāha. Second were Yogendra's octogenarian parents, who had traveled for two days from a village near Agra to attend. Yogendra's sprightly father was an active participant in many aspects of the event's rituals. Yogendra and his own wife, who was constantly by his side during the fire sacrifice and the kathā and all the rituals associated with both, were the third generation. The fourth generation was represented by Yogendra's son and daughter-in-law, who had come from Australia especially for the week. As we shall see later, Yogendra also attributed the conception of his grandson, the fifth generation, to the success of the saptāha.

In addition to the family aspect, there is the social nature of the saptāha from the sponsor's point of view. This was an important community event in the district, and the impact of the saptāha on the local villagers and the participation of the community made a strong impression on Yogendra and served to deepen his faith. While it is true that the saptāha was organized nominally for "honoring" his own grandfather, Yogendra was pleased and proud to see the impact it had on the local community. As a major benefactor in the neighborhood over many years, Yogendra had provided financial and material support to numerous families, by supplying clothes, assistance with education, employment, and housing. Organizing this saptāha was part of a larger pattern of this social service. As sponsor, he provided an opportunity for local people to experience and express their faith, to take part in a socially sanctioned form of entertainment, and to enjoy a free meal. In providing a saptāha for the local community, Yogendra added to his already considerable stock of social capital in the district.

Brisbane Organizers

It would have been interesting to interview the organizers of the Canberra saptāha, but at that stage in the project, I was caught up in the intricacies of the text and the use of the verses. It was only later that the importance of interviewing organizers and sponsors began to take shape. The saptāha in Brisbane in June 2014 provided the perfect opportunity to fill this gap. The two shorter narratives below are from organizers of saptāhas held in Queensland. These were less formal in the sense that they were niṣkāma and lacked a specific goal or outcome. We saw earlier that Yogendra Yadav was deeply involved in the daily ritual side of the event, and his reflections were largely based on the impact on himself and on his family. In common with the saptāha described by Yogendra, however, the social and community aspects of the Brisbane events were also significant. For these two organizers, the primary impression, the most significant outcome was the pleasure of providing a rich experience for members of their social circle. The two events in Brisbane played a strong role in bringing members of the Indian community together and enabling them to share and deepen their experience of "Indian-ness" in a new environment. The first respondent, who asked to remain anonymous, said this of her experience as an organizer:

> I feel great. I feel so good. I don't want to boast, but today I felt so good doing it. It's a different feeling, and you just have to experience that feeling. When people appreciate and when people are happy, you can see, like today, such a nice kirtan, and everyone is enjoying it, then a little bit of *ahaṁkāra*—ego—comes in, that the Lord used us as an instrument in organizing this saptāha, and these people are relishing that. Just as Maharaj-ji was explaining yesterday, the Lord comes to make other people relish the stories, and then he wants to relish them himself. Until the time that you serve, then

> you feel that, when other people are happy, that is the highest happiness, I believe.

I asked Shulakshna, another of the leading members of the Brisbane Bhakti Yoga Centre and co-organizer of a number of saptāhas, about her experience:

> Oh! Oh! It's just like your body has got this extra energy, and with my saptāha at my place, it was heart-warming. I did so much. At that time, we did not know most of the people. When they came and saw the Bhāgavata stage and the deities, they just said, "Wow! Who did this?" I did this wonderful decoration, and people were so attracted. Just like they do it in Vrindavan, . . . not that much, but still it was worth looking at, and people said, "My God!" It was so beautiful. The hall was decorated. . . . It was so well decorated, and I was so happy. We did all the shopping for ourselves, saying that this many people would come. We didn't want any shortages. And anybody coming, we fed them and gave them prasād to take home for the rest of the family. And people coming to help us, we just told them, "This is your house. For seven days, you do your cooking here. Whatever you feel like eating, cook and eat." Those people were so happy. Some places you go, you can't do this; you can't do that. At my place, it was just open, so it was so nice. I felt very warm inside. To me, it was just like someone was always with me. The energy in myself was humongous, three or four times what I usually had, and everybody kept saying, "My God, how can you work like this? How can you do this?" And I'd say, "It's all been Rādhā-Kṛṣṇa.[2] He's the one, and she's the one who's taking care of this."

In this chapter, we have explored the saptāha from the point of view of the sponsor and organizer. We have seen that a wide variety of individuals choose to sponsor or organize saptāhas. Varṇa (caste) is not a significant barrier, but because the contemporary saptāha is an expensive undertaking, most organizers and sponsors tend to be financially well off. Among the motivations for organizing a saptāha are the traditional grounds, the "liberation" of the soul of a deceased ancestor, but we have also seen individuals who wanted to fulfill personal wishes, some mundane and some otherworldly. Sponsors report finding that organizing a saptāha is fulfilling and enriching, either as a result of benefits to themselves or from the pleasure they see in members of their communities. In addition to these intangible, numinous benefits, sponsors acquire considerable social capital. As mentioned at the start of this discussion of sponsors, perhaps the most crucial of all their decisions is the choice of exponent, and it is to the exponents that we turn in the next chapter.

4

The Exponent—Hotṛ

IN THE VEDIC yajña, the chief priest who carries out the act of worship is called the hotṛ, literally the "sacrificer" or "worshiper." It is the hotṛ who pours the oblation of clarified butter into the sacred fire on behalf of the sponsor while intoning the appropriate mantras to ensure the success of the ritual. Traditionally, the role of hotṛ is highly specialized. He must be trained in ritual theory and practice, especially in the recitation of mantras. It is the power of his spoken words, the mantra, that lends the sacrifice its efficacy. Just as the hotṛ presides over the yajña and activates it with mantras, the exponent presides over the Bhāgavata-saptāha and vivifies the event with the spoken word. In this chapter, I attempt to open a door into the world of the exponents. What are their backgrounds? What was their vocation? How were they trained, and how do they experience the process of saptāha?

Exponents of the Bhāgavata are usually known by Hindi versions of various Sanskrit terms. Heard in conversation and seen in advertising, these terms include *vyās* and *kathā-vyās*, after the sage Vyāsa, the traditional author of the Bhāgavatapurāṇa. Other common terms include *āchārya* (teacher), *kathā-kār* (storyteller), *shāstrī* (possessor of scripture, holder of the traditional equivalent of a master's degree), and *pravacak, pravaktā,* or *vaktā* (speaker). Bonazzoli (1983, 273) adds several other, more literary Sanskrit terms, which appear in text but not in common parlance: *purāṇajña* (knower of the purāṇas), *paurāṇika* (purāṇicist), *vyākhyātṛ* (narrator). Copywriters in the saptāha advertising industry sometimes achieve great heights of lyricism. One speaker, for example, was billed as *kathā ras pravahak, vishva-pravaktā, bāl-shuk,* "conveyor of the essence of the narrative, universal narrator, a young Śuka," after Vyāsa's son.

In broad terms, contemporary Bhāgavata exponents come from one of three backgrounds. Some are born into families of the hereditary priesthood associated with the major temples in Vrindavan and inherit a long family tradition of Bhāgavata exposition. These lineages stretch back as far as the 1570s. Many of the leading exponents in Vrindavan are in this category and use the Hindi honorific title *Goswami*. A second group of exponents are those who have risen through the traditional guru-kula, or "guru family," system of education. Students in this group hail from a variety of backgrounds and, responding to a spiritual thirst, have sought out gurus to whom they apprenticed themselves. They live with their spiritual masters, traditionally for twelve years but in practice sometimes less, receiving close personal tutelage. A third group of exponents are graduates of dedicated Bhāgavata colleges. Young boys, and a much smaller number of girls, mainly from poorer Brahmin families, come from all over North India and Nepal to study in one of the many institutions of this kind in Vrindavan. These students graduate after two to five years of study, by which time they are supposed to have acquired sufficient skills to earn a living with their religious expertise. Bhadri Prasad, the exponent at Naluna, was the graduate of one such institution. Speakers from all three backgrounds, but especially the guru-kula and college graduates, may append the honorific *Maharaj* to their names.

Of the exponents I have interviewed, I have selected several for this chapter to illustrate the diversity of their backgrounds and fortunes. Three are members of the hereditary priesthood associated with the Radha Raman Temple: Shrivatsa Goswami, Abhishek Goswami, and Chandan Goswami. Shrivatsa, although of the older generation and of impeccable lineage, is particularly interesting for his unorthodox approach to the tradition. The two younger goswamis exemplify a generation seeking to balance the pressures of modernity and the call of tradition. I also introduce two exponents who have risen through the guru-kula system: Radhikadas Maharaj, a "sole operator" working from a small ashram in Vrindavan, and Siddhanti Maharaj, who has the backing of a large and successful international organization. I conclude this section with an account of a visit to the Vedic Yatra Pathashala, a small training college for Bhāgavata exponents. The interviews with the goswamis and Siddhanti Maharaj were conducted in English; those with Radhikadas Maharaj were in a mixture of Hindi and English; and the conversations with the staff and students of the Vedic Yatra Pathashala were conducted in Sanskrit.

The Goswamis of Vrindavan

November is not a bad time to be in Vrindavan. The days are pleasantly warm but no longer hot; the nights are cool and not yet cold. Moreover, it is under the autumnal full moon that Kṛṣṇa dances with his beloved gopīs. November also marks the end of the busy pilgrimage month of Kartik, and the dense masses of visitors start to disperse. The sun, sometimes struggling to penetrate the North India haze, shines in the palest of blue skies. We arrived in Vrindavan in November 2013 with a list of potential contacts generously provided by my friend and colleague Ilona Wilczewska Avadhuta. By the end of the month, we had interviewed representatives from several of the most important lineages of hereditary priests, graduates from guru-kulas, and students from a leading college in which the next generation of Bhāgavata exponents was being trained.

Shrivatsa Goswami

Through a massive wooden gate in a towering masonry wall sat Jai Singh Ghera, an oasis of calm, sequestered from the chaos of Vrindavan's monkey-infested lanes and traffic-choked bazaars. Pressing in on the medieval structures in the original sixteenth-century compound were three modern multistory buildings topped with glistening white pavilions in the Bengali style. These handsome mansions accommodated the guru's family, guests, and a large cultural center, respectively. Inside the compound, two large, friendly dogs bounded up to be patted. Busy retainers crisscrossed broad brick pathways bordered with neat gardens. On the ground floor of the guru's residence was a large, airy vestibule set with cane chairs. Shrivatsa Goswami appeared for our interview, a towering man in an orange wrap and cream dhoti, warm, generous, modest, but at the same time commanding and magisterial. While the house crows croaked, parrots squealed, and motorbikes tooted outside, we spoke for nearly an hour.[1]

Shri Shrivatsa Goswami was born in 1950 into a long and illustrious lineage founded by Gopala Bhatta Goswami (1501–c. 1591), one of the six founding fathers of Vrindavan and a disciple of the great Bengali Vaiṣṇava saint Caitanya (1486–1533). For sixteen generations, Shrivatsa's family has been the custodians of the Radha Raman Temple, one of the famous "seven temples" in the town. Shrivatsa's father, Purushottam Goswami, was a great advocate, innovator, and champion of the culture and traditions of Vraja.[2] The father's work has been continued, deepened, and broadened by the son as director of Sri Caitanya Prema Samsthana, an institute for Vaiṣṇava culture and studies, and through the Vraja Research Project, both of which are housed in the Jai Singh Ghera compound.

Shrivatsa is an important international interpreter of the religious and cultural traditions of Vrindavan and Vraja through his books, *At Play with Krishna* (Hawley and Goswami 1981) and *Celebrating Krishna* (Goswami and Beeche 2001), and his numerous other writings on Vaiṣṇava traditions and Hinduism more broadly. He is also the editor of a volume on Caitanya traditions in the *Encyclopedia of Indian Philosophies*, and has become a sort of international "go-to" spokesman for Hindu traditions. Shrivatsa had just returned from a Universal Peace Federation meeting in Amman when I interviewed him, and he had represented Hindus at the World Interfaith Harmony Week at the United Nations in New York in 2012. Pope Benedict invited him to the twenty-fifth anniversary of the World Day of Prayer at Assisi in 2011. He is also connected with several international peace organizations, including Religions for Peace and the Interreligious Federation for World Peace, the Elijah Interfaith Institute, and the World Council of Churches.

Following his early schooling in Vrindavan, where he was born, Shrivatsa studied at Benares Hindu University, and he had held positions as a visiting scholar at Harvard, Heidelberg, and several other universities in Europe, the United States, and Japan.

There is a strong tradition of Bhāgavata exposition in Shrivatsa's family. Both his father and his brother were highly respected Bhāgavata speakers. Shrivatsa's father, whom he described as "an amazing man," initiated many trends, including the incorporation of music into Bhāgavata events. This practice had been unknown until the 1950s, when he began combining sacred song with the spoken word. Shrivatsa's brother, Sant Venugopal, followed in their father's footsteps as a committed Bhāgavata exponent who dedicated his life to the practice. Shrivatsa explained that his brother was practically married to the text and, as a result, never took a worldly wife. Sant Venugopal travels the world giving Bhāgavata-saptāhas:

> Practically every week, he is delivering a Bhāgavata, like Mahāprabhu Vallabhācārya.[3] He had also this practice. He would stay in a place, do a Bhāgavata-saptāha, and when the saptāha is over, then he will travel to another place, reach there, do a Bhāgavata-saptāha, and then after seven days, move from there. That was his life. He started

> much before me. He is much younger than me but much older than me in Bhāgavata.

Shrivatsa spoke of his own introduction to the practice of Bhāgavata-saptāha exposition:

> I started in the 1990s, I started late.... It was my mother's arm-twisting. She was a terrorist [laughter]. Unfortunately, she is not with us anymore. Once she said, "I want to hear Bhāgavata-saptāha from you." I said, "Your other son is already doing that. So why do you want to make a redundant practice?" [laughter]. "I want to hear from you." I said, "All right, let me study." So I studied at her behest. I studied for some time with some gurus, and with my father I studied the most. Then I said, "All right, if you are intent upon listening, then you have to become the yajmān." So she was the yajmān of my first Bhāgavata. My parents were the yajmān of my first Bhāgavata. They played the part of Parīkṣit, and it took place in Dwarka in Gujarat. It was a great pleasure, but there when I did it, it was a coup. When I started, everyone was shocked, because I asked my wife to sit with me, and we made it a joint venture. And it is still a joint venture. I have not given any Bhāgavata without her. I studied with gurus, and my father is basically my guru, and the text is the guru.

The text was indeed his guru. Shrivatsa's father stipulated that for his sons to qualify as exponents of the Bhāgavata, they must complete fifty-one pārāyaṇas. Accordingly, the two brothers read the Bhāgavatapurāṇa from cover to cover once a week for a year. Having completed this rigorous introduction to the text, Shrivatsa developed this approach to giving saptāha performances:

> I create my own understanding of a particular reading, and I make some notes, and I keep the text and the notes together. I don't repeat. Something should evolve in each Bhāgavata. Mostly, my saptāhas would be different. The whole stories will be the same, because you can't deviate from that. You have to be faithful to the stories. But Bhāgavata is an amazing thing. It is like an Indian sweet called *sohan papdi*.... It is like a small cake, but it has layers after layers after layers. And that is Bhāgavata. The more you read

> the Bhāgavata, the more layers appear. That is my experience, my humble experience, with Bhāgavata. The more you peel, the more it gives you something, like a *kalpa-vṛkṣa* [wish-fulfilling tree], like a *kāma-dhenu* [wish-fulfilling cow]. It always gives—the cow that always gives. But it will give only when you surrender. If you are out of milk, then this cow won't give, but if you just surrender and pray, it automatically drops the milk, and that is amazing. I cannot put that into words, but that is my experience. And especially when you sit on that ritualistic throne, the throne itself makes you speak. You bring a set of notes, and you find out that you have not even looked at those notes. You have said something really different. So it is the seat, the *vyās-pith*, that makes you speak. It is really ineffable.

The concept that the *vyās-pith*, the "throne of Vyāsa" on which the exponent sits, provides some form of divine inspiration during a saptāha is shared by a number of speakers, as we shall see. Shrivatsa went on to express his preference for smaller audiences:

> Although I have also given kathās to ten thousand people, I dislike that. I completely dislike it. I would like to give my kathā to a maximum of a hundred people. Maximum. Because to me, it is a spiritual journey. It is something significant. It is not a "show-off" business. Once, for the first time in my life, I was in Raipur, and people were sitting as far as I could see. I said, "To whom shall I talk?" I was sitting fifteen feet up on the stage, people all over, so whom am I talking to? Bhāgavata is a dialogue textually, and also in performance it is a dialogue. In my kathā, I usually invite responses from people. I make them come up with some statements or answers to my questions or teasers or things like that. So what I did, the first bamboo pole of that canopy, I made that my listener—I am not joking—and I talked for seven days to that bamboo pole [laughter]. I want one-to-one. I want one-to-one.

For most speakers, and indeed for sponsors, there is great prestige in attracting mega-audiences of ten thousand, twenty thousand, or thirty thousand to stadium-style events. A saptāha attended by one hundred thousand people was mentioned in Vrindavan. For Shrivatsa, whose lineage, reputation, and track record are already peerless, there is no allure in addressing such big crowds. The quality of communication between speaker and listener is paramount, and this quality is inversely proportional to the size of the audience. The bigger the crowd, the poorer the communication.

Shrivatsa differs from other speakers in this, and he differs in a number of other ways as well. We have already seen how he created a stir by inviting his wife to accompany him onstage. As a matter of pride, most speakers maintain a precise tally of how many saptāhas they have given, whether tens, hundreds, or a thousand. Shrivatsa expressed complete disdain for this subject, remarking in an offhand manner that he had no idea how many saptāhas he had given, but perhaps his son would remember, adding that he did saptāhas "very selectively." He had declined to give a saptāha in his hometown: "I have never done a Bhāgavata in Vrindavan. I feel myself very unfit to do that. I feel I still have to learn more." Furthermore, he refused to travel internationally to give saptāhas. All speakers expressed disdain for money and for so-called professional speakers who were said to be motivated by material gain.[4] Shrivatsa took this a step further:

> I have missed many kathās because the sponsor comes to ask me how much the expenditure will be. My standard rule is, any organizer who asks me what the expenditure in Bhāgavat will be, I never do that [event]. I never ever do that. Because Bhāgavata is not something for money. It will give you money, but don't ask. Don't ask.

In addition to the fact that he turns down invitations when the question of remuneration is raised, most interesting perhaps is Shrivatsa's attitude toward the Sanskrit language and its role in Bhāgavata discourses. I return to his unconventional and challenging views on this subject in chapter 8.

Abhishek Goswami

Not far from Shrivatsa Goswami's compound was the temple precinct of Radha Raman, dedicated to Kṛṣṇa in the form of the "Delighter of Rādhā." Inside a splendid pink sandstone portal, a paved footpath led past lofty old mansions that leaned in on either side. A steady stream of devotees flowed between the gate and the temple. Passersby warned of "monkey danger" and advised visitors to hide their valuables. Around a corner at the end of the footpath, another ancient gateway opened directly onto the temple forecourt. I climbed a narrow set of marble steps on the right and stooped to pass through the front door of an ancient edifice. A small, dark antechamber surrounded by red stone pillars led to a central atrium lit from above. As my eyes became accustomed to the dark interior, I noticed that the walls were covered with gorgeous murals from floor to ceiling, showing herds of cattle, gopīs, peacocks, and parrots. Incongruously in these rarefied surroundings, a brand-new children's bicycle was propped against an armchair, as if proclaiming that this was also a family home.

Abhishek Goswami came down the stairs, appeared from behind a curtain, and ushered me into a further chamber off the atrium. He sat regally against cushions on the floor, with his back to the wall on which more gopīs sported in a sylvan glade. Shriman Madhava Gaudeshvar Vaishnavacharya Maharaj Shri Abhishek Ji Goswami, to give him his full title, was in his late thirties. He was related to Shrivatsa Goswami but was of a younger generation. Steady, dignified, helpful, highly articulate, and thoughtful, Abhishek spoke perfect English. The house was two hundred fifty years old, he explained, and his family, as traditional goswamis of the Radha Raman Temple, had lived there for perhaps ten generations. As we settled in, an assistant set up an iPad to record video of our interview.

Bhāgavata exposition ran in Abhishek's family—his great-grandfather was a highly renowned Bhāgavata exponent—but his own path to the vocation was by no means straightforward. Abhishek's father, his father's cousins, and their children were all religious and were serving in the Radha Raman Temple. But Abhishek's father felt that the younger generation, even in priestly families like his own, were drifting away from spiritual practices and rejecting a lifestyle that had been structured around the Bhāgavata for generations. When Abhishek was just five years old, his father resolved to send him to boarding school in far-off Dehradun. As a young student, Abhishek was always fascinated by Vrindavan. He used to feel that his cousins back home were having much more fun than he was. He joked that of course, his cousins all felt that he was the one who was having all the fun. After graduating, he did higher studies in Ahmedabad, Gujarat. With a degree in business administration in hand, he and some friends planned to start up a factory or some other enterprise. They formed a company, but just before launching the business, Abhishek wanted to spend some time back in his hometown. In Vrindavan, his parents asked what he intended to do. He replied, "I want to read something." That was when he received his first copy of the Bhāgavatapurāṇa. For the twenty-three-year-old, this was a life-changing event:

> If you ask somebody from Bombay or Delhi, there are cults around novels; Ayn Rand is a cult, and other people are a cult. Bhāgavata actually washed off everything till that day I had read, achieved, or understood, and I used to just cry reading it. It was unstoppable. I was basically born in the Radha Raman family, and you were actually getting connected to your roots. The genes had started giving answers to what you were reading, and I just loved every moment.

At first, Abhishek read the Bhāgavata with the help of a Hindi translation, but soon the family invited an instructor to come and give him some training in Sanskrit grammar, beginning with the foundational grammatical text, *Laghu-siddhānta-kaumudī*.

Speaking of his training, Abhishek described the approach adopted by his teachers for making sense of the Bhāgavatapurāṇa, a sprawling and difficult text of fourteen thousand verses. His instructors divided the text into groups of similar units, such as the panegyrics known as *stutis* and the songs of praise, or *gītās*. These are the most important devotional elements of the text, in which bhakti receives its fullest expression. The Bhāgavata thus becomes more manageable. This seems to be a common approach in expositions of the text, as many speakers structure their entire discourses around these two elements, skipping from one stuti or gītā to the next, remaining less concerned with the interconnecting narrative. Abhishek said:

> Those traditional teachers who have taught me how to do my preparation for a Bhāgavata, they always tell me that Bhāgavata becomes very easy when you divide it. I asked them, "How do you divide it?" "It is so easy. Bring all the stutis separately, right from *Kuntī-stuti* to *Bhīṣma-stuti* to *Dhruva-stuti* to *Prahrāda-stuti*. So in the entire Bhāgavata, whoever has done a stuti, from Brahmā doing a stuti to Indra doing a stuti after committing mistakes, everybody has done a stuti. So bring all the stutis in one corner. OK, now let's work on gītās—*Gopī-gītā, Yugala-gītā, Bhramara-gītā*, there are so many gītās there. Now bring all the gītās together at one time. Just at the moment you start dividing Bhāgavata, you will see that Bhāgavata actually contains somebody who has been blessed by the Divine Presence and has actually done a stuti, and your entire Bhāgavata is complete. Otherwise, you go through the Māhātmya and then Bhakticaritra ["The Story of Bhakti"] and then Gokarṇa talking.

> But then don't just go the way it has been written originally in the Bhāgavata script. Go by making your own meanings of it.

Abhishek explained that for a person with a modern education such as himself, and indeed for many in his audience, it is difficult to accept the concept that Gokarṇa, one of the central figures in the Māhātmya, really had the ears of a cow, as the text states. In his expositions, Abhishek suggests that rather than "ears of a cow," Gokarṇa, a virtuous and saintly man, had "ears for a cow," that is, he was sympathetic to the suffering endured by cattle, a common concern shared by many Hindus, especially in Vrindavan. By skillfully reinterpreting the narrative in this way, Abhishek converted the story from something the audience might simply reject as fantasy to something that aligned with their own lives and concerns and with broader public discourses.

After immersing himself in the Bhāgavata in his hometown, Abhishek experienced a change of heart and informed his prospective business partners that he would not be joining them:

> I told my friends, "Friends, I don't think that I can continue with any other thing because I actually want to be in Vrindavan, and there is so much here that I don't want to come back." And everybody there at that point in time said to me, "You are a fool." They did not know what the Bhāgavata is. "This is just a book that you are reading." I said, "No, it's not just a book."

Now committed to Vrindavan and Bhāgavata exposition, Abhishek began a quest to attend as many saptāha events as possible in order to understand how various speakers narrated the text and to learn as much as he could. Before he gave his first saptāha, he underwent a period of intense preparation. He traveled to Haridwar at the foot of the Himalayas, where, according to tradition, Śuka narrated the first saptāha to Parīkṣit. In Haridwar, he took up residence in an ashram, bringing with him only his copy of the Bhāgavata. Every day on the banks of the Ganga, he made this supplication to the river: "Bless me so that I can, like you, have millions of waves, and if I am wrong, then correct me." Abhishek sat and rehearsed the entire Bhāgavata with no audience except the Ganga itself for ninety days, stopping only for prayers at dawn, midday, and dusk.

After he completed his practice in Haridwar, he returned to Vrindavan, where he soon received his first invitation to give a saptāha. Although he had two months' lead time, he still felt mentally unprepared. He had rehearsed the text a number of times and knew all the key verses, but he had never faced an audience other than the river. His first Bhāgavata was initiated by various Nepali organizations and Vaiṣṇava committees and was in held Kathmandu. In Abhishek's words, "It actually changed everything because . . . I was first introduced to what simple words can do to a person's heart when you relate Kṛṣṇa-līlā [the past-times of Kṛṣṇa]."

Like Shrivatsa, Abhishek was selective when it came to sponsors for whom he would conduct a saptāha. Before accepting an invitation, he preferred to meet the entire family in their home to assess the depth of their commitment:

> Are they ready to welcome it? Because from my point of view, it should not just be as if some entertainment is going to happen for seven days, and you are going to invite everyone from friends to your relatives, and you are going to set up a really beautiful *pandal* [tent], and it will be more like a socializing event. I don't think Bhāgavata should be an entertainment or that [such an] invitation should be accepted. But somebody [can accept] an invitation, meeting the whole family and thinking that they are bringing festivity to their lives—not entertainment, festivity, because Bhāgavata brings festivity. It is a transformative thing, yes it is. It just changes you. It can transform you. It is exactly how you drink this nectar. You have to be prepared. So if that preparedness is happening, you see the mood of the people in the house, even the youngsters.

The younger generation of Indians have experienced Western influence, and some have comparatively more money and freedom. Abhishek maintained that Bhāgavata was a means to bring young people back into the spiritual fold and return them to their family traditions. Abhishek claimed that an important realization from his first Bhāgavata was that an exposition should not simply follow the written text. The exponent should seek to visualize the events described in the narrative and recount these in a way that will engage and inspire his audience. For him, as for many other speakers, the vyās-pith exerted an inspirational, almost mystical power:

> It is not necessary only to speak what you have read. Because the moment you have gone through Bhāgavatas, I think that vyās-pith where you sit and narrate the kathā becomes such a sacred place

> that whatever you have accumulated in your brain, it becomes so active, that the moment the delivery of these words starts, it is actually God's grace. One won't be able to describe it in words. But you should be able to see it.... So that is why *ṛṣis* [sages] were called seers. So in my point of view, in a Bhāgavata, I would sit on the vyās-pith, and I would actually like to see it, because when you start seeing it and narrating it, everything changes.

To illustrate further the importance of visualizing the narrative episodes as he expounds on them, Abhishek told the story of a learned man, a "pandit-ji," who had only read the textual sources but had never meditated and had therefore "never drunk the nectar of the essence of the scriptures." Such a pandit might say in his saptāha, "The Bhāgavata says this, this says this, this mantra should be fitted in here, and this should be said there. This is in this Bhāgavata, this is in that Bhāgavata. That is in the Māṇḍūkyopaniṣad or Kathopaniṣad and other places." Abhishek's point was that a person who has "lived and drunk this nectar" will actually say in his exposition, "I am saying this." He is liberated from the need to quote from other scriptures, because he can speak from his own intuition, insight, and experience.

> My basic idea of Bhāgavata is, if I am thirty-eight or thirty-nine years now, I have lived my life, that complete richness of life, what I call life, what I call enriched life, when I definitely sit on the vyās-pith and narrate the kathā. Because that is blissful. Words will not be able to do justice to it. But I think once we started narrating the first Bhāgavata, that happened, I think it is your heart pouring out. I actually call the Bhāgavata-saptāha pouring out your heart and filling up so many earthen pots that are there in the form of human beings, just ready to fill their heads and take the garbage out.

Abhishek had given about one hundred fifty saptāhas to date; his most recent event had been held in Delhi a few months before our interview and was attended by twenty-five hundred people every day.

Chandan Goswami

Vaishnavacharya Chandan Goswami, another descendant of the Radha Raman lineages and a cousin of Abhishek Goswami, was born in Vrindavan in 1983. The first time I met him, he and his elder brother were on temple duty. Gorgeously dressed in silk kurtas, dhotis, and wraps, the two young men were responsible for opening the door of the inner sanctum to reveal the deity to the host of devotees gathered in the temple court, performing āratī before the deity for his pleasure, and distributing prasād at the close of the ceremony. His family home, where we later sat and talked, was also in the Radha Raman Temple compound, almost next door to Abhishek's family.

Chandan Goswami first studied the Bhāgavata from the age of fourteen under his late guru, Tulsi Charan Swami, for three or four years. Tulsi Charan Swami had a deep knowledge of the Bhāgavata and, according to his student, could identify any of its fourteen thousand verses by canto, chapter, and number. His teacher came to Chandan's home every day, and for two to three hours, he would lead his student systematically through the text, starting from the Māhātmya. Although Chandan studied very little grammar at that time, they would analyze one or two verses in depth, and a further five verses would be set for memorization. These might be drawn from anywhere in the text, or they might belong to specific prayers that the guru chose to emphasize, especially the gītās or stutis. As mentioned earlier, the older school of teachers holds that these prayers encapsulate the essential devotional philosophy of the Bhāgavata, while the purely narrative elements are secondary. Chandan still remembers today the verses he memorized in his youth: "He used to give me the essence of it at that time. He was making me prepare for the Bhāgavata-saptāha, a bit in a commercial way, but what he had given is something I never lost, and I always respect that."

After the death of his first guru, Chandan "took refuge" with his own father as guru and continued his study of the text. The young student began to develop a deep affection for the Bhāgavata, especially the tenth canto, set in Vrindavan.

Chandan's career experienced what he described as a "bump." He had not originally intended to become an exponent at such an early age but planned to postpone that career until he was thirty-five or forty, as do many speakers in Vrindavan. Chandan went to his father one morning as he was taking his "bed tea." He paid obeisance, sat on the floor, and said to his father, "I have three career options. Can you just tell me which one I can go for?" "Yes, you can ask," his father replied. Chandan said that some disciples who were in the film industry had offered him roles in Bollywood. His father put down his cup and asked, "So do you want to run around the bushes and the trees singing a song with the heroine?" "No, I don't want that." That was the end of the first option. Chandan then asked, "How about trying for modeling?" His father said, "Would you like it if after ten years your disciples would do āratī to a photograph on the altar of you in swimwear?" Chandan replied, "I can't imagine that." So the second option was finished. Finally, he said, "OK, I have a third option. One of my cousins is a flight attendant. He is also calling me to come. Do you mind if I go and join him?" His father asked, "So you want to become a waiter?" Chandan said, "No, I don't want to become a waiter." His father continued, "If that's what you want, I can ask one of my disciples to put you in a five-star restaurant, and you can work there. You can serve all the people nicely. Why do you want to go to forty thousand feet to do this waiter work?" Chandan was speechless, and, realizing the truth of his father's words, he felt that all three of his hopes had been "nicely, very sweetly crushed."

Heartbroken, he retreated to his room, where a photograph of the deity Kṛṣṇa in the form of Radha Raman was hanging on the wall. He locked the door, lay down on the bed, and, with his pillow on his head, cried himself to sleep. A strange and powerful dream came to him. He was running through the jungle playing hide-and-seek with a beautiful girl. Chandan followed the girl into a cave, but it was pitch-black inside, and he was unable to find her. Instead, he came across a young boy, five or six years old, holding a stick like a cow-herd. In the local Braj-bhāsā dialect, Chandan asked, "What are you doing here, young fellow? What are you doing, so small, and in this cave in the jungle?" The boy replied, "I was waiting for you." "Waiting for me? Go back home, and tell me where that girl is." The boy said, "I'm waiting for you. Didn't you recognize me?" Chandan peered into the boy's face, thinking that he recognized him from somewhere, and suddenly he realized that it was his own deity Radha Raman. Chandan made his obeisance, and the deity said, "I gave you a birth in a family to serve me and to preach my name, and what you are doing is chasing after *māyā*, illusion. This girl is māyā." Chandan continued:

> All of a sudden, I woke up, and this photograph was lying next to me. And everything got changed afterward. Radha Raman Dev maybe wanted to give me a sign that this dream was real—it was not any of my emotional creation or something. So at the time I saw that, I thought, "I know my path. It is so clear." That was the time I decided, "OK, no more Bollywood [laughter]."

FIGURE 4.1. Radha Raman. The image of Kṛṣṇa as he appeared to Chandan Goswami in his dream.
Source: 4krsna.wordpress.com

Like many speakers, Chandan described the process of exposition as a transcendental experience of divine inspiration:

> I personally do not feel that I give the kathās, because these are our teachings and this is what I have got from our āchāryas. Also, when you sit to give the kathā, ask your Lord only to deliver that kathā, and ask your Lord only to listen to that kathā. You are not speaking, nor are you giving the kathā to the ordinary audience.

Chandan gave his first saptāha in 2008 at the age of twenty-five and had since given around sixty. In 2013 alone, he gave week-long expositions in the United Kingdom, Argentina, Brazil, the United States, and Canada. At other times, he taught in the United Arab Emirates, South Africa, and many places in India.

Speakers of this younger generation, such as the cousins Abhishek and Chandan, are firmly embedded in digital culture and make extensive use of websites, blogs, Facebook, Twitter, and YouTube.[5] At the time of this writing, Chandan's Facebook page already had several thousand "likes" and "followers." Not only did Facebook facilitate direct communication between Chandan and his devotees all over the world, but his team uploaded a fresh image of the deity Radha Raman every day, displaying his ever-changing apparel and offering virtual darshan to any devotee who logged in.

Chandan's Facebook page is also a place for personal reflection. Regarding the challenges of his vocation as a Bhāgavata exponent, he posted this poignant personal note on the first day of the new year in 2014:

> There are moments in life that make me realise how challenging this preaching path is; one which Radharaman-ji has bestowed upon me. There are times where I wish I had taken birth in a Sudra [low-caste] family since I love the simplicity of the instructions from Shastras specifically related to the devotional practice of Sudras, which keep them free from twice-born rules and only ask them to chant His Holy-Name to attain perfection.[6]

I turn now from the hereditary goswamis of Vrindavan to introduce two Bhāgavata exponents who are products of the traditional guru-kula, or "guru family," system. As boys, they experienced a thirst for spiritual knowledge that led them to seek out gurus with whom they could live and study. The first, Radhikadas, found his guru in Mumbai, while Siddhanti Maharaj settled in Vrindavan.

The Guru-Kula Path

Radhikadas Maharaj

I first contacted Acharya Shri Chandradas-ji Maharaj "Radhikadas" having seen his billboard on the main street of Vrindavan. I cold-called him, introduced myself and my project, and arranged to meet him at the ISKCON shelter for abandoned cattle the following morning. He arrived right on time and ferried us by motorbike down a network of sandy lanes between the circumambulatory path and the Yamuna River to his residence/ashram, a modest three-room apartment in a concrete blockhouse. Double steel doors opened into a spacious but unfurnished hall with a shrine at the far end, overseen by a large garlanded image of Rādhā.

Radhikadas appeared to be in his mid-forties and was of medium build, with close-cropped hair and the single lock, or *śikhā*, typical of orthodox Vaiṣṇavas. Dressed in orange robes, he had a friendly but modest

FIGURE 4.2. Radhikadas Maharaj with his daughter Poonam at his ashram.

disposition. His nineteen-year-old daughter Poonam, a second-year student at the local university, brought chairs, snacks, and tea for us, while her father sat on a raised platform in front of the altar. He recounted his early life in halting but expressive English, which I have edited lightly:

> My mother and father lived in a village. I was reading a lot. So when I was reading, I was thinking: What is the sun? What is the world? What is man? What is lady? What is death? What is birth? What is happiness, and what is sadness? Who is giving happiness? Who is giving sadness? Who is giving money? Who is giving poverty? Who gives death? So I was thinking all the time.

Impelled by these existential questions and finding no answers at home, he sought instruction elsewhere. His quest led to a guru-kula in Mumbai, where he studied for the requisite twelve years. He described his training:

> Bhāgavata-saptāha classes, training, very difficult subjects, but all the time, *brahmacarya* [celibacy], mantra meditation, chanting mantras,

> chanting the guru mantra, reading Śrīmad-bhāgavata *granth* [text] and Veda and others, Bhaktamālā, Śrīmad-bhagavadgītā, purāṇas, Mahābhārata, Padmapurāṇa, and other granths. Long time reading. Twelve years reading. Twelve years reading granths. Chanting the guru mantra and *brahmacarya pālana* ["adhering to the rules of celibacy"]: no sex, no drinking, no smoking, no meat. All the time thinking about God and meditation. So afterward, it came into my heart. Afterward, I was always feeling joy. I did not want other *indriyas* [sense-objects] and *vṛttis* [activities], I did not want other beautiful girls, other foods. I didn't want them. All the time, I enjoyed Lord Kṛṣṇa. He is real knowledge. He is real life. He is the real *upalabdhi* [achievement].

Since Radhikadas gave his first saptāha in 2003 in Vrindavan, he has given an average of four or five saptāhas per year and a total of forty or fifty to date. His most recent saptāha, the one advertised on the billboard we had seen, finished only ten days before our first interview and was sponsored by a group of his disciples from Orissa. It had been held in the hall in which we were sitting and was attended by about two hundred people daily from 2 to 6.30 p.m. Like many exponents, Radhikadas traveled all over India to give saptāhas. The event before the most recent one was in Allahabad; his next event would be in Mumbai. Of his experience as a Bhāgavata exponent, Radhikadas said, "All saptāhas are different. Śrīmad-bhāgavata granth is very big. Like the rays of the sun. All rays give light. The Śrīmad-bhāgavata is the same as the sun. The Śrīmad-bhāgavata has all knowledge. So, as the sun gives light, in the same way Śrīmad-bhāgavata gives knowledge."

Radhikadas explained that during each of the seven days of the saptāha, one negative state is dissolved: ignorance, egotism, attraction, repulsion, clinging to worldly life, self-consciousness, and possessiveness. If one listens wholeheartedly, personal transformation is achievable: "How much you listen, one hundred percent listen with your heart, so after seven days, you change your life. But listen. Listen. One hundred percent listen. Listen with your heart."

After the death of his father, Radhikadas returned to his village to conduct a saptāha. His daughter proposed that she accompany him back to Vrindavan, as she wanted a "spiritual life." She had kept house for her father for the past two years, and, as Radhikadas explained, "doing sādhana, chanting mantras, sevā, singing—nice singing—and experiencing Śrīmad-bhāgavata. . . . My daughter is *brahmacari*. No boyfriends, no other eating, only eating this prasād," he said, indicating the meal of consecrated vegetarian food that Poonam had just served us. Did Radhikadas hope that his daughter would become an exponent one day? "At this time, she is not ready, but after reading Śrīmad-bhāgavata."

At the end of a follow-up visit a few days later, Radhikadas invited us into a chamber off the main hall that doubled as his bedroom and office. Stacks of DVDs of his recent saptāhas were piled on the desk and on the floor, the beginnings of a modest retail enterprise. He suggested a price of 1,100 rupees (US $20) for a set of twenty DVDs of a saptāha he had given in Mumbai, explaining that the price only covered the cost of production, adding apologetically that he was no businessman. Poonam helped sort out the DVDs while he showed me a forty-page booklet he had written and published. He proudly pointed out an account of his guru lineage; it showed Radhikadas as the ninetieth member in a line of succession stretching back twenty-seven hundred years to Lord Krishna himself.

Siddhanti Maharaj

It was a mild mid-morning, with the winter sun struggling through the haze. We were stuck in gridlocked traffic on the outskirts of Faridabad, a satellite city on the edge of New Delhi. Although we had set out from Vrindavan some three hours earlier, we were still running late for our ten o'clock appointment. My cell phone rang at 10:02. It was our prospective host, Siddhanti Maharaj, chivalrously ringing to check that we were all right and offering us help, "as you are new here." We eventually located his residence down a side street in an affluent new suburb of upper-middle-class homes set around a rectangular park of lawns and trees.

Siddhanti's ashram, the Sri Radha Madhav Gaudiya Math, was in a new marble-lined building of three stories. The interior was cool and dark, with a generous entrance hall opening into a shrine room on one side. An assistant ushered us in and directed us up a sweeping white-marble staircase. At the top, Siddhanti welcomed us and embraced me warmly. In his simple but comfortable living quarters, we accepted water and guava juice. Siddhanti, about forty years old, wore the tonsure and salmon-colored robes of a Gauḍīya Vaiṣṇava renunciant. His demeanor was calm and quiet, friendly and accommodating without being effusive, yet he appeared entirely confident in his role and knowledge.

According to his website, Bhaktivedanta Siddhanti Maharaj was born in Delhi in 1972, and at the age of twenty-three, in 1995, he left home to live in Vrindavan. In 1997, he met his guru, Srila Bhakti Pramod Puri Goswami Maharaj, from whom he received is primary initiation, or dīkṣā. Following his guru's death in 1999, he "took shelter" with Srila Bhaktivedanta Narayan Goswami Maharaj and was engaged in the publication of Narayan Goswami's books and magazines. Siddhanti took vows of renunciation, or *sannyāsa*, in November 2010 and went on to establish the ashram in Faridabad, where he now holds regular weekly programs. Siddhanti travels all over India, particularly North India, and has been as far away as Australia, "spreading the message of Sri Caitanya Mahaprabhu, especially the message of Śrīmad Bhāgavata," and is well known for his Bhāgavata-saptāhas.[7]

During the ten years Siddhanti spent with his guru, he only heard occasional saptāhas from him, but "every class, every lecture," was based on the Bhāgavata, even if it was not in the form of a saptāha. His guru provided the original inspiration for him to become a Bhāgavata speaker: "I used to see my spiritual master, he was very expert in giving saptāhas. He could bring out so many hidden secrets, so I was inspired just by seeing him. I was inspired in my heart. One day, I wanted to be a speaker like him." Regarding his experience of saptāha and the process of giving saptāhas himself, Siddhanti said:

> There are different categories of speakers. Some speak for others but are not inclined to follow the teaching themselves. They are only speakers. There is another category. They also want to get inspiration in their own hearts. They follow what is written. The speaker is the first audience, because the mouth is very close to the ear. With this, the speech goes to the heart.
>
> I'll tell you one secret. Kathā does not mean that we just study something and speak about it. Sometimes when we speak, something miraculous happens. This is the mercy of kathā. If the speaker is very confident and is speaking from the heart, then by the mercy of kathā, some new things that we have not even heard of come, which is one of the miracles of kathā. Some points come out of our mouths which we never even thought about. It is kind of a surprise; then we have so much respect for the Bhāgavata-kathā. It is by its mercy that we are able to speak about this.

Siddhanti's description of the "miracle" that befalls speakers during a saptāha is similar to the sensation of "divine inspiration" alluded to by many exponents, the mystical power of the vyās-pīth to inspire speech, the grace of God, and, as Siddhanti put it, the mercy of the Bhāgavata itself.

A young person from Delhi had earlier suggested to me that his generation was not especially interested in religion, being too busy with their own lives. Siddhanti has a reputation for appealing to younger people, so I asked him how he went about attracting and retaining such an audience. He explained that he sought to inspire them by beginning with what he called the "very basics," before speaking in any depth about devotion:

> We get friendly with them, and when they are friendly with us, then we try to make our points. Some of them like it, and some of them, even if they don't dislike it, they become neutral. Bhāgavata-saptāha is a festival time [*utsav*], so if not for a three- or four-hour session, they come for one or two hours. They come at the last session and enjoy the dancing and all. So we have to create that environment which is comfortable for the young people, by telling them that it is a festival: "Don't think it is anything that is only meant for religious people. It is a carnival. You come, and you'll see yourself." So they come.

Since Siddhanti gave his first saptāha in 2010, he had given forty or fifty in all, sometimes conducting as many as four events back-to-back in a month. His most recent saptāha was a month or so before our interview, in Ambala, Kurukshetra. That event was attended by about thirteen hundred people and was jointly sponsored by eight families. He has traveled to Australia on a number of occasions and gave the performance in Brisbane that I will describe in chapter 7.

Vedic Yatra Pathashala

Having introduced speakers of the goswami lineages and the guru-kulas, I will now give an example of the third pathway to the vocation of exponent: the Bhāgavata college system. After a long, bumpy auto-rickshaw ride through the clogged lanes of the medieval heart of Vrindavan, the road opened out as it approached the outskirts of the town. After many inquiries and a number of false leads, I eventually found the Vedic Yatra Pathashala, a training college for Bhāgavata exponents, next to Vrindavan's only railway line.[8] The school consisted of a group of modern one- and two-story concrete buildings. An obliging watchman seated outside an iron gate signed me in, and a huddle of young male students in smart uniforms of white kurtas and crimson dhotis led me across an open courtyard into a long, narrow vestibule.

Seated on the floor were several young students stripping tulsi leaves off their stalks and dropping them into a large wicker basket. Between them was a forty-year-old man with soft brown hair and a wispy beard, in the robes of a renunciant. I introduced myself, asked to speak to the guru, and was shown into a small, dark, crowded room. Perched on the edge of a bed in the inner sanctum was a diminutive, very elderly gentleman in a white nightgown and nightcap. He apologized in Sanskrit for being in poor health and was obviously having trouble breathing, but he still managed to make me feel welcome. We spoke briefly, but he indicated that as all the teachers were having a day off, there was no one for me to talk to. On reflection, he suggested that I should talk to Madhukanthadas, the older person in the vestibule, so I joined the little group on the floor stripping tulsi leaves.

Madhukanthadas took a while to warm up but eventually began to tell me about himself and the history and routines of the college. We sat in the middle of a growing circle of students who listened eagerly to our conversation and contributed the odd word of English, Hindi, or Sanskrit to the exchange. Madhukanthadas was originally from Orissa, had been in Vrindavan for twenty-one years, and had been associated with the college for fifteen years. He was a celibate renunciant and filled a role similar to that of a housemaster in a British-style boarding school.

The college was established in 1964, specifically to train boys in the Bhāgavatapurāṇa, by the guru Bhagavat Bhushan Shri Shrinathji Shastri Puranacarya (b. 1924), the elderly gentleman I had met inside. The college accepted one batch of twenty-five students every other year. The youngest students were fourteen to fifteen years old, and the oldest were twenty-one. Most were from Brahmin families in North India and Nepal. My question about whether girls were admitted was briskly dismissed.

The aim of the "gurudev" was to enable students to be self-sufficient by the time they graduated at the end of their two-year training period. Each graduate should be able to support himself financially by one or more of four practices: as a professional reader of the Bhāgavata (*Bhāgavata-pārāyaṇa*), as a Bhāgavata exponent (*Bhāgavata-kathā pravacaka*), as an expert in the ritual worship of Rudra (a form of Śiva, a practice known as *Rudrābhiśeka*), or as a practitioner of *karma-kāṇḍa*, that is, as an officiating priest in a range of other ritual practices. Over the decades, the school claimed to have produced two thousand graduates, of whom at least one thousand have become Bhāgavata exponents. The college's website mentions Shri Krishna Chandra Shastri "Thakurji," Shri Badrishji, and Shri Girishnandji among the "luminaries" it has produced.[9] All three are well-established Bhāgavata speakers, and the first, Thakurji, is indisputably one of the superstars of the profession. According to Madhukanthadas, there were fifteen other similar schools that specialized in Bhāgavata training in Vrindavan. This school, with twenty-five students, was considered to be among the larger ones.

The students' day started at 5 a.m. with an hour-long session of chanting the Gāyatrī-mantra, a traditional requirement for all Brahmins, and was followed by two hours of yoga. From 9 to 10 a.m. each day, the students chanted eleven chapters of the Bhāgavatapurāṇa. As the complete text was 355 chapters long, a full recitation took just more than one month. Over the two-year period of training, each student completed about twenty full recitations. From eleven until noon, the students studied Sanskrit grammar. While some had already studied Sanskrit before they joined the college, many were starting from scratch. In Vrindavan in general, Bhāgavata exponents did not necessarily have a deep knowledge of grammar but simply studied the Sanskrit text with a parallel Hindi translation. At this school, in contrast, the students were required to attain a good command of the grammar as part of their training, although how far they progressed in two years was unclear. The rationale for grammatical knowledge was given in an aphorism by Madhukanthadas: "Without salt, curry has no taste; without grammar, the Bhāgavata has no taste."

After lunch, the students studied *nītiśāstras*, the well-known treatises on conduct, including Cāṇakyanīti. Once a week, they had English classes and Sanskrit conversation classes. All the students I encountered were competent in spoken Sanskrit, and the boys and I laughed together as we corrected one another's little grammatical failures. At least some classes were conducted in Sanskrit; the students spoke Sanskrit in the classroom, but they spoke Hindi in the courtyard and elsewhere. The older boys knew English well. At 3 p.m. each day, there was an hour-long session of Bhāgavatapurāṇa study. This was open to the public, and as many as two hundred or three hundred people came from outside to audit the classes. Finally, every evening, there was a one- to two-hour discourse on the Bhāgavata conducted by the guru. Classes were held on this pattern every day of the week, with rest days on the first, eighth, and twelfth days of the lunar month. In addition to this formal instruction, students also undertook service for their "guru-mother and -father" and helped to look after the school's cattle.

Hanging on the end wall in the vestibule was a photo portrait of a handsome, clean-cut young man. This was the guru's grandson, Bhagwatkinkar Shri Anurag Krishna Shastri "Kanhaiyaji," now a successful and well-known speaker in his own right. Typical of the younger generation of contemporary speakers, Kanhaiyaji also gave discourses on Rāma, Hanumān, and the Great Goddess Devī, in addition to the Bhāgavatapurāṇa. He has also assumed overall management of the school, and the income from his kathā performances was its sole source of income, as the students paid no fees. The college's financial self-sufficiency was a point of pride, and, as Madhukanthadas remarked, "We are not begging; we are not demanding fees from parents."

Just as I was leaving, I was summoned back to the guru's den, where Shrinathji moved with difficulty from his bed to an armchair. He kindly gave me some prasād in the form of chunks of crystallized sugar, with the words "This is to be taken to your own country." After my conversation with Madhukanthadas and my final audience with the guru, the boys

FIGURE 4.3. Students at the Vedic Yatra Pathashala, Vrindavan, with three of the college's newborn calves.

insisted that I should visit the cattle stalls. They excitedly led me past the school pump and along the courtyard under a huge old neem tree to the far end of the compound. The cattle stalls occupied the ground floor of one multistory block. They proudly introduced me to the twenty-one cows that provided milk for the school. The boys crowded around three fifteen-day-old calves, hugging and petting them while I took their photos. On my way out of the college, the older students proudly displayed their school ID badges on scarlet lanyards and the name of the school embroidered on their kurtas. They were very eager that these should also be photographed. A cheerful entourage of students escorted me to the gate, where we parted on the friendliest terms.

My visit to the Vedic Yatra Pathashala provided a preliminary glimpse into the previously opaque world of Bhāgavata training. This was my closest approach to seeing how students learned to recite, study, understand, and discourse on the Bhāgavata. In addition, I enjoyed the traditional atmosphere of the college, the obvious affection and reverence the boys had for their elderly guru and for the housemaster, and the way they lavished affection on the calves. It was also significant because schools like these are a major source of new Bhāgavata exponents.

The Crowded Marketplace

The world of Bhāgavata-saptāha exponents is a crowded marketplace. The billboards that line the streets of Vrindavan promoting individual speakers and their saptāhas clamor for attention. The number of potential sponsors and the amount of wealth they are prepared to invest in saptāhas are substantial but not infinite. Hundreds of newly minted exponents enter the market every year. Prospective exponents are in unspoken competition with one another for audiences, devotees, and sponsorship. Not all new speakers succeed in establishing themselves, and many fail to gain a foothold. The goswamis from the prestigious lineages enjoy considerable advantages bestowed by names, titles, and in some cases financial resources. The institutional backing of a temple or a well-known family may provide a lifeline, while independent new speakers must strive to build their own followings.

The guru-kula graduates inherit some of the prestige of their gurus, whose names and images are often featured in their promotional materials. While the first of these speakers introduced here, Radhikadas, was more or less a "sole operator," Siddhanti Maharaj had a substantial organization, the International Pure Bhakti Yoga Society, behind him. Such institutions provide Internet presence, expertise, publishing services, publications, and access to a larger public beyond their own devotees and supporters.

Another point raised by my visit to the Vedic Yatra Pathashala is the ethical relationship between giving Bhāgavata-saptāha performances and the necessity of earning a living. Bhāgavata college graduates, especially those lacking significant social connections, must rely on their own talents to build their reputations and support bases, often in the face of prejudice expressed by other speakers that they are only in it for the money. Yet even in the college system, well-known and highly respected teachers such as Shrinathji lend credibility, support, and encouragement to their protégés.

Everyone within the tradition, exponents and audiences alike, agree that the sacred narratives of the Bhāgavatapurāṇa should not be sold for money. As an anonymous devotee in Vrindavan remarked, "It is very sinful. There should not be commercialization. Saptāha gives you love. You cannot sell this thing. Those professionals, they charge huge amounts, ten to fifteen lakhs of rupees." And yet, of course, most, if not all, speakers accept donations, and nearly all have families, charities, and institutions to support. While people are scathing about those who give saptāha performances for money, particular criticism is aimed at "professional" speakers who graduate from Bhāgavata schools. They are held to be distinct from speakers from family lineages and those associated with the major temples or guru-kulas, whom they call "spiritual" speakers. Siddhanti expressed a commonly held view:

> There are two categories of speakers: one is those who are spiritually inclined; others are materially motivated. . . . By performing Bhāgavata-saptāhas, they get a lot of donations. There is a lot of money involved. There are so many speakers, especially in places like Vrindavan, who are professionals. They are only conducting saptāhas for money. So in the kathā, they inspire people in so many ways to come forward and give so many things [i.e., large donations].

Siddhanti backed this up with a quotation: *śrīmad bhāgavata-mahapurāṇaṁ yad vaiṣṇava-priyam* (BhP 12.13.18), the Bhāgavata is "beloved of Vaiṣṇavas" not just common devotees but those who are purely devoted to Kṛṣṇa and who have the highest motives. Speakers who are materially motivated will never be able to activate *śabda-brahman*, the numinous power of the spoken word, and their saptāhas will never be truly transformative. As Siddhanti said:

> There is one verse that says kathā is only for Vaiṣṇavas to speak, not professionals. A Vaiṣṇava is a devotee who has surrendered his life to a spiritual master. If Bhāgavata is heard from the lips of a pure devotee, this gives so much change for the audience. Bhāgavata given for inferior motives does not affect the heart at all. An example is given: milk which is touched by the lips of a snake . . . still appears to be milk, but if you drink that, it would give a poisonous effect and would harm us. If a nondevotee or a professional [gives a saptāha], then it gives a poisonous effect. All other material desires get more and more. This is evidenced by the scriptures.

There is a general consensus that, unlike "spiritual" speakers, the "professionals," or "those who speak with the lips only," are not bona fide. A similar point of view was expressed by Abhishek Goswami:

> Now there are hundreds and hundreds and hundreds of speakers. But some are very famous, and some are not so famous. Some are just doing Bhāgavata for their livelihood. So once your own principle for doing a Bhāgavata is for creating a livelihood from it, then you have lost it. Then even wanting your śabda-brahman to be reignited in a Bhāgavata, you've lost it. You've lost it. Everybody needs resources to run their family or to run their household, but when you are there in the Bhāgavata, just forget it. And the moment you really forget it, then material possessions and materialistic pursuits should not be of any importance to you. The moment they are not—the moment they are not really—I am telling you Bhāgavata itself starts blessing you.

One of the explicit aims of the Vedic Yatra college was to enable the boys to become self-sufficient, that is, to make a living from their expertise as specialist religious practitioners. Having spent time at the school and having met the guru and the students, I was feeling much more sympathetic toward this cohort of speakers, and my understanding of the ethical issues became more nuanced, but outside the colleges themselves, I sought in vain for sympathy for this approach, which offers children from poor families an opportunity to make a living as professional Bhāgavata exponents.

One informant remarked that the crux of the matter was not the amount of wealth that exponents accumulate but their motivation. "It is more an attitude thing," she said. "Some rich and successful exponents are not attached to wealth and are otherworldly. It is not the money but the attitude to money." There is a long-standing skepticism among non-Brahmins and among nonreligious people in general regarding Brahmins' attitude toward money. As another informant remarked, "As soon as those goswamis get into your home, they are charging extra for this and extra for that." It is certainly true that the most financially successful exponents have very considerable wealth. One famous speaker lives in a palatial residence with sweeping lawns right in the middle of Vrindavan itself. It is so prominent that, as someone said, "Every parrot and every crow knows it." This exponent, though apparently very rich, is also highly respected.

The marketplace is not only crowded, but it is also becoming increasingly diverse. There are new classes of exponents entering the fray. For example, Radhanath Swami, an ISKCON devotee originally from the United States, is, as far as I know, the first non-Indian speaker on the saptāha circuit. Ilona Wilczewska informed me of a Bhāgavata training school for girls at Barsana, not far from Vrindavan. A small number of female exponents are now giving saptāhas. One professor, Prema Pandurang, is well established and highly esteemed (Desai 2013). Indeed, some male exponents already feel threatened by the advent of female competition: "They are pretty, they wear makeup and beautiful clothes. Of course, people will choose to see them," one insider complained.

I conclude this section with a reflection on the question of vocation. In his study of exponents of the Rāmcaritmānas tradition, Lutgendorf (1991, 173) found that "most performers . . . described their choice of vocation as the result of spiritual experiences or as a response to an inner summons." The two younger goswamis, Abhishek and Chandan, both responded to powerful spiritual experiences. Abhishek, in the interval between college and a career in business, was profoundly moved by reading the Bhāgavata, which "washed off everything till that day I had read, achieved, or understood." Similarly, Chandan experienced a life-changing dream in which he was presented a mission by his deity Radha Raman, which emphatically put an end to his Bollywood fantasies. Satchitananda Sai, the exponent at the saptāha in Canberra, described his experience of vocation: "I worked in IT as a business analyst. The call came from the Divine that I should take up this mission. When he gives the command, he gives the skills, the resources, the knowledge—all of them."[10] The exponent from the guru-kula system,

FIGURE 4.4. A female exponent, Sadhana Shakti-ji, advertising in Vrindavan.

Siddhanti Maharaj, was moved to become a speaker by his spiritual master. Siddhanti reported that he was "inspired in his heart" by his guru's teachings and resolved to become an exponent himself. Radhikadas's vocation was not explicit; it may have been a continuation of the spiritual thirst that drew him to the guru-kula in the first place, coupled with the demands of making a living. Shrivatsa Goswami, again, proves the exception. Of all the speakers, he was the most down-to-earth and the least likely to romanticize. The impulse for him was his mother's arm twisting.

These exponents are all extraordinary individuals, each in his own way. Most have undergone years of training and have acquired a profound knowledge of the text and the philosophies of their respective lineages. They have the ability to extemporize for hours on end, for seven days straight, and to hold an audience's attention throughout. Some have the stamina to maintain this discipline week on, week off, not just for months or years but in some cases for decades on end. All have demonstrated the ability to survive and thrive in a crowded, highly competitive marketplace. The vocation of the exponent only acquires expression through the performance of the text, which is the subject of chapter 5.

5

The Text—Veda

AS EARLY AS four millennia ago, the sacred songs offered during Vedic fire rituals were grouped together in *maṇḍalas*, or cycles, each traditionally preserved by a specific priestly lineage. The ten maṇḍalas together, consisting of just more than one thousand songs, are known as the Ṛg Veda. As these songs invoke the deities to maintain the universe, they came to be invested with awesome authority and terrible power. The Vedas were preserved orally and passed from generation to generation, and they have come to signify supreme sacred knowledge in the Hindu world. As the symbol of the ultimate storehouse of knowledge, *Veda* provides the metaphor for this chapter. Indeed, the Bhāgavatapurāṇa, in common with a number of other texts in the Sanskritic archive, even refers to itself as the "fifth Veda." This chapter summarizes the main narratives of the Bhāgavatapurāṇa and illustrates how exponents arrange their spoken discourse around the text.

The structure of the Bhāgavatapurāṇa is very complex; it consists of a set of narratives made up of stories within stories within stories. A skillful exponent may occasionally remind the audience which character within the narrative is addressing whom. While it is desirable to maintain this sense of clarity, it is perhaps less important than the overall discursive thrust of the performance. The general impression gained by the audience during a saptāha is of a set of free-standing narrative units strung out along a single chronological thread or, to use a more Indic metaphor, like pearls on a string. The audience may also become aware of a degree of congruity among the units: in the majority of narratives, especially in the skandhas preceding the Kṛṣṇa avatāra, a great bhakta (a devotee of the Lord), either an avatāra himself or a partial avatāra (*aṁśa*) of the Divine, extols Viṣṇu, receives instruction on the true nature of all things, and achieves a state of unity with the Absolute. As the Melbourne-based exponent Satchitananda Sai remarked, "The Bhāgavatapurāṇa is a scrapbook filled what Bhagavān's devotees. Some people collect stamps, some collect coins. Bhagavān collects devotees and puts them in his scrapbook." Each narrative unit is thus a story of redemption which reflects in miniature the process of the Bhāgavatapurāṇa as a whole.

In the following account of the narratives of the Bhāgavatapurāṇa, I use four broad categories: mythology, history, cosmology, and theology. The mythological sections deal primarily with deities, the historical narratives mainly treat human characters, the cosmological passages describe the creation and constitution of the universe, and the theological sections are primarily didactic and philosophical in character. Of course, there is much intermixing of these subjects; human characters pop up in mythological sections, and vice versa, and theology pervades the whole work. These categories are merely intended to be a rough guide to the dominant themes of the various sections.

It is not possible for an exponent to cover every episode of the Bhāgavatapurāṇa in a week, nor is it possible to summarize all fourteen thousand verses in a few pages; some process of selection is necessary. All exponents have their own ways of choosing appropriate episodes for exposition and apportioning the content of the twelve skandhas over the seven days. As mentioned in chapter 1, performance theory sensitizes us to the fact that oral performances are emergent; no two saptāha events are identical. Each develops independently in accordance with the predilections of the performer, the responses of the audience, and any number of other ambient influences on the day. Comparison of audio recordings of successive saptāha performances by the same exponent reveals a similar overall structure but considerable differences in content and emphasis. Although the narratives are usually treated in the order in which they appear in the original text, some exponents may choose to omit certain skandhas (for example, the largely cosmological and historical second and sixth books) or to treat them very cursorily.

Exponents like to claim "divine inspiration" when it comes to selecting narratives for a performance. Some say the exposition comes to them spontaneously, simply as the result of ascending the vyās-pīth, the speaker's throne. Only one speaker, Shrivatsa Goswami, admitted to making some cursory notes before a performance, but many exponents keep a notebook in their laps during a performance, which they glance at from time to time. Before he gave his first saptāha, Abhishek Goswami attended many events in Vrindavan to learn from other exponents. There is also a certain degree of imitation among speakers. I have noticed trends of quoting particular verses, even ones that do not appear to be very significant. For example, many speakers dwell on the verse from the Māhātmya in which the young girl Bhakti says to Nārada, "Hail, hail, O holy man! Wait a while. Put an end to my worry" (BhP 0.1.42). This could only be the result of speakers learning from one another's performances.

In terms of dividing the text over the week, the Sanskrit edition of the Bhāgavatapurāṇa published by the Gita Press suggests this program, giving the end point for each day:

Day One. The dialogue between Manu and Kardama (3.21).
Day Two. The story of Bharata (5.15).
Day Three. The end of the seventh skandha (7.15).
Day Four. The advent of Kṛṣṇa (10.6).
Day Five. Kṛṣṇa's marriage with Rukmiṇī (10.55).
Day Six. The Haṁsākhyāna, better known as the Uddhava-gītā (11.16).
Day Seven. The remainder of the text (12.13).

It is apparent from this scheme that much more time (four of the seven days) is dedicated to the final three skandhas alone, especially the much-loved tenth skandha, in which the pastimes of Kṛṣṇa are recounted. This is indeed typical of most saptāha performances; audiences and exponents especially look forward to the "sweetness" of the narratives relating to the youthful deity.

The summary of the narratives of the Bhāgavatapurāṇa provided here largely follows the performance given by Acharya Sri Satchitananda Sai in Canberra in April 2013, which I describe in chapter 2. This breakdown differs from the one given above in the Gita Press edition. One unusual feature of this event was that the exponent covered the Māhātmya in a preliminary session held on the evening before the saptāha began, so this event actually ran over a total of eight days.

Preliminaries: The Māhātmya

Most saptāha events begin with a session devoted to the Śrīmad-bhāgavata-māhātmya, "The Greatness of the Glorious Bhāgavata," which consists of about five hundred verses in six chapters. The purpose of expounding on the greatness of the Bhāgavatapurāṇa is, as one exponent put it, "to put people in the right frame of mind for the next seven days" or, more specifically, to impress on the audience the salvific and transformative potential of the main text.

The Māhātmya consists of two "case studies," one nested within the other. In the first, the peripatetic sage Nārada meets a young woman named Bhakti ("Devotion") and her two sons, Jñāna and Vairāgya ("Knowledge" and "Detachment"). While the boys are young in years, they have the appearance of decrepit dotards. Wishing to assist Bhakti and her sons, Nārada seeks advice from the Sanatkumāras, the four divine mind-born sons of the god Brahmā. The Sanatkumāras recommend a saptāha and give an example of its redemptive power by relating the story-within-a-story of the terrible sinner Dhundhukārī. This miscreant drives his father from his own home, causes his mother to throw herself into a well, lives off the proceeds of crime, and is eventually murdered by a gang of prostitutes. His troubled ghost returns to haunt his virtuous brother Gokarṇa. Even the most efficacious funerary rites fail to emancipate his spirit. In desperation, Gokarṇa conducts a saptāha, with the result that his wicked brother's ghost is liberated. Hearing this story, Nārada becomes convinced of the efficacy of the Bhāgavata-saptāha, and the Sanatkumāras narrate the Bhāgavatapurāṇa for Bhakti and her sons. At the end of the performance, all three, thoroughly rejuvenated, sing and dance for joy. The take-home message is that anyone who listens to a saptāha with devotion will at least experience a rejuvenation of his or her faith and, possibly, liberation, or mokṣa.

Day One: Skandha 1

The first skandha provides a narrative frame for the entire Bhāgavatapurāṇa and explains how the text itself came into existence. Like many other great texts in the Sanskritic corpus, the Bhāgavatapurāṇa is cast as a dialogue between a wandering bard named Ugraśravas and a community of sages headed by Śaunaka in the legendary Naimiṣa forest. In the opening passages of the Bhāgavatapurāṇa, Śaunaka welcomes the bard and requests an account of the deeds of the Lord. In response, Ugraśravas briefly describes the avatāras of Viṣṇu and relates how the Bhāgavatapurāṇa was originally composed by the sage Vyāsa. Vyāsa, according to this tradition, had arranged the Vedas and composed many of the earlier purāṇas and the Mahābhārata but still felt no satisfaction. Nārada, calling at Vyāsa's hermitage, diagnoses the cause of his dejection: none of Vyāsa's earlier works had fully praised the Lord, and none had truly addressed the question of bhakti. To remedy this, and to dispel his melancholia, Nārada advises Vyāsa to compose the Bhāgavatapurāṇa.

To demonstrate the power of this spiritual knowledge, Nārada tells Vyāsa his own backstory. In a previous life, he was born as the son of a serving woman. At the age of five, he became the servant of a community of holy men devoted to singing the praises of the Lord. As the result of hearing their songs from an early age, he gained a true knowledge of the self and achieved a state of transcendental bliss. In due course, at the end of his allotted years, he gave up his body and many eons later was reborn as the divine sage.

This is the first of many narratives in the Bhāgavatapurāṇa in which we see a "cult of youth." In much of the Sanskrit archive, wisdom is correlated with age, and the great sages are usually either mature, elderly, or incalculably ancient. In contrast, many characters in the Bhāgavatapurāṇa demonstrate prodigious religious understanding at the precocious age of five or six years. Nārada's previous incarnation as the serving woman's son, Bhakti's two sons, the Sanatkumāras, Dhruva, Prahrāda, the young Kṛṣṇa himself, and many others also fit this description. These younger characters embody and express the youthful vigor of the cult of devotion that colors the whole of the Bhāgavatapurāṇa and set it apart from the two epics and most other purāṇas.

At the end of Nārada's account, Vyāsa is convinced that composing a purāṇa filled with bhakti and praise of the Lord will dispel his gloom. As he does so, his mood lifts, and he subsequently teaches the entire narrative to his son Śuka, who in turn relates the story to the king Parīkṣit.

In order to contextualize the descent of Parīkṣit, the main narrative introduces a flashback to the end of the Mahābhārata war, the cataclysmic struggle between the five Pāṇḍava brothers and their one hundred avaricious cousins, the Dhārtarāṣṭras. In a final act of vengeance, the warrior Aśvatthāman murders the Pāṇḍavas' sons in their sleep, leaving their family without a living heir. Arjuna's son Abhimanyu had perished earlier in the battle, leaving behind his pregnant wife, Uttarā. To complete the annihilation of the Pāṇḍava lineage, Aśvatthāman discharges a magic weapon to destroy the fetus in Uttarā's womb, but Kṛṣṇa subdues the weapon, saves the unborn child, and rescues the dynasty. As a result of this act of mercy, the Pāṇḍavas' mother, Kuntī, and their grandfather figure, Bhīṣma, sing fulsome praise to the Lord. These two panegyrics (Bhīṣma-stuti, BhP 1.9, and Kuntī-stuti, BhP 1.10) and other similar songs of praise provide much of the raw material reproduced and elaborated during saptāha performances.

Uttarā's baby (Abhimanyu's son and Arjuna's grandson) is born as Parīkṣit, the central character to whom Śuka eventually relates the Bhāgavatapurāṇa. The earlier narrative creates a link between two of the great Sanskrit literary traditions, the Mahābhārata and the Bhāgavatapurāṇa. As the sole descendant of the Pāṇḍavas, Parīkṣit is eventually installed on the throne and rules gloriously. One day, while he is out hunting, he approaches a sage to ask for a drink of water and a place to rest. The sage, being deep in meditation, fails to respond to his request. Parīkṣit takes offense, picks up a dead snake with the tip of his bow, and drapes it around the sage's shoulders. When the sage's son sees this outrage, he curses Parīkṣit to be bitten by the great serpent Takṣaka and die within seven days. On learning of this terrible curse, Parīkṣit repairs to the banks of the Ganga, where he vows to wait for death, surrounded by a host of sages and other dignitaries. Vyāsa's wandering son, Śuka, arrives at the river, and Parīkṣit asks this seminal question:

> Tell me all that is to be done in this world by a person who is about to die. What should people hear, what should they recite, what should they do, what should they bear in mind, and what should they avoid? Surely, O Brahmin, no one has ever seen you remain in the homes of householders for longer than it takes to milk a cow. (BhP 1.19.37–39)

Śuka's short answer is to listen to, recite, and reflect on the stories of the Lord; his long answer, given over the following seven days, fills the next eleven skandhas of the Bhāgavatapurāṇa.

Day Two: Skandhas 2–4

The second day of the Canberra saptāha was devoted to the next three skandhas. The second skandha is partly theological and partly cosmological. Śuka explains to the king the means of worshiping Viṣṇu, including meditation on the syllable *Oṁ*. This is followed by a description of the creation of the universe and the various avatāras of the Lord. It concludes with a summary of the ten topics that are conventionally covered by a purāṇa, known as the *lakṣaṇas*, or characteristics. These include the various stages of creation, the deeds of the gods, and genealogies of the mythical progenitors of humankind.

The third skandha is the first of the "historical" books. Śuka tells Parīkṣit about his great-great-uncle, the sagely Vidura, a central figure in the Mahābhārata, who had gone on a pilgrimage to avoid taking sides in the terrible internecine war. On the banks of the Yamuna River, Vidura meets Uddhava, one of Kṛṣṇa's closest disciples. Uddhava informs Vidura that the great war is over and that most of the heroes, including Kṛṣṇa himself, are no more. At Uddhava's suggestion, Vidura proceeds to the ashram of the sage Maitreya at Haridwar in pursuit of the highest wisdom. The latter sections of this skandha consist of cosmology and mythology. Maitreya describes to Vidura the process of creation and the divisions of time. Maitreya also recounts the myth of Viṣṇu's attendants, Jaya and Vijaya, who were cursed to be born as the demon twins Hiraṇyakaśipu and Hiraṇyākṣa. The latter conquers the whole world but is defeated by Viṣṇu in the avatāra of Varāha, the Divine Boar.

Maitreya's exposition now switches to history and describes the Svāyambhuva *manvantara*, the first age of humankind. As is well known, the Indic scheme of time is cyclical. Each cycle has a human progenitor called a Manu, a set of gods led by a king called an Indra, a set of sacred texts called the Vedas, and a set of seven sages. In each cycle, the Manu, the Indra, the Vedas, and the sages have different names.

The account of the first manvantara opens with the story of Kardama and his consort, Devahūti, two of the progenitors of humanity during that particular cycle. Following their honeymoon in an airborne palace, the couple produce nine daughters and a divine son, Kapila, who is a partial embodiment of the Lord. In response to his mother's request, Kapila teaches her about the true nature of existence and the means of achieving liberation by becoming one with the Divine. This is the first of many thematically related subnarratives (*upākhyāna*) in the Bhāgavatapurāṇa in which an exemplary devotee (*mahābhakta*) of the Lord gives a teaching on the nature of existence which results in liberation (*mokṣa*) for the listener. Indeed, the whole Bhāgavatapurāṇa can be seen as a fractal set of this theology. Whether "zooming in" to the scale of individual narrative units or at the level of the intermediate framing narratives or "zooming out" to view the entire text as a whole, this self-similar pattern of liberation through devotion is constant.

In the fourth skandha, a historical book, the sage Maitreya tells Vidura a number of well-known stories. In the first of these, the great human progenitor (*prajāpati*) Dakṣa conducts a sacrifice but, in contravention of normal Vedic practice, neglects to offer a portion to the deity Śiva. Śiva's spouse, Satī, who happens to be Dakṣa's daughter, is furious at this insult and immolates herself. In revenge, Dakṣa is beheaded by one of Śiva's emissaries, but the other gods intervene on Dakṣa's behalf, his head is restored, and the sacrifice is completed. Nārāyaṇa (Viṣṇu) appears in person and pronounces himself nondifferent from all other deities, declaring, "I am myself everything." In a happy ending, Satī is reborn as Pārvatī and is reunited with Śiva.

In the next narrative, Manu's grandson Dhruva, a five-year-old prince and one of the purāṇic child prodigies mentioned earlier, is slighted by the queen, his stepmother, and leaves home for the wilderness, where he encounters the sage Nārada. At this point, according to Satchitananda Sai, the sage's first words to the boy were "Picnic in the forest?" This kind of humorous interpolation is an example of the Brechtian juxtaposition of sacred and profane by which skillful exponents may keep their audiences engaged for hours on end.[1] Nārada teaches Dhruva how to meditate on Viṣṇu in order to overcome all suffering. After six months of great austerities, Viṣṇu appears in person, and the child sings a great song for the Lord, known as "Dhruva's Praise" (Dhruva-stuti, BhP 4.10), another of the text's more famous passages. The boy eventually returns to his repentant parents. Like Kapila in the previous skandha, Dhruva is held up as a model devotee.

Day Three: Skandhas 4–6

On the third day, Satchitananda Sai completed the fourth, fifth, and sixth skandhas. The first of these introduces the king Pṛthu, a descendant of Dhruva and a prudent and successful ruler. One day, Pṛthu's subjects come to him and complain of a terrible famine. The earth is no longer sufficiently productive to meet their needs. Mother Earth in the form of a cow appears to the king and promises that she will provide all necessities on the condition that the inhabitants exert themselves. The king, Pṛthu, therefore teaches his people the arts of agriculture, animal husbandry, and industry. Villages, towns, and cities develop, all thanks to the bounty of Mother Earth, and the king leads his subjects in a great sacrifice. So pleased is Viṣṇu with the offerings that he appears in person to Pṛthu and gives him instructions on the nature of the self as unchanging, absolute, and one with the Divine. Subsequently, the Sanatkumāras appear at the court of Pṛthu and deliver a discourse on the means of attaining the Divine.

The king duly passes these sublime teachings to his subjects. In the passage of time, once his own five sons have assumed their inheritance, the king is relieved of his mundane responsibilities and moves to the forest. These two embedded discourses of Viṣṇu and the Sanatkumāras are favorites among many exponents, as they encapsulate the key teachings of the Advaita Vedānta view that the self and the Divine are one.

Another favorite in saptāha performances is an allegory told by Nārada to a descendant of Pṛthu. In highly simplified form, the story is as follows. A king, Purañjana (representing the soul, or ātman), resides in a city with nine gates (the body). He takes a beautiful woman (the intellect) as his principal queen. His city is destroyed by a great general (death), but in his next life, the king is led to realization of the true nature of reality by a wandering Brahmin (a guru). This allegory is much more elaborate in its original text, and exponents display their virtuosity and engage their audiences by developing it even further. At the end of the fourth skandha, Vidura, having received all these sublime teachings from the sage Maitreya, bows to him and returns to his residence in Hastināpura.

In the fifth skandha, a largely historical book, we return to the banks of the Ganga, where Śuka is telling Parīkṣit the story of another of the progenitor Manu's descendants. Āgnīdhra rules the world and enjoys both earthly and heavenly pleasures for one hundred million years. Āgnīdhra's son Nābhi worships Viṣṇu, who then manifests on earth in the form of a son, Ṛṣabha, who is the perfect devotee. Having instructed his own one hundred sons in true knowledge, Ṛṣabha takes up the life of an ascetic. Naked, he wanders all over South India with a stone in his mouth to suppress his thirst. He sings an exemplary song of praise to the Lord known as Ṛṣabha-gītā (BhP 5.4–6), which is often repeated to saptāha audiences. Ṛṣabha places his son Bharata on the throne and finally surrenders his body by walking into a forest fire. This narrative purports to show that it is possible even for a householder to be perfectly devoted to Viṣṇu-Kṛṣṇa and to attain the highest truth. Liberation is not solely the province of the renunciant.

Ṛṣabha's son Bharata rules as a great emperor over the land that eventually receives his own name, Bhārata, "India." After ten million years, he retires to a hermitage in the Himalayas, where he continues to propitiate the Lord. Bharata is so overcome by attachment to an orphaned fawn that he is reborn as a deer. In a later birth, he is again born into a Brahmin family. While he pretends to be dull-witted, his perfect equanimity enables him to escape from becoming a human sacrifice at the hands of some tribal people. This apparently foolish fellow is nicknamed Jaḍabharata,

"Stupid Bharata." A certain king comes to realize Jaḍabharata's superior inner qualities and requests a teaching on the nature of existence, which Jaḍabharata duly delivers. The fifth skandha concludes with Śuka's "cosmological" description of the continents, mountains, and rivers, the paths of the sun, moon, and planets, the twenty-eight hell realms and all their respective colorful torments.

The sixth skandha interweaves strands of theology, history, and mythology. Śuka's description of the hell realms in the previous skandha rouses Parīkṣit's concern, and he asks the sage how a person might avoid such a fate. Śuka's short answer is atonement, but the king is unconvinced and compares atonement to an elephant bathing in dust—the animal is just as dirty at the end of the process as it is at the start. Śuka illustrates the power of atonement with the story of a fallen Brahmin, Ajāmila. After eighty-eight years of immoral life, the servants of Yama, the Lord of Death, arrive to take the old man to hell. On seeing them, Ajāmila calls out for his son, who happens to be named Nārāyaṇa, which is also one of the names of the Lord. Hearing this cry, the beneficent emissaries of Viṣṇu, who are now also on the scene, assume that the old man is calling out in repentance. They wrest him from the clutches of Yama's messengers and convey him to heaven. Such is the power of the divine name, even if it is only enunciated by accident. In the subsequent theological section, Śuka recounts how Indra, the king of the gods, first learns the mantra *Oṁ namo nārāyaṇāya* and how he defeats the great demon Vṛtra in combat. In a typically purāṇic inversion of the older Vedic myth, Vṛtra turns out to be a mighty devotee of the Lord and delivers a discourse to Indra (BhP 6.11). Vṛtra's teaching is held up by exponents as yet another important statement of bhakti. This demon's backstory is explained in the myth of Citraketu, the lord of the *vidyādharas*, a species of celestial musician. This king once saw Śiva openly embracing his consort Pārvatī—or having intercourse with her (the Sanskrit is ambiguous). Citraketu mocks the deity for this public display of affection and is cursed by Pārvatī to be born as the demon Vṛtra.

Day Four: Skandhas 7–8

At the beginning of the seventh skandha, a largely mythological book, Parīkṣit asks Śuka how the Lord, who is the friend of all, would kill demons, such as the brothers Hiraṇyakaśipu and Hiraṇyākṣa. Śuka responds by recounting a conversation between Parīkṣit's great-uncle Yudhiṣṭhira and the sage Nārada. Yudhiṣṭhira, the king who emerged victorious at the end of the Mahābhārata war, asks Nārada how such reprobates as Śiśupāla (who had insulted Kṛṣṇa) and the blaspheming King Vena had achieved a state of union with the Divine. In reply, Nārada relates the story of Jaya and Vijaya, the two gatekeepers in Viṣṇu's paradise Vaikuṇṭha, to which I alluded earlier. Brahmā's four sons, the Sanatkumāras, although fully adult, still have the appearance of five- or six-year-old boys. One day, Jaya and Vijaya fail to recognize the boys and refuse them entry. The Sanatkumāras then curse the gatekeepers to be reborn as demons and to be slain by Viṣṇu in various forms thrice over. Jaya and Vijaya are then born as Hiraṇyakaśipu (killed by Viṣṇu in the form of Narasiṁha, the Lion-man) and Hiraṇyākṣa (slain by the boar avatāra, Varāha). Next, they are reborn as the demon-king Rāvaṇa and his brother Kumbhakarṇa (both killed by Viṣṇu in the form of Rāma). Finally, they are reborn as Śiśupāla and Dantavakra, who are slain by Kṛṣṇa, who is, of course, also a form of Viṣṇu. Once their sins in the form of their impure bodies have been destroyed thrice over by the various forms of the Divine, the curse is lifted, and they return to their old jobs guarding the entrance to Paradise.

Nārada now returns to the narrative of the slaying of the demon Hiraṇyakaśipu at the hands of Narasiṁha, the Lion-man avatāra. Impressed by Hiraṇyakaśipu's austerity in standing on one toe for thirty-six thousand years, Brahmā offers him a boon. Hiraṇyakaśipu asks that he be free from death at the hands of any living thing, indoors or outdoors, by day or by night, by any weapon, in the air or on the ground, or by any man or animal. Hiraṇyakaśipu subsequently has a son, Prahrāda, who grows to become another perfect devotee of Viṣṇu-Kṛṣṇa. Because the Lord in the form of the Boar had killed Hiraṇyakaśipu's brother Hiraṇyākṣa, Hiraṇyakaśipu is the sworn enemy of Viṣṇu. Prahrāda's faith and eloquence in the cause of the Lord grow in spite of his father's objections, admonitions, and punishments. When Prahrāda begins to teach the dharma to the other demon boys, his father decides to dispose of him. At dusk one day, Hiraṇyakaśipu swings his sword to kill the boy but accidentally strikes a stone pillar nearby. The pillar slits open, and Viṣṇu, in the form of Narasiṁha, half-man and half-lion, springs out. Narasiṁha lays the demon across his lap and disembowels him with his claws. The pillar, on the threshold of the palace, is neither indoors nor out. Because he is killed by the Man-lion (neither man nor animal), at dusk (neither night nor day), on his lap (neither on the ground nor in the air), and with claws (without a weapon), Hiraṇyakaśipu's boon has not been invalidated. Now that the young demon boy Prahrāda has been delivered from his brutal father, he gives a long eulogy to Viṣṇu. Like Vṛtra, the demon in the sixth skandha, Prahrāda's perfect devotion to the Lord is particularly poignant, as he was born in the race of demons. This story of Prahrāda's deliverance and devotion is also a great favorite among saptāha exponents and audiences.

The final section of this skandha is largely theological: Yudhiṣṭhira asks Nārada about the respective dharmas or traditional codes of conduct in idealized Brahminical society for each of the four social divisions, or varṇas (Brahmin, warrior, citizen, and servant), and for each of the life stages, or *āśramas* (student, householder, anchorite, and renunciant). Nārada's reply fills the remainder of the skandha and concludes his dialogue with Yudhiṣṭhira.

The eighth, largely historical, skandha deals with human characters with some additional divine mythology. The duties and functions of the Manus in administering the universe and propagating dharma are briefly described, as are the details of their respective epochs. Interspersed among these accounts are three well-known narratives, those of the Elephant-king, the Churning of the Ocean, and the dwarf avatāra known as Vāmana.

The Gajendra-mokṣa narrative, "The Liberation of the Elephant-king," is very famous and much loved. When a herd of elephants descends to bathe in a lake, a crocodile seizes the leg of their leader. The two great beasts are locked in an equal contest for a thousand years, but neither is able to overcome the other. In desperation, the elephant offers a great prayer of devotion to Viṣṇu. In response, the deity appears on the back of the divine bird Garuḍa and rescues the elephant from the crocodile's jaws. For his piety, the elephant attains liberation and is borne to heaven. His great encomium, known as *Gajendra-mokṣa-stotra* (BhP 8.3), is another favorite that is said to function as a powerful mantra itself; hearing or reciting it with devotion is said to free an individual from fear, sin, and so on.

The second important narrative in this section is the Churning of the Ocean, or *Samudra-manthana*. The gods, sorely pressed and exhausted in their endless war against the demigods, praise the Lord at great length and implore him to give assistance. Viṣṇu instructs them to make peace with the demigods, as together they might obtain the nectar of immortality by churning the Ocean of Milk. The gods take the sacred Mount Mandara as their churning stick and rest it on the back of the Tortoise-avatāra. Vāsuki, the king of the serpents, becomes the cord with which the churning stick is rotated. The first result of the churning is the poison known as *kālakūṭa*, which spreads across the world. In desperation, Śiva agrees to hold the poison in his throat, with the result that his neck is permanently stained blue. Next, all worldly treasures, including the sacred cow, horse, and elephant, are churned forth. Finally, a divine figure arises with a pitcher of nectar. The demigods attempt to snatch the pitcher away, but it is restored to the gods by Viṣṇu. The gods drink the nectar and then resume their cosmic struggle with the demigods. This famous narrative, like many others in the Bhāgavatapurāṇa, is also found in less-developed form in the Viṣṇupurāṇa and the Mahābhārata. The earlier versions lack the strong element of devotion and the profuse praise of Viṣṇu found in this later, more elaborate text.

The third important mythological narrative in this section concerns Bali and Viṣṇu. The demigod king Bali attacks Amarāvatī, the city of the gods, and forces all the divinities to flee. Diti, mother of the gods, is deeply concerned for the welfare of her offspring and consults her husband, Kaśyapa. He confers a vow on her, which she follows assiduously for twelve days. At the end of this period, Viṣṇu appears to her and agrees to intervene. In the form of the dwarf avatāra Vāmana, Viṣṇu goes before Bali and requests the gift of a piece of land, a mere three paces in length, as measured by his own stride. Bali consents to this apparently modest request, but Viṣṇu then reveals his true cosmic form and makes three giant steps that cover the three worlds. Bali, bound to keep his word, gives up the whole universe, the demigods are driven from Amarāvatī, and the gods regain their old home.

The eighth skandha ends with a chapter in which Viṣṇu appears as the Fish-avatāra. In this purāṇic equivalent of the Noah's ark story, a certain fish warns the righteous king Satyavrata of the impending deluge. The king loads a ship with specimens of each of the plants and animals in the world. When the great flood arrives and covers the earth, Viṣṇu in the form of a giant fish, Matsya, tows the ship across the ocean to safety.

Day Five: Skandhas 9–10

The ninth skandha is largely historical and is concerned with the current epoch. The present Manu, Śraddhadeva, is the progenitor of two dynasties: the Solar, which is descended from his son Ikṣvāku, and the Lunar, descended from his daughter Ilā. As part of the history of the Solar dynasty, this skandha includes a shortened version of the story of Rāma. Here the great epic has a happy ending, with Rāma and Sītā reunited in

Ayodhyā, unlike the better-known text attributed to Vālmīki which ends with the couple's ultimate separation. The ninth skandha also includes an account of the descent of the Ganga River from heaven and the sage Paraśurāma's repeated attempts to rid the world of the warriors on account of their arrogance. Genealogies of many famous figures are given. These include Yayāti (who exchanges his old age for the youth of his son Puru) and the king Duṣyanta (with a condensed version of the famous love story between this figure and a sage's daughter, Śakuntalā). The skandha also documents the lineages of the Pañcālas, the Kurus, the Yadus, the kings of Magadha, the Pāṇḍavas, and the Dhārtarāṣṭras, all of whom are important characters in the Mahābhārata. This section concludes with the events that lead up to the birth of Kṛṣṇa.

One thread unites all the narratives of the Bhāgavatapurāṇa up to this point: the role of devotion as a means of salvation. Time and again, the great devotees, the mahābhaktas, find themselves in extremis. Through their songs of praise to Viṣṇu-Nārāyaṇa, they are able to win divine grace and liberation: Bhīṣma on the battlefield, Kuntī on learning that Kṛṣṇa had saved the Pāṇḍava lineage, Dhruva the five-year prodigy who went without food and water for six months, Ṛṣabha the wandering ascetic, the demons Vṛtra and Prahrāda, and the king of elephants rescued from the crocodile. Through these stories, the central discourse of devotion is imparted to the audience.

The entire Bhāgavata up to this point, much like the Old Testament, completes the history of the world as far as "the present," that is, up to the birth of Kṛṣṇa and Parīkṣit's immediate forebears. The stage is now set for the tenth skandha, which, like the New Testament, is filled with the advent and activities of the Divine.

The first three or four days of most saptāha performances, during which the initial nine skandhas are covered, often seem like little more than a preamble to the later days, when narratives from the tenth skandha are told. There is a palpable sense of rising expectation as the week progresses. The tenth skandha is the best-loved and most widely read section of the entire work, as it deals with Kṛṣṇa's advent, boyhood, and youth. Especially prominent are his romantic dalliances with the cowherding girls and women, the gopīs, which are endlessly portrayed in art, music, song, dance, and literature. This is perhaps the key narrative of the Bhāgavatapurāṇa and the high point of every saptāha. As Satchitananda Sai put it, the tenth skandha is like the sweet dessert that follows the main course of the earlier books.

The story of Kṛṣṇa begins with Kaṁsa, the tyrannical king of Mathura, a city on the Yamuna River. After the wedding of his young cousin Devakī to Vasudeva, a nobleman of that city, Kaṁsa is driving the couple home in their bridal carriage. Suddenly, a celestial voice warns Kaṁsa that Devakī's eighth child will be his killer. Kaṁsa promptly leaps at Devakī with his sword, but he is dissuaded from killing her by her new husband, who promises to surrender all the children that she will bear in the future. The first six babies are duly handed over and dispatched by the tyrant, who imprisons the hapless couple. Three significant births now take place. First, an aspect of Viṣṇu known as Śeṣa enters Devakī's womb. Viṣṇu commands the goddess Yogamāyā to transfer this embryo from Devakī to the womb of Rohiṇī, another of Vasudeva's wives who lives safely outside the prison, beyond the grasp of Kaṁsa. Śeṣa is eventually born as Kṛṣṇa's elder brother Balarāma, Devakī's seventh child. Next, the goddess Yogamāyā herself enters the womb of Yaśodā, the queen of Gokula, the cow-herding community on the other side of the Yamuna River. Yogamāyā is born to Yaśodā as a baby girl. Third, the Lord himself then enters the womb of the imprisoned Devakī and is born as Kṛṣṇa, Devakī's eighth child. With divine protection, Vasudeva is miraculously able to leave the prison and carries the baby Kṛṣṇa to safety across the river to Gokula. He then swaps the divine child Kṛṣṇa for Yaśodā's baby girl and takes the female infant back to the prison cell. Hearing that the eighth child has been born, Kaṁsa enters the prison to kill the baby. The infant is instantly transformed back into her divine form and ascends to heaven unharmed. Meanwhile, there is great rejoicing in Gokula at the advent of the baby Kṛṣṇa. Much of the remainder of the tenth skandha deals with three subjects: the mischievous antics of the divine child and his brother Balarāma, Kṛṣṇa's prodigious acts in slaying multiple demons sent by the evil king Kaṁsa, and his romantic love games with the gopīs.

Day Six: Skandha 10 Continues

The image of the sweet toddler—irresistible chubby cheeks, huge dark eyes, golden earrings, soft curls falling across his forehead, wearing a garland of forest flowers and a headdress of peacock feathers—evokes powerful emotional responses across the Hindu world, among saptāha audiences in particular. Hanging on these stories, devotees sit rapt, laughing, cheering, and sobbing as the narrative unfolds during the sixth and seventh days.

The young Kṛṣṇa and his brother Balarāma exasperate and enchant the cow-herding community in Gokula with their pranks: stealing milk, untying cattle, teasing the women. Kṛṣṇa's divine nature becomes manifest: he uproots two great añjana trees, he overturns a fully laden cart with his bare feet, he reveals the entire universe within his mouth, and he lifts the mountain Govardhana to provide shelter for the community from a cataclysmic storm. In one famous narrative, he deceives parents, herdsmen, and even the god Brahmā by creating doubles of all the boys and cattle of the community.

The tyrant Kaṁsa learns that he was cheated at Kṛṣṇa's birth and dispatches numerous demons to kill the boy. These include Pūtanā, a witch who nurses the baby Kṛṣṇa with poison on her breasts. Realizing the trick, Kṛṣṇa sucks the life out of her. Other demons attack in the forms of whirlwind, calf, heron, python, donkey, bull, horse, and cow-herd. All are defeated by the deity merely by the touch of his body. Saptāha audiences laugh and clap as one foe after another is destroyed. As Satchitananda Sai put it, "Kaṁsa's phone book is getting very thin: Delete. Delete. Delete."

The most famous passages in this skandha describe Kṛṣṇa's romantic/erotic dalliances with the gopīs. Kṛṣṇa plays his flute in the forest of Vrindavan on moonlit autumn nights. The gopīs, whose minds have already been captivated by his beauty and antics, are irresistibly drawn to the sound and abandon whatever they are doing. The divine youth attempts to send the women home, warning of the dangers of adultery and adding that true love arises through devotion rather than physical attachment. The gopīs chide him for his heartlessness, praise him lavishly, but refuse to leave. Kṛṣṇa relents and leads them through the forest to the banks of the Yamuna, where he disports himself with them on the cool sands, playfully touching their hands, hair, thighs, skirts, and breasts. When he suddenly renders himself invisible, the love-maddened women vainly search the forest for him, singing his praises and calling on him to revive them with "the nectar of his lips." Kṛṣṇa eventually reappears, explaining that he had vanished only to teach them the virtues of constant love. He now creates multiple forms of himself so that all the gopīs are able to dance the famous Raslīlā with Kṛṣṇa simultaneously. After the dance, they all bathe together in the Yamuna. Exponents often dwell on a number of famous songs of praise, devotion, and longing associated with these narratives, including the Song of the Flute (Venu-gītā, BhP 10.21), the Song of the Gopīs (Gopī-gītā, BhP 10.31), and the Song of the Bee (Bhramara-gītā, BhP 10.47).

Two points need to be made here. First, these narratives provide an excellent opportunity for audience participation. At the larger, musically oriented saptāha events, both men and women spring to their feet and take part in the Raslīlā, dancing either alone or in rings. Participants are said to experience the actual Raslīlā itself, and some may enter an ecstatic, trancelike state. At Mridul Krishna's saptāha in Mumbai in 2009, twenty small stages had been set up along length of the tent, where pairs of girls and women, in imitation of the gopīs, performed a folk dance known as Dandiya-ras.

Second, a popular tradition arising in the sixteenth century within the Gauḍīya Vaiṣṇava school recognizes a particular favorite of Kṛṣṇa among the gopīs, the princess Rādhā. Although she is not named in the Sanskrit text, she is believed by followers of this tradition to have enjoyed an especially close relationship with her divine lover. The exquisite yearning of Rādhā and the other gopīs for their absent paramour is taken by this school to be the highest form of love for the Divine. A great body of narrative, both textual and oral, has developed around the figure of Rādhā, and at saptāha events with strong Gauḍīya leanings, praise of Rādhā-rāṇī, "Queen Rādhā," is a constant theme. As an extension of this philosophy, Rādhā is sometimes elevated even further: some traditions teach that Kṛṣṇa and Rādhā are simply two aspects of a single unified Divine entity that bears both their names, Rādhā-Kṛṣṇa.

At this point in Śuka's narrative, King Parīkṣit interrupts to ask how Kṛṣṇa, who manifests in the world to establish dharma and to extirpate its opposite, adharma, could commit such an immoral act as enjoying himself with other men's wives. Śuka was the first of many, including the nineteenth-century savant Vivekananda and numerous contemporary exponents, who have sought to explain away the explicit nature of the Raslīlā (Paranjape 2004, 176–181). The original Sanskrit, which I have followed closely here, is more explicit than the versions usually narrated in contemporary saptāhas. Most speakers and commentators go to great pains to play down its sexual nature. The idea that the highest form of the Divine would have multiple adulterous relationships is both theologically and socially challenging. Exponents warn audiences that only ignorant and "unrealized" individuals would interpret this episode in erotic terms. The apparent paradox of the perfect divine being indulging in seemingly immoral behavior is sometimes explained by the fact that Kṛṣṇa, as the Ultimate, is untouched by any virtue or sin.

After the Raslīlā, Kṛṣṇa's nemesis, the tyrant Kaṁsa, is still intent on destroying him. The king sends a messenger, Akrūra, to invite Kṛṣṇa and his brother Balarāma to a wrestling match in Mathura with the intention of having them both murdered. The lamentations of the people of Vraja at the departure of the two precious boys, the heartbreak of Kṛṣṇa's surrogate mother, Yaśodā, and the eulogy of the messenger Akrūra are often elaborated by exponents. At Satchitananda Sai's saptāha, one devotee was so deeply moved by the account of Yaśodā's grief that she sobbed uncontrollably and wailed, "Kṛṣṇa! Kṛṣṇa!" while the exponent himself and many others in the audience were also moved to tears.

When Kṛṣṇa arrives in Mathura, he defeats four wrestlers and an elephant and then dispatches Kaṁsa by throwing him from a high building. Kṛṣṇa is reunited with his natural parents, Vasudeva and Devakī, restores to life his six brothers who had been killed by the tyrant, and performs a number of other feats.

After the sustained fever pitch and emotional outpouring of the first half of the tenth skandha, the remainder of the book seems anticlimactic. Kṛṣṇa, grown to manhood, establishes his own city of Dvārakā, overcomes various adversaries, abducts and marries Rukmiṇī, and takes sixteen thousand secondary wives. One incident that often assumes a central role in the final day or two of the saptāha is the narrative of Sudāmā, a childhood friend of Kṛṣṇa's from Mathura who comes to visit him in Dvārakā. Sudāmā is so poor that the only gift he can afford to offer Kṛṣṇa is a handful of parched rice. On his return home, he finds that his hovel has been converted into a magnificent mansion. Sudāmā's act of piety is another favorite story among contemporary exponents, and brief dramatic performances of this narrative are occasionally included in saptāhas. The last part of the skandha describes Kṛṣṇa's visit to Indrapraṣṭha, the city of the Pāṇḍavas, and to Hastināpura, which again links the narratives of the Bhāgavatapurāṇa and the Mahābhārata. Curiously, Kṛṣṇa's central role in the Mahābhārata, a text of one hundred thousand verses, including his enunciation of the Bhagavadgītā, is summarized in a single verse in the Bhāgavatapurāṇa:

> Having slain many highly irreligious kings, and having caused others to be slain by those led by Arjuna, he brought about the establishment of dharma through the agency of Yudhiṣṭhira and the rest. (BhP 10.89.66)

The skandha ends with a rerun of the Raslīlā of Vrindavan. This time, it involves Kṛṣṇa's love games with his sixteen thousand wives and their songs of yearning when they are separated from him. Each of his wives bears ten sons, and we are told that it would take more than ten thousand years to count them all, in addition to the 38.8 million teachers required for their education. Eventually, Kṛṣṇa's clan, the Yādavas, grows so large that it could field an army of ten trillion warriors.

Day Seven: Skandhas 11–12

The great Mahābhārata war had relieved the earth of its burden as Kṛṣṇa had originally promised, but as the Yādavas had multiplied and grown arrogant and unruly, the world was now groaning again under their weight. Day seven begins with the eleventh skandha, in which Kṛṣṇa vows again to lighten the earth's load, this time by annihilating his own clan. As a prank, some Yādava boys dress up one of their fellows, Sāmba, as a pregnant woman. The boys lead Sāmba before some sages and cheekily ask the wise men to predict if the baby will be a boy or a girl. The sages see through the trick and curse Sāmba to bear an iron pestle, which will eventually destroy their race. The terrified boys examine Sāmba's belly and find a pestle; they grind it into pieces and throw it into the sea. The fine particles of iron eventually wash ashore, where they become embedded in a sort of reed called *erakā*. A fish swallows one of the larger fragments of metal and is eventually caught by a fisherman. In time, that piece of iron is made into an arrowhead. The import of all this becomes clear at the end of the skandha.

Much of the remainder of the book, known as the Mukti-skandha or "Book of Liberation," contains philosophical discourses on the attainment of union with the Divine through devotion, knowledge of the self, and yoga. These discourses are couched in the form of dialogues between Nārada and Kṛṣṇa's father, Vasudeva, and between Kṛṣṇa and his closest devotee, Uddhava. This latter discourse is known as the Uddhava-gītā (BhP 11.6–29). These contain reprises of the duties of each varṇa and āśrama, a chapter on how to differentiate good from bad, how to put up with indignities, the role of worship and good conduct, and the nature of māyā or illusion. Among the stories that Kṛṣṇa imparts to Uddhava is the famous narrative, always popular among exponents and audiences, of Avadhūta's gurus. This wise young Brahmin, when asked about the source of his wisdom, lists twenty-four unusual "teachers," including the earth, from which he learned forbearance; a python that taught him to take sustenance wherever he found it; and the prostitute Piṅgalā, from whom he learned that the Lord is the only constant lover. Many of Kṛṣṇa's teachings in this section cover territory similar to that in the Bhagavadgītā, including the imperishable nature of the ātman, or soul, the paths of action and devotion, and the Sāṁkhya system of yoga.

As the hour of doom approaches, the Yādavas, drunk on a powerful liquor called *maireyaka,* fall upon one another with all the weapons at hand. When they run out of weapons, they fight with the iron-filled erakā reeds until eventually they all lie dead. Kṛṣṇa alone remains, reclining under a banyan tree. A passing hunter, mistaking his foot for a deer, shoots him with the fated arrow. Thus, the Kṛṣṇa avatāra draws to a close, and Kṛṣṇa-Viṣṇu ascends again to his divine realm of Vaikuṇṭha.

In the short final skandha, the twelfth, Śuka lists the names of the kings who will rule the world after Parīkṣit dies and describes the evils of the present era, the Kali-yuga. He also relates how the Lord will return once more in the form of Kalki to cleanse the earth. Riding a white horse and wielding a sword, Kalki will annihilate tens of millions of bandits in the garb of kings. With a description of the final dissolution of the universe, Śuka completes his narrative and assures Parīkṣit that only his body will die: his ātman, his true inner self, is indestructible. The king salutes Śuka one last time, and the sage departs. At that moment, Takṣaka, the king of serpents, approaches Parīkṣit in the form of a Brahmin and bites him on the foot. The virulence of the serpent's poison instantly reduces the king's body to ashes, but his soul, purified by the narratives of the Bhāgavatapurāṇa over the last seven days, is released and merges with the Absolute. Later, Parīkṣit's son, Janamejaya, enraged to hear that his father has been killed by Takṣaka, sets about immolating every serpent in the world. The site of his great snake sacrifice becomes the place where another sage, Vaiśaṁpāyana, relates the great epic of the Mahābhārata, but that is another story.

With the death of Parīkṣit, the Bhāgavatapurāṇa arrives at a rather anticlimactic conclusion. One exponent likened the text to a jam sandwich. The philosophy—the bread and butter—at either end is important, but the sweetness, the jam in the middle, is experienced in the stories of Kṛṣṇa's childhood and youth in the forests of Vraja. Some exponents, Satchitananda Sai among them, prefer to leave their audiences with a more upbeat ending and conclude the final session with a flashback to the middle of the tenth skandha, in which Kṛṣṇa weds Rukmiṇī. A theatrical reenactment of the wedding, as described in chapter 3, transforms the final session into an auspicious occasion filled with joyous sights, sounds, and emotions. This way, the whole week finishes with a bang.

Some exponents cover each day's content in a single session of three or four hours. Satchitananda Sai spoke for a total of about six hours a day during his saptāha in Canberra. However exponents choose to divide the material, they invariably include verses in Sanskrit from the Bhāgavatapurāṇa. The number of verses introduced in a session varies greatly, from half a dozen to as many as a hundred or more. The ways the verses are employed and the role they play in the audience's reception and experience of the performance are explored in chapter 6.

6

The Verses—Mantra

THE MANTRA IS the hymn of praise sung during the Vedic act of worship as the ritual substances are offered into the fire. These songs eulogize the deities and contain supplications for the mainstays of Vedic society: productive cattle, sunshine and rain in due proportion, strong sons to protect the herd, and victory over one's enemies. Only when the hymns are correctly intoned will the deities be gracious. Thus, the sound of mantra has the power to move the gods and sustain the universe. Similarly, in the minds of many saptāha participants, the sound of the individual Sanskrit verses intoned by the exponent lend authenticity, power, and dignity. My aim in this chapter is to show how the Sanskrit verses contribute to the experience of the saptāha as a powerful and authentic event. Most exponents and audience members believe that the Bhāgavatapurāṇa has power, but how is this power constituted? What role do the Sanskrit verses play? How do exponents employ Sanskrit verses in their oral delivery and to what effect?

Satchitananda Sai gave a saptāha in English in Melbourne in November 2012, for which a complete audio recording is available (Satchitananda Sai 2013). In order to explore how Sanskrit verses are used in oral performance, I analyzed the introductory session on the Māhātmya. I summarized the exponent's spoken discourse, noting the Sanskrit verses he used, transcribing and translating them, and locating each verse in the text of the Māhātmya. I also identified the primary doctrinal points made and analyzed how the exponent interpreted each verse. Finally, I attempted to identify the function of each verse and the role it played in the overall narrative.

Twin processes of entextualization and contextualization provide a productive theoretical framework for understanding how authority and hence transformative power are produced in performance (Demmer and Gaenszle 2007; Bauman and Briggs 1990). According to Bauman and Briggs (1990, 73), entextualization is “the process of rendering discourse extractable, of making a stretch of linguistic production into a unit—a *text*—that can be lifted out of its interactional setting.” Entextualization is a strategy to shift the focus of the spoken word away from the immediate context toward a greater discursive universe. This process causes a unit of discourse to appear constant across different contexts. Audiences usually expect that a given passage from a canonical text is fixed and immutable. Entextualization also engenders the perception that the speaker has no control over the substance of the textual utterance.

Entextualization also involves the elevation of “ordinary speech” into something extra-ordinary; that is, it brings about the reimagining of speech as “text.” By the use of particular strategies, including stylistics, figurative language, and changes in tempo, pitch, and oral quality, speakers signal that the discourse is part of a time-honored tradition. This has a marked impact on the perception and imagination of the audience and on the reception of the discourse. This strategy “decenters” the discourse from the social context in which it is delivered and, as Gaenszle (2007, 113) suggests, creates a transcendent, ideal, timeless, normative order. This is also a question of power, and the speakers appear to be speaking no longer on their own behalf but on behalf of a greater collective agency, thus endowing the spoken discourse with special authority.

Entextualization has also been called “decentering” by Kuipers (1990, 4), as it removes the ritual discourse from the central context in which it is made, and repositions it in timeless, universalized space. As Gaenszle (2007, 114) says, entextualized discourse sounds as if it is no longer the words of the speakers themselves but emanates from some transcendent sphere, which he terms the “offscape,” “a time and place beyond the contingencies of the present.”

The complement of entextualization is contextualization. According to Gaenszle (2007, 104–107), this is the process by which a ritual performance is “grounded, embedded, or ‘anchored’ in a situational context” and is the “ongoing connection of texts to their performative contexts.” It is the “flexible, adjustable uses of ritual speech in performance through which the textual tradition is tied up with the particularities of the performers, clients, and audience, and is thus provided with contextual meaning and relevance.” One example of this process was observed in a wedding ritual in Tamku, India, which was performed without a groom. In this case, the normal utterances made by the officiating parties had to be modified to fit the context in which the groom was absent.

Bauman and Briggs (1990, 69) suggest that the agents in a performance assess the discourse as it is emerging and embed assessments of its structure and significances into the discourse as it is being produced. In saptāha performances, exponents critically assess audiences and the way the spoken discourse is being received, and they make adjustments as they proceed. Bauman and Briggs list communicative competence, personal history and social identities among the variables that performers need to consider when shaping their performances.

I use *entextualization* in the sense that the exponent draws on the authority of the Bhāgavatapurāṇa in the use of verses extracted from the text. I use *contextualization* in the sense that the exponent adjusts or adapts his spoken discourse to the context in which it is produced, that is, the way it is "keyed" to a particular audience in a particular time and place. Within the matrix of entextualization and contextualization, the verses fulfill two main functions: they may be used as evidence of certain doctrinal points, or they may be used to signal the start of a new direction in the narrative. Some verses appear to fulfill both functions simultaneously.

Few of those who attend saptāha performances, in India or elsewhere, know enough Sanskrit to access the verses on a semantic level. For example, only one of the attendees I approached at Satchitananda Sai's saptāha in Canberra claimed to be able to understand Sanskrit. He was an older man who had moved from India to Australia after he retired, and he stated that he could understand twenty-five percent of the Sanskrit, "or fifty percent if Guru-ji speaks slowly." He was certainly an exception. Several of the goswamis in Vrindavan confirmed this view.

During the two-hour session devoted to the Māhātmya, Satchitananda Sai incorporated about forty verses in his spoken discourse. With the exception of a single verse from the Bhagavadgītā and another from elsewhere in the Mahābhārata, all verses were drawn from the Māhātmya itself. As six chapters of this section have a total of about five hundred verses, this represents a usage rate of less than ten percent.

When first introducing a Sanskrit verse into the discourse, Satchitananda Sai would usually chant or intone it in an elevated, artful mode, typical of entextualized speech in this and other traditions. The great majority of verses were introduced in the order in which they appear in the text. In the next section, I give several examples of each function, evidential and narrative, in chronological order.

The Avatāras of Kṛṣṇa

The opening words spoken by Satchitananda Sai in the first session of the saptāha were as follows:

> Śrī Kṛṣṇa, in the Bhagavadgītā, says,
> *yadā yadā hi dharmasya glānir bhavati bhārata |*
> *abhyutthānam adharmasya tadātmānaṁ sṛjāmy aham ||*
>
> "Whenever there is a decline in dharma, by my own *śakti*, by my own power, I create myself—*sṛjāmy aham*. I give myself a form, I give myself a name, so that I may restore the dharma back to its pristine glory." (1.1.1.3:05–3:45)[1]

This verse (BhG 4.7) is one of the most famous in the Hindu world. In contrast to what I suggested earlier, it is one of the verses that many people would understand, even if they did not know Sanskrit. As a result of its ubiquity, or perhaps as a partial cause of it, it was chosen as the theme song for B. R. Chopra's perennially popular television version of the Mahābhārata. It was spoken by Kṛṣṇa to his friend and confidant Arjuna at the start of the war, just as Kṛṣṇa was about to reveal himself as Bhagavān, the Ultimate Divine, or God manifest in human form.

Before considering the function of this verse in the spoken discourse, let us see how the exponent handled it phrase by phrase. The original Sanskrit might be translated literally as follows:

> *yadā yadā hi dharmasya glānir bhavati bhārata |*
> *abhyutthānam adharmasya tadātmānaṁ sṛjāmy aham ||*
>
> Whenever there is a decline in dharma, O Bhārata,
> [and] an increase in nondharma, then I create/manifest myself.

Comparing the exponent's rendering above with the original Sanskrit, we see that the first phrase, *yadā yadā hi dharmasya glānir bhavati*, is translated literally as "Whenever there is a decline in dharma." The word *bhārata*, simply meaning "O Bhārata" and referring to Kṛṣṇa's interlocutor Arjuna, is elided. The additional phrases in the exposition, "by my own *śakti*, by my own power" and "so that I may restore the dharma back to its pristine glory," are interpolations. "I give myself a form" and "I give myself a name" are glosses on *sṛjāmy aham*, "I create/manifest myself." Thus, the exponent's rendering of this verse consists of a blend of translation, interpretation, and interpolation. This is a common approach in oral expositions of this kind. In the saptāha tradition, exponents are not expected to deliver strict word-by-word translations, nor do audiences expect to receive them. Rather, exponents offer a free, vivacious interpretation that retains the spirit of the original, if not the precise wording.

In the tradition of which Satchitananda Sai's exposition is an example, the deity Kṛṣṇa is not different from Viṣṇu or Nārāyaṇa. All forms of the ultimate deity are referred to interchangeably as Bhagavān, Lord or simply God. The import of this verse is that the Lord appears on earth periodically to restore dharma and to erase anything contrary to dharma. The exponent used this verse as evidence of the doctrinal point he was about to convey: that the Lord not only manifested as Kṛṣṇa but also appeared as an avatāra in the physical form of the Bhāgavatapurāṇa.

The Bhāgavata as an Avatāra

The exponent used the canonical reference BhG 4.7 as the basis for an exposition on the avatāras of Bhagavān, or, to put it another way, he used the verse as scriptural evidence that Kṛṣṇa manifests in various forms. Having established this point, his next doctrinal move dealt with the nature of the current avatāra. The exponent first described some of the previous manifestations of Bhagavān. These included Paraśurāma, the Brahmin who exterminated the Kṣatriyas; Kṛṣṇa; Narasiṁha the Lion-man; Varāha the Boar; and so on. He then explained how each avatāra appeared to reestablish a particular form of dharma in earlier eras:

> When Bhagavān takes an avatāra, he restores all of these dharmas, but what about mokṣa-dharma, Bhāgavata-dharma, the dharma of a bhakta, of a Bhāgavata? . . . What is the highest dharma? Mokṣa-dharma. How does Bhagavān protect it? Bhagavān himself thought about it. He says, "I have taken so many different avatāras to protect all the other dharmas. What avatāra shall I take to protect this Bhāgavata-dharma, this mokṣa-dharma?" Thinking about this, Bhagavān took an avatāra: the avatāra that Bhagavān took is the Śrīmad-bhāgavata-mahāpurāṇa. . . .
>
> The Padmapurāṇa, one of the eighteen purāṇas, speaks about the glory of the Śrīmad-bhāgavata-mahāpurāṇa, which is also one of the eighteen purāṇas. The Bhāgavata-māhātmya, which is

> what we are going to be discussing today, speaks about the glory of the Śrīmad-bhāgavata, and it is contained in six chapters within the Padmapurāṇa. And within that Padmapurāṇa itself is this statement:
>
> *śrīmad-bhāgavatākhyo 'yam pratyakṣaḥ kṛṣṇa eva hi* | (BhP 0.6.30)
>
> This Bhāgavata is not different from Kṛṣṇa. It is *sākṣāt śrī kṛṣṇa svarūpa* itself. Among all the avatāras that Bhagavān took, the Bhāgavata-avatāra is the one that fosters mokṣa-dharma, Bhāgavata-dharma, bhakti-dharma, the greatest dharma of all. . . . In all of the other dharmas, Bhagavān had to come back repeatedly to protect them. He thought, "All those dharmas are OK. I can let them go in the declined state for a while, but mokṣa-dharma, I cannot afford to let it decline at all. I cannot wait for Bhāgavata-dharma to decline and then take an avatāra." He thought about it, and he said, "I will take such an avatāra that will always be there. There is no disappearance to this avatāra: Bhāgavata-avatāra. The physical forms of other avatāras will fade, but Śrīmad-bhāgavata will not fade. It is śabda-brahman. It is Bhagavān himself in the form of the Word." (1.1.1.6:48–10:16)

The literal meaning of the verse *śrīmad-bhāgavatākhyo 'yam pratyakṣaḥ kṛṣṇa eva hi* is: "This [purāṇa] known as Śrīmad-bhāgavata is Kṛṣṇa himself in manifest form." This is similar to the first part of the gloss given by the exponent earlier. The word *pratyakṣaḥ*, which I have translated as "in manifest form" means literally "before the eyes" and, by extension, "manifest," "visible," "real," and so on. The second part of the exponent's gloss is "It is *sākṣāt śrī kṛṣṇa svarūpa* itself." The Sanskrit word *sākṣāt* is a synonym for *pratyakṣaḥ* and is found in many Indian vernacular languages. The phrase "It is *sākṣāt śrī kṛṣṇa svarūpa* itself," or "It is the manifest form of Śrī Kṛṣṇa," would be understood by most of the Tamil and Hindi speakers in the audience.

The function of the verse in the middle of this section is to provide scriptural evidence for that second doctrinal point: that the Bhāgavata-purāṇa is an avatāra of Bhagavān/Kṛṣṇa.

The Naimiṣa Forest

Now that Kṛṣṇa's appearance as an avatāra had been introduced and validated with reference to scripture, and he had appeared as the Bhāgavatapurāṇa in the present decadent era of the Kali-yuga, two fundamental doctrinal points had been established. They are critical for understanding the discourse that follows. The exponent then began his narration of the Māhātmya proper.

> In the Padmapurāṇa, the six chapters that detail the Māhātmya, the glory of the Bhāgavata, start off, like all the other purāṇas, in one particular location called Naimiṣa. Naimiṣa-araṇya in India is the place where all of these holy texts are always expounded. Here, this Naimiṣādri is also no less: Wheelers Hill this place is called. The word *Naimiṣa* means "that which is circumscribed with a wheel." . . . Brahmā created a *manocakra*, a mental wheel, and sent it rolling, and he said, "Wherever that wheel will come to a stop, know that place which is within the circumference to be free from the pernicious influence of the Kali-yuga." . . . That place which is encircled by the circumference of the wheel, *nemi*, is called Naimiṣa. Interestingly, this suburb is also called Wheelers Hill. I have changed it to Naimiṣādri—Naimiṣācala [laughter]—and this is the Naimiṣa-kṣetra where Bhāgavata, Rāmāyaṇa, etc., will all be conducted in the presence of these divinities that are constantly living, breathing, present here. (1.1.12:29–14:28)

This is one of the popular folk etymologies of the toponym *Naimiṣa.* From the Sanskrit *nemi*, meaning the outer rim of a wheel, he derived Naimiṣa to give "that which is encircled by the circumference of a wheel." With mock seriousness, he equated the name Naimiṣa with Wheelers Hill, the suburb of Melbourne where the saptāha was being conducted. This is a good example of contextualization, where the exponent takes a textual element and playfully manipulates it in response to the context of the performance. The parallel between the names of the two locations suggests a parallel between the sanctity and profundity of Ugraśravas's recounting of the Bhāgavatapurāṇa in the Naimiṣa forest and the current event. It also suggests a further parallel in the passage that followed, in which the exponent drew an analogy between the assembly of sages in the forest and "all of you," the audience. *Naimiṣe* is the first word of the opening verse of the narrative of the Māhātmya, which the exponent then recited aloud:

> *naimiṣe sūtam āsīṇam abhivādya mahāmatim* |
> *kathāmṛta-rasāsvāda-kuśalaḥ śaunako 'bravīt* || (BhP 0.1.3)
> (1.1.1.14:30–14:47)

A literal translation of this verse might be:

> In the Naimiṣa forest, having saluted the wise *sūta* as he was sitting, Śaunaka, who was experienced in enjoying the essence of the nectar of stories, spoke.

The exponent did not translate this verse directly but introduced most of the important individual terms from the verse and expanded on them. He began with the word *sūta*:

> All the stories of the purāṇas were told by a person call the *sūta*. . . . A sūta is a bard, a person who tells stories. In terms of caste, they were a little bit lower [than Brahmins]. This particular person was called Ugraśravas. *Śravas* means "fame"; *Ugraśravas* means "divine or terrific fame." The fame that he attained was due to his chanting of the holy purāṇa, which he narrated to the sages who had collected together in Naimiṣa, such as all of you. All these sages got together and said, "We will isolate ourselves from the world, . . . we will stay only in this Naimiṣa-kṣetra which is free from Kali's influence. All we will do here is conduct a *dīrgha-satra*, a long sacrifice." Every morning, a yajña, a sacrifice, was performed, and in the afternoon, they would all sit down and listen to stories told by this sūta Ugraśravas. (1.1.2.0:00–1:29)

Having glossed on the word *sūta*, he explained the name *Ugraśravas* and interpolated some materials about the sages, their location, and their occupation. The exponent then turned to the phrase *abhivādya mahāmatim*, "having saluted the wise," from the original verse and alluded to the word *āsīṇam*, "sitting," in the following section. The word *ṛṣi* means "sage."

> All the ṛṣis were headed by a ṛṣi called Śaunaka. When this particular Bhāgavata-māhātmya starts off, all the ṛṣis had gathered together and gave a seat of respect and honor to the sūta Ugraśravas. *abhivādya mahāmatim* ["having saluted the wise"]—Śaunaka, a great ṛṣi, came and saluted Ugraśravas. Although by birth and age Ugraśravas was lower than this ṛṣi Śaunaka, he comes and salutes Ugraśravas, because Bhāgavata resides in him. That place or person in whom the Vedas or Bhāgavata reside is a temple, and therefore

> that person is worthy of salutation, and so Śaunaka, the great ṛṣi, salutes the sūta, *mahāmatim*, "of exalted wisdom." (1.1.2.1:29–2:27)

Here the Sanskrit text serves two functions. First, it pushes the narrative forward in a small way as it describes how the sages in the forest welcomed the sūta Ugraśravas. To an Indian audience, "saluting" in this context would conjure up an image of the forest sages greeting the newly arrived Ugraśravas with joined palms, perhaps stooping to touch the feet of their guest. Second, the exponent uses the term *abhivādya mahāmatim* to make a doctrinal point. In traditional Hindu legal texts, sūtas are said to be the product of miscegenation between members of the Kṣatriya (warrior) and Brahmin (priestly) castes. As such, a sūta would be considered "lower" in the social hierarchy than the sages, who would normally be of unsullied Brahmin stock. Yet the sages honor him, in spite of his inferior social position, because the sūta is one "in whom the Bhāgavata resides." The fact that the Brahmins honor the sūta indicates the prestige and potency of the text. The exponent continued:

> What kind of person was Śaunaka? The Māhātmya says he is a person who is *kathāmṛta-rasāsvāda-kuśalaḥ*—he who is capable of extracting the *rasa*, the essence, of the stories and enjoying them. *kuśalaḥ*—one who is skilled. There is a beautiful word in Sanskrit, *kuśalatvam—kuśalaḥ*. "Dexterity" or "skill" is the usual translation. It comes from the root *kuśān lātīti kuśalaḥ*. . . . "He who attains the skill to remove the grass [bladelike leaves of the *kuśa* grass] but without cutting himself on that grass is kuśalaḥ." (1.1.2.2:34–3:56)

Literally, *kathāmṛta-rasāsvāda-kuśalaḥ* might be translated as "skilled or experienced (*kuśala*) in the enjoyment of the essence (*rasa-āsvāda*) of the story nectar (*kathā-amṛta*)." The sense is that Śaunaka is a discerning listener, a connoisseur, who appreciates the deeper import of the narratives but does not get distracted by superficial details. The exponent cited a popular etymology for the word *kuśala*, deriving it from *kuśa*, a grass used in many sacred rituals. Anyone who is able to pluck the sharp-edged kuśa grass without cutting his or her fingers is said to be *kuśala*, or skillful. The exponent's technique here was to extract a Sanskrit phrase from the verse, and, rather than simply or directly translating it, he expanded on it.

Using this evidence from the verse, the exponent established that Śaunaka was a person who was able to appreciate the essence of a story.

The sage is held up in the following section as a paragon for everyone who attends a saptāha. The speaker entextualized the discourse in selecting the verse to make a doctrinal point that the story is to be received by connoisseurs like Śaunaka. He then contextualized it by expanding on the folk etymology of *kuśala* for the audience. This harks back to a point the exponent made in his opening remarks: the purpose of this introductory session was to put devotees "in the right frame of mind" for listening to the narratives over the next seven days. He went on:

> Like that, here, these *Bhāgavatāmṛtam kathā* ["Bhāgavata nectar stories"] that we are going to listen to will have so many different stories, so much symbolism and expression, but you must be clever enough, skillful enough, to extract the *rasa* [juice, essence] of it, but you should not ask silly questions: "Ah, but this happened there, that happened there." For these questions there is no room here. If you have those questions, you will not enjoy it. A glass of good fruit juice is kept in front of you. All you have to do is drink it and enjoy it. If you look into the chemical composition, the analysis of it—how much of this is present, how much of that is present, and so on and so forth—you will never end up drinking it. Drink it! Enjoy it, then look at all that stuff.... Don't analyze too much....
>
> Śaunaka is *kathāmṛta-rasāsvāda-kuśalaḥ*—one who is capable of enjoying the rasa, taste, the essence of it.... Just as when you eat a banana, you throw away the peel, you only eat the fruit. Like that, these great truths are going to be enshrined in the Bhāgavata, and it comes with a packaging, it is going to come with a covering. Sometimes the covering is only there to facilitate the easy transportation of the stories from the *vaktā* to the *śrotā*, from the speaker to the listener. Don't get overmuch engrossed in the packaging, the peel of it. Although I say peel, Bhāgavata does not have any peel. All of Bhāgavata is only *rasam—pibata bhāgavataṁ rasam* ["Imbibe the nectar of the Bhāgavata"]. No peel, no pit, no pulp, only juice.... Drink only that which is good for you, what is essential for you. (1.1.2.4:03–6:06)

The term *Bhāgavatāmṛtam kathā* (Bhāgavata nectar story) links this section of the discourse back to the root verse through the phrase *kathāmṛta* (story-nectar). Similarly, there is a reprise of the phrase *kathāmṛta-rasāsvāda-kuśalaḥ* (skilled in enjoying the essence of story nectar). Like Śaunaka, devotees are urged to concentrate on the essence of the narratives, not to get trapped in the fine mesh of superficial detail, which the exponent characterized as "packaging" or "peel." It is the essence, the juice or rasam, which the audience is enjoined to drink. To underline this point, he cited the famous line from the Bhāgavatapurāṇa, *pibata bhāgavataṁ rasam,* "Imbibe the nectar of the Bhāgavata" (BhP 1.1.3). In effect, this section provides the scriptural authority for the exponent's instruction to devotees that they must focus their minds on the main thrust of the discourse.

Vaikuṇṭha: The State of Bliss

The exponent now returned to the discourse in the Naimiṣa forest. At this crucial point, in response to the sages' question about the best way of attaining Kṛṣṇa in the Kali-yuga, the exponent, now channeling Ugraśravas, introduced the Bhāgavatapurāṇa and its powers:

> In this world there is only one thing that can bring us solace from all these troubles. It can take us right up to the state of the Supreme Being. It can give us supreme ānanda [bliss]. That path, that sādhana, is listening to stories of the Lord, the description of his deeds and his attributes, which alone can be called the panacea to all worldly ills. Such a holy scripture, which is a culmination, combination, collection, and compilation of all the stories of the Lord, composed by the sage Vyāsa, narrated by Śrī Śuka, is called the Śrīmad-bhāgavata. It is filled with those tales of the Lord which are all equal to or greater than nectar in their sweetness and in their ability to give us everlasting ānanda.
>
> *menire bhagavad-rūpaṁ śāstraṁ bhāgavataṁ kalau |*
> *paṭhanāc chravaṇāt sadyo vaikuṇṭha-phala-dāyakam ||* (BhP 0.1.20)
> (1.1.2.10:40–11:38)

I will insert my own literal translation of this verse to provide a reference point for what follows:

> They [the wise] regard the Bhāgavata as the scripture that is the embodiment of Bhagavān in the Kali[-yuga], [and] which

> immediately bestows the reward of Vaikuṇṭha by reciting it or listening to it.

This is one of the most important doctrinal points to be made in this context. The Bhāgavata is the best means or, to use the technical expression, the best sādhana, for achieving unity with the Divine in this degenerate age, Vaikuṇṭha being the name of Viṣṇu-Kṛṣṇa's paradise. The exponent first introduced this point in his oral discourse, then cited the verse from the Bhāgavata as scriptural evidence in support of the proposition. That is to say, he made an important doctrinal point first and then supported it with the text, on which he glossed phrase by phrase in the following section. But before he did so, the exponent reprised an earlier quotation from the Bhāgavatapurāṇa. This is still the voice of Ugraśravas:

> O Śaunaka, you said, *prayacchati guruḥ prītaḥ vaikuṇṭhaṁ yogi-durlabham* [BhP 0.1.8], "If the guru is pleased, then Vaikuṇṭha itself can be had." How do you think the guru is going to give you Vaikuṇṭha? Vaikuṇṭha is not somewhere there. He is not going to take a group on a tour to Vaikuṇṭha. He is not going to arrange a big tour, saying, "On this day we will all fly out to Vaikuṇṭha, see Vaikuṇṭha, come back." No—what is this Vaikuṇṭha? This is this Vaikuṇṭha: *menire bhagavadrūpaṁ śāstraṁ bhāgavataṁ kalau*. There is a *śāstra*, there is a scripture, in this Kali-yuga called the Śrīmad-bhāgavata. *menire bhagavad-rūpaṁ*—understand this to be the very form of the Lord itself. Listening to this, studying this, narrating this—if someone narrates it to you and you listen to this—*sadyo vaikuṇṭha-phala-dāyakam*—instantaneously you will get Vaikuṇṭha. Immediately—*sadyo*. It won't happen after some time. It's not going to happen after a few years. Immediately, even as you are listening to it, you will be in Vaikuṇṭha. (1.1.2.11:42–12:41)

After the reprise and the lighthearted interpolation of the guru as travel agent, the exponent glossed on each phrase from the root verse. Here the text makes two more key doctrinal points: the Bhāgavatapurāṇa is Bhagavān in physical form, and listening to it or reciting it will lead to Vaikuṇṭha. In both cases, the points are backed up by scriptural evidence extracted directly from the root text. In the following passage, the exponent provided an explanation of Vaikuṇṭha. The "Swami" referred to below is the exponent's own guru, Sathya Sai Baba.

> Now you should understand what Vaikuṇṭha is. Vaikuṇṭha is not a place; it is the ānanda that comes naturally to us when we listen to the stories of the Lord. Recently, about two days ago, Swami in his thought for the day had said how listening to the glories, the deeds of the Lord, fills us with ānanda because of his omnipresence within us. We are from him. We are part of him. We are him. Therefore, when we listen to the stories of the Lord, we find such great ānanda coming into our hearts. That ānanda is the Vaikuṇṭha-loka. (1.1.2.12:44–13:20)

The concept of attaining Vaikuṇṭha has evolved over time. The concept of heaven is an ancient one in the Indic imaginary. In the Vedas, warriors who die in battle proceed to a glorious heaven. This originally predated the concepts of karma and rebirth and in later times coexisted with them. In older purāṇic literature, Vaikuṇṭha was the heavenly abode of Viṣṇu, where he resides with his consort, Lakṣmī, either reclining on the serpent Śeṣa in the middle of the cosmic ocean or, alternatively, on the eastern slopes of Mount Meru. Another sense of attaining Vaikuṇṭha is exemplified by King Parīkṣit in the Bhāgavatapurāṇa. As the result of hearing the Bhāgavatapurāṇa from Śuka, Parīkṣit was "liberated" on his death and ascended to Vaikuṇṭha. In this context, Vaikuṇṭha implies liberation from cyclical existence after death. The next step in the evolution of the concept is seen in the Māhātmya. Those who are fortunate enough to listen with devotion to an entire saptāha are carried to Vaikuṇṭha in divine chariots by the servants of the Lord. That is to say, after a saptāha, they go straight to heaven without the inconvenience of dying. A further stage in the evolution of the concept is apparent in Satchitananda Sai's exposition: Vaikuṇṭha is not only to be understood as a heavenly abode of Viṣṇu. No one is going to be carried to heaven, dead or alive. Vaikuṇṭha is the ānanda, the bliss, that is experienced when reciting or listening to the Bhāgavatapurāṇa. Overlaid on this is the Advaita position that we are all nondually one with the Divine. Vaikuṇṭha finally becomes the realization of this state of unity.

Nārada and Bhakti: Two Narrative Verses

After Ugraśravas tells the sages in the Naimiṣa forest about the Bhāgavatapurāṇa, the head of the community, Śaunaka, asks about the origins of the text. Ugraśravas then begins to relate the embedded narrative of the Sanatkumāras, the divine sage Nārada, and the young woman

Bhakti, which was outlined earlier. The Sanatkumāras ask Nārada why he looks so miserable. He explains that while roaming the world, he had found only corruption. The exponent, now channeling Nārada, said to the Sanatkumāras, "'My masters, my gurus, what shall I say? I went on a *tīrtha-yātrā*—I went around all over the place—all over the earth I went around—pilgrimage.' A lot of people go on these pilgrimages now. They book from here itself. They go. Package tour—they book and go like this. Nārada went on his own package tour" (1.1.3.5:09–5:30). The exponent then recited three lines from the Māhātmya that list the places Nārada visited:

> *puṣkaraṁ ca prāyagaṁ ca kāśīṁ godāvarīṁ tathā* ||
> *harikṣetraṁ kurukṣetram śrīraṅgaṁ setubandhanam* |
> *evamādiṣu tīrtheṣu bhramamāṇa itastataḥ* || (BhP 0.1.28–29)

He then gave an almost word-for-word translation of this verse as follows:

> Here and there I wandered to all these holy places. I went to Puṣkara, Prayāga, Godāvarī, Haridvāra, Śrīraṅga, Kurukṣetra, Rāmeśvara—all of these different places I went. (1.1.3.5:44–5:58)

This verse makes no particular doctrinal point, and after the above translation, the exponent passed over it without further comment or elaboration. Yet it has a particular purpose and fulfills a function in terms of the structure of the whole Māhātmya. As stated earlier, the overall composition of the Māhātmya is as follows. The outer framing story is the dialogue between Ugraśravas and the sages in the Naimiṣa forest. Within that outer frame is this embedded narrative of the Sanatkumāras and Nārada. Within that second framing story, the Sanatkumāras tell Nārada the story of Gokarṇa and Dhundhukārī. This verse in which Nārada recounts his itinerary stands at the beginning of the second framing story. It flags a transition in the narrative between the outer frame and the second frame. The Sanskrit verse not only marks a new starting point in the structure and pushes the new narrative unit forward, but it is also a conspicuous way of signaling to the audience that this story and the exponent's spoken discourse are still firmly embedded in the authority of the Sanskrit text.

We see something similar in the following verse, another important juncture in the narrative, where the sage Nārada first encounters the young woman Bhakti. She introduces herself and explains why her sons appear so much older than she does. Literally, the verse could be translated as follows: "I am called Bhakti. These are my two sons, Jñāna and Vairāgya by name, grown decrepit through the workings of fate." Here the exponent recited the Sanskrit verse and expounded on it by embedding individual phrases extracted from the verse into a lighthearted imagined dialogue between Bhakti and Nārada:

> *ahaṁ bhaktir iti khyātā imau me tanayau matau* |
> *jñāna-vairāgya-nāmānau kāla-yogena jarjarau* || (BhP 0.1.45)
>
> "Hey, *devarṣi* Nārada—have you not recognized me? Don't you know who I am? You are an authority on me, you are an expert on me. I am Bhakti."
>
> "Which Bhakti? What Bhakti? Did your parents name you Bhakti? Very nice name."
>
> "I am Bhakti herself! I am Bhakti-devī herself. *ahaṁ bhaktir iti khyātā*. I am Bhakti herself."
>
> "Uh-huh, and who are the old men, father and uncle?"
>
> "*imau me tanayau matau*—These two are my sons."
>
> " 'These two are my sons'? How can that be possible! You are sixteen years of age. These fellows are ninety years of age. How can they be your sons?"
>
> "*jñāna-vairāgya-nāmānau kāla-yogena jarjarau*—They are called Jñāna and Vairāgya: *jñāna*, wisdom; *vairāgya*, detachment. These two sons of mine have become old. Affected by the Kali-yuga, they have become so old."[2] (1.1.3.10:26–11:39)

The divine sage (*devarṣi*) Nārada is regarded as an "expert" on Bhakti because he is traditionally held to be the author of the Bhakti-sūtras, one of the most important texts on devotion in the Vaiṣṇava tradition. Bhakti would naturally expect Nārada to recognize her. The seamless integration of the Sanskrit text drawn from the root verse into the humorous spoken exposition is typical of the South Indian Kathā-kāla-kṣepa style of oral performance (Ananth Rao 2011). Satchitananda Sai's spoken discourse was at once translation and commentary, but even more, it was an excellent example of how the exponent injected levity, along with contemporary concerns and diction, into his oral performance. Imagine this as a rapid-fire delivery, with the exponent clearly enjoying the humor as much as the audience did. The exponent went on to make the doctrinal point that in the Kali-yuga, one may find devotion—the temples are always full—but devotion must be accompanied by spiritual knowledge and worldly detachment, both of which are deficient in the present age.

In summary, this verse serves two functions. First, it highlights an important point in the narrative as it introduces Bhakti and her two sons, the key characters in this narrative unit. Second, it serves as the basis for an important doctrinal point on the relationship between devotion, spiritual knowledge, and worldly detachment.

Of the forty-odd Sanskrit verses in this two-hour session, about half were primarily used as scriptural evidence for doctrinal points, and half were used to push the narrative forward and anchor the spoken discourse in the written text, while a small number performed both functions. The exponent did not treat all verses in the same way. The treatments varied from a simple literal translation with no elaboration, to translation with some additional interpretation, to interpretation only with no attempt at translation, and finally to the Kathā-kāla-kṣepa-style treatment in which each phrase of Sanskrit is repeated and followed by a translation and an elaboration.

Audience Reception

Entextualization, the use of the text to reinforce discursive points and to advance the narrative, and contextualization, the weaving of the text into the context of the spoken narrative, both serve to endow the discourse with the authority and authenticity that are held to be inherent in the root text. Evidence for the affective reception of the discourse may be found in the responses of the audience to the verses.

In Indic terms, the verses add *rasa*—"juice" or "succulence"—to the spoken discourse. From the audience's point of view, they add interest and aesthetic appeal to the exposition as a whole. During one break at the Canberra saptāha, an Indian attendee in his late forties remarked that without the Sanskrit, the saptāha would be "just like reading a book." He continued, "We know the stories from plays and books, but this is different. It is not possible to have a Bhāgavata-saptāha without the Sanskrit verses." An Australian-born Indian girl in her late teens said this of the Sanskrit verses: "They are poetic. I don't get bored. They mean something to the people who can understand them. Guru-ji connects with them." Two points are noteworthy here. First is the aesthetic function the Sanskrit verses play in elevating and enriching the discourse. Second, even though this young woman did not understand them herself, she appreciated the fact that the exponent "connects with them," and she seemed to be touched by the verses vicariously through him. An older attendee, born in India and in his seventies, said the Sanskrit verses were "important for the teacher and for the message." Another Indian man, in his fifties and having lived in Australia for many years, observed, "The Sanskrit verses bring the stories alive. They are the Vedānta, Vedas, and stories speaking." A Sri Lankan woman also about fifty years old said, "Because of the āchārya's *bhāva* [emotion], it touches my heart, but I feel sad that I have to wait for the translation before I can drink it."

The inclusion and explanation of the Sanskrit verses give the audience the sense of being in direct contact with the original text, accessing the Sanskrit directly, and achieving a vicarious understanding and enjoyment of the Bhāgavata. Even if one does not know the language, it is possible to enjoy the aesthetic experience of the sound and at the same time to have the intellectual experience of making meaning from the discourse. Audiences are thus able to engage with the text at a semantic and affective level through the mediation of the exponent.

In addition to the aesthetic reception, there is a more profound response to the Sanskrit verses. As Coburn (1984, 445–447) observed:

> [F]or many Hindus, the holiness of holy words is not a function of their intelligibility. On the contrary, sanctity often appears to be inversely related to comprehensibility.... Simply hearing this cultured language bordered on being a numinous experience.... [T]he propensity to memorize and to recite holy words—perhaps as a manifestation of devotion (*bhakti*), perhaps with the aspiration of having one's consciousness transformed by the mantras, ... runs very, very deep in Hindu life.... Hindus have affirmed that the holiness of the Word is intrinsic, and that one participates in it, not by understanding, but by hearing and reciting it.

Untranslated, the verses may not be understood semantically but are experienced as *śabda,* sacred sound, like mantra. When they are re-presented in the vernacular, they become accessible as *artha,* or meaning. And yet, as the Māhātmya and exponents repeatedly remind audiences, hearing the narratives themselves is enough to lead to mokṣa, Vaikuṇṭha, and "bliss." The transformative qualities usually attributed to the sound of mantra are also experienced by many devotees as abiding in the stories. One young woman at the Canberra saptāha observed, "The Sanskrit Vedas existed before time. They have the power to transform. Guru-ji has said that even if you cannot understand them, they can transform you." Another Anglo-Australian in her sixties said that she could not understand the Sanskrit, but it was like music: "It enters my heart. Sometimes I feel my heart will burst." When asked about the Sanskrit component, a man in his thirties said, "It is the language of the Vedas. Even if we cannot understand it, it enters our inner being, and we become attuned to the truth." Mackenzie Brown (1986, 75) calls this the "Purāṇic synthesis of sound and meaning":

> In the Purāṇas, the narrative or story literature has become the primary holy word, reincorporating the old mantric tradition under new terms. The saving story itself has taken on the character of mantric efficacy though not mantric immutability.

We see in the combination of the Sanskrit verses, chanted in the original and translated and expanded in the vernacular, the twin desires of what Coburn (1984, 450) terms "literal preservation" and "dynamic recreation." That is, the original text is preserved and maintains its mantra-like qualities of authority, yet in the vernacular narrative, the desire for understanding is met, and the transformative power of the narrative is activated.

Ways of Understanding the Verses

What is the difference between mantra and the Sanskrit verses in a saptāha? They certainly share some characteristics: both mantra and the verses are regarded as sacred sound by many within the tradition, powerful enough to effect transformation. But there are also important differences. The frameworks for understanding mantra developed by Gonda (1963), Staal (1989), Alper (1989), and others are not particularly helpful for understanding how Sanskrit verses "work" in the context of a saptāha. For one thing, mantras are *apuruṣeya*; that is, they do not have a human author but are of cosmic origin, whereas the verses of the Bhāgavatapurāṇa are conventionally ascribed to Vyāsa. Second, the aesthetics that surround the two are quite different. Mantras are sacred, divine, and powerful, but they are not uttered for their inherent beauty. The Bhāgavatapurāṇa, on the other hand, is a highly sophisticated composition that has much in common with the courtly poetry of the first millennium CE. It is considered to be a beautiful, highly sophisticated literary creation, and as the text itself frequently reminds us, it to be savored by *rasikas*, connoisseurs who are able to appreciate its flavor or essence, its rasa. It is to be sung and enjoyed for its beauty and poetry, something that could not be said of Vedic mantra.

The concept of ritual speech may provide a useful insight here. Ritual speech is a specialized register within a given linguistic repertoire. This form of verbal art may be distinguished from "plain speech" (Kuipers 1990). Like the Sanskrit verses, ritual speech as practiced among the Weyewa people of Indonesia is authoritative, powerful, and potentially transformative in that it may dispel a variety of malign influences that affect individuals or families. Unlike ritual speech in the sense used by Kuipers, the Sanskrit verses are further removed from plain speech, as they are not intelligible at a semantic level for most people who attend saptāhas. In fact, the exponent who chants Sanskrit verses is effectively using a foreign language as far as most attendees are concerned. Sanskrit is not just a variation on plain speech, not merely a change in register, but a shift into another linguistic realm.

Studies of sacred languages elsewhere in the world indicate many similarities with the Sanskrit verses in saptāha events and with the role of Sanskrit in Hindu traditions and practices more generally. With reference to the early Christian church in particular, Sawyer (1999, 23, 164–165) describes a situation analogous to the role of Sanskrit in Hindu practices:

> Common to many religions is the tradition that rituals must be performed in a particular language, frequently a language clearly distinguished from the language of everyday use. In some cases it is a special variety of the participants' own language, perhaps an obsolete, forgotten dialect, while in others it is a completely different language which is totally unintelligible to the worshippers.
>
> [L]anguage is an expression of a worshipping community's identity, and those responsible for preserving or controlling that identity use the traditional forms of language and ritual to do this. Priests may also use their own exclusive expertise in an ancient sacred language to maintain their dominant role in the community.... [Faith communities] are moved by the familiar sounds of the traditional language, even if they do not always know what it means, and argue for its superior beauty or mystical power. In other words, unintelligibility is sometimes associated with sacredness, and translation with modernization and secularization.

The problem here is that this approach tells us what we already know: that sacred language is powerful. The question that remains, however, is what makes it so? We return to this problem in a later chapter.

Scripture, Evidence, Faith, and Truth

Some final observations on scripture, evidence, faith, and truth are in order. Most, if not all, literate faith traditions share a concept of scriptural authority. To a greater or lesser extent, the words of the Bible, the Qur'an, the Torah, or the Analects are held by the faithful to be true and are the yardstick by which other statements may be evaluated. There is a long tradition of *śabda-pramāṇa*—literally, "measuring by the word"—or scriptural authority in Hindu epistemology (Matilal 1986, 21–45; Adluri 2014). While this originally applied to the authority of the Vedas, within Gauḍīya Vaiṣṇava circles, the Bhāgavatapurāṇa has also attained the status of Vedic infallibility. Scriptural authority, along with perception, inference, and others, are all recognized as valid ways of establishing "true knowledge." Members of all faith communities are, of course, just as capable of undertaking independent critical thought as are nonmembers, yet in certain situations, such as during a saptāha, at the feet of a guru, in *satsang* (gathered for religious instruction) with fellow devotees, *śabda* (the Word) is the dominant *pramāṇa* (measure), scripture is "truth." This is easy to verify in the field: for every devotee, in those circumstances, at that time, the verses drawn from the Bhāgavata are incontrovertible.

It took me some time to realize that many audiences already know the main narratives. At first, I thought that exponents had to convince their audiences of the truth of their positions. I slowly came to see that the audiences are already in the fold. In general, they already want the discourse to be true. As a result, the exponents are in every sense already preaching to the converted. On the first day of the Canberra saptāha, the exponent made an interesting point. He told the audience that they could choose to believe the stories of the Bhāgavata or not. The essence was bhakti, jñāna, and vairāgya—devotion, spiritual knowledge, and worldly detachment. The teachings on these are still valid, even if the rest are only stories. "But believing is extra sweetness," he added.

7

The Audience—Viś

THE METAPHOR FOR this chapter on the audience is *viś*, a term that originally referred to a settlement or a dwelling and later by extension to "settlers," "people of the tribe," and the "community" of Vedic society. The viś included the class of producers—farmers and graziers living in villages—in contrast with the ruling class of warriors (the *rajanya* or *kṣatra*) and the priestly caste of Brahmins. In this chapter, I explore the Bhāgavata-saptāha from the point of view of the community. Who attends these events? What attracts audiences? Do attendees come with specific wishes or desires that they hope will be fulfilled? To what extent are the prescribed traditional vows and restrictions still followed? What do audiences experience, and what do they take away from these events? I draw on interviews with audience members at a range of saptāhas, including many English-speaking members of the Indian community in Australia.

I had made some tentative progress in gathering material from audience members at the saptāha at Naluna and later in Canberra, but to understand the performances from the point of view of attendees, it was clear that I needed more data. Bhaktivedanta Siddhanti Maharaj, one of the exponents I had interviewed in India, mentioned that he had been invited by some devotees to conduct a saptāha in Brisbane, Australia. I contacted the organizers, the Brisbane Bhakti Yoga Centre and, having received a warm invitation, found myself at the Paloma Reception Centre in the suburb of Sunnybank as dusk was falling on a mild winter's day in June 2014. The two-story community hall, which belonged to the local Catholic church, sat under spreading tropical trees at the side of a railway-station parking lot. Four lanes of rush-hour traffic roared past on a major suburban highway. Only three other people were there for the advertised starting time of 5 p.m. on the first day of the saptāha. Laughing, we agreed that the event was probably running on "Indian time." One of the other early arrivals was a woman in her thirties who described herself as *nāstik*, or nonreligious. She was only there, she said, because her aunt had previously heard a talk by the speaker and recommended him. The other early arrival was an energetic and outgoing woman in her late thirties, who expressed great devotion and spoke fervently about her experiences at other saptāhas. I saw her as a good potential interviewee.

As we chatted in the parking lot, people began to appear out of the gloom in twos and threes, mostly in traditional Indian dress, some in street clothes, a number of non-Indians among them. The speaker, Siddhanti Maharaj, eventually got out of a devotee's SUV and greeted me warmly. It was a pleasure to see him again, and we chatted briefly about his trip, his teachings, and his travel plans.

The key to the venue had gone astray, and as a growing crowd waited under the portico, a young male vocalist playing a mridanga and two older men with hand cymbals led bhajans. Nobody minded waiting, and after an hour of energetic singing and dancing, the front door was finally opened. The exponent, bearing a copy of the Bhāgavatapurāṇa on his head, led a procession of around forty devotees up the stairs to the second floor. A large meeting room had been set up with rows of stackable plastic chairs at the back and mats on the floor at the front. An altar laden with images and offerings and a beautifully decorated throne for the speaker stood at the front of the room. The mridanga player, Gaura Raj Prabhu, who had accompanied Siddhanti Maharaj from India, led an extended āratī. Siddhanti began his exposition at about 7 p.m. with the Gokarṇa story from the Māhātmya. As he spoke rapidly in Hindi, a handful of non-Hindi speakers huddled around a female devotee at the back of the hall who provided seamless simultaneous interpretation in English.

Each evening for the next week, while junior tae kwon do classes were held in the community hall downstairs, Siddhanti discoursed on the Bhāgavata upstairs for about two hours. Numbers of attendees ranged from about one hundred to one hundred fifty, with a core of around thirty who attended every session. Every evening, the exposition was followed by an hour of energetic singing and drumming, kirtans and bhajans, led by Gaura Raj Prabhu, who was something of a costar at the event. During these musical interludes, most of the women danced together in large circles in the center of the hall. After āratī at the conclusion of each session, everyone lined up at the back of the hall to receive prasād. This took the form of substantial plates of rice, rotis, vegetables, and fruit, all of which had been brought in by devotees. By the time dinner was over and I had completed one or two interviews (in English) with members of the audience, I just had time to catch the ten-thirty train.

In terms of content, this saptāha was unlike any other I had attended. While most exponents adhere closely to the structure and content of the Bhāgavatapurāṇa, Siddhanti Maharaj made only occasional references to the root text. Instead, he used its narrative structure as a broad framing device for a stream of anecdotes and interpolations from other sources and from oral tradition. His entire discourse over the seven days included barely a handful of Sanskrit verses from the Bhāgavata. The main topics for each day were the Gokarṇa story from the Māhātmya, Vyāsa's despondency, the story of Dhruva, the advent of Kṛṣṇa, folk and oral narratives concerning Rādhā, the story of Mount Govardhana, and, finally, Kṛṣṇa's destruction of various demons.[1] This simplified structure was the result of two factors. First, the schedule was organized so that the Govardhana narrative was recounted on the very day of the lunar year when Kṛṣṇa's raising of the mountain is traditionally celebrated. Second, only limited time was available each evening, because many of the participants were working full-time. Early on, Siddhanti took me aside and said half-apologetically words to the effect of "Of course, this is not how we usually do it in India."

In addition to the evening sessions, Siddhanti also gave discourses each day from 10.30 a.m. until about 1 p.m. in the homes of various members of the organizing body, the Brisbane Bhakti Yoga Centre. Seated in an armchair with twenty to thirty devotees at his feet, Siddhanti would invite the assembly to suggest a theme from the Bhāgavatapurāṇa for the morning. He would then deliver an impromptu discourse on the topic until lunchtime.

My primary goal in attending the saptāha in Brisbane was to understand the experience of audience members. I was curious to learn what attracted audiences to these events and whether they observed any particular vows or restrictions. One of the claims often made about these events is that they exert a transformative and life-changing effect on those who attend. How might these claims be understood? Is it possible to isolate those factors that enable audiences to experience saptāhas as authentic and powerful? In exploring these questions, I have allowed my informants, as far as possible, to tell their own stories.

The Brisbane Bhakti Yoga Centre

The Brisbane Bhakti Yoga Centre is a nonprofit organization that developed around a nucleus of Gujarati-speaking families who emigrated from Fiji to Australia in the late 1980s and early 1990s. Most of the society's members received initiation from Srila Bhaktivedanta Narayan Goswami Maharaj, founder of the International Pure Bhakti Yoga Society (IPBYS). Narayan Goswami visited Australia about a dozen times between 1998 and his death in 2010. The group was formed in 1999 following his first visit and was legally incorporated in 2010.

In addition to the four saptāhas that Brisbane Bhakti has organized over the years, as many as six sādhus are invited from India each year to give teachings in Brisbane, either in the homes of members or, like the saptāha I attended, in a rented hall. All speakers who had been invited to date were disciples of Narayan Goswami and are described by group members as "our god-brothers."

Brisbane Bhakti's parent organization, IPBYS, holds two main events in India every year: a seven-day pilgrimage to Mayapur, the birthplace of Caitanya in West Bengal, and a month-long pilgrimage in and around

FIGURE 7.1. Bhaktivedanta Siddhanti Maharaj giving an impromptu Bhāgavata talk in a private home during the saptāha, Brisbane, April 2014.

Vrindavan. Some members of the Brisbane society have taken part in these pilgrimages and have developed close relationships with various IPBYS teachers during their time in India. Two younger members of the group are now living in the society's ashrams in India. These contacts facilitate communication between the parent body and the Brisbane branch.

The group, which has also attracted members from other communities, both Indian and non-Indian, maintains links with several Gauḍīya Vaiṣṇava organizations in Queensland, including ISKCON. It provides a framework in which members expand and deepen their spiritual practice through weekly meetings and pass on their religious and cultural observances to their children. They do this chiefly by encouraging practices such as singing bhajans and kirtans, reading the Bhāgavatapurāṇa and the Bhagavadgītā, adopting a *sattvik* vegetarian diet, and fasting on Ekādashī, the eleventh day of each lunar fortnight.

What Attracts Audiences?

There will always be worldly reasons for attending a saptāha. One of the leading exponents in Vrindavan, Shrivatsa Goswami, an "insider" whose credentials are impeccable, made this down-to-earth observation:

> First of all it is the organizer. There is a social obligation: "Oh, my first cousin is organizing a Bhāgavata, so I must go" [laughter]. Or to show off: "I will wear my best sari, best necklace, best this, best that" [laughter], and things like that. That is to a larger degree, but having said that, the ulterior motives, it is like whether with love or hate you handle fire, it will burn you. Same as Bhāgavata-kathā. I have seen people, they say, "Oh, just to fulfill my social obligation I came for one hour, but I could not leave." Most of the testimonies are like that. Bhāgavata sucks them in. So they come with ulterior motives, and then they get sucked in. Or "The *kathā-vacaka* [exponent] has fantastic music" or "He has the best oratory skills," so all these recommendations have drawn an audience to come.

Ignoring these worldly motives, it is primarily the desire for religious knowledge that is frequently mentioned by attendees. Most of the members of Brisbane Bhakti had followed some forms of Hindu practice in Fiji before migrating to Australia but without a deep understanding. Moving from a large, long-established Indian community in Fiji to become dislocated newcomers in Australia, they experienced a need to reestablish a sense of community and create a new identity for themselves. Emigration also provided an opportunity for discovering a reinvigorated "Indian-ness" and "Hindu-ness" not previously accessible.

Karuna Raniga and her husband, Prakash, were leading members of the Brisbane Bhakti Yoga Centre. Karuna, a third-generation Gujarati born in Fiji, described her family as very religious, following the customs and culture of her tradition. Before she emigrated, Karuna had wanted to learn more about the rituals her family practiced in Fiji. Out of curiosity, she had joined the Ramakrishna Mission in Nadi but received few and unsatisfactory answers. Karuna and her family migrated to Brisbane twenty years ago, and, like many immigrants before her, she was concerned that her children would lose their culture and traditions. She began taking her family to the local ISKCON temple. These visits stimulated her own spiritual interests, as she began to find answers she had been seeking: "All the practices there had reasons, so that really interested me. Then I got deeper and deeper, and went more and more into it."

That Karuna should also be involved in organizing saptāhas in Australia was hardly surprising, given her long family association with the practice in Fiji. From a very young age, she watched her socially active aunt organizing similar events, and she recalled attending saptāhas from around age eight with her grandmother. She had attended at least one a year, sometimes two or three, and helped organize many saptāhas in Fiji as a girl. "So I have been attending these basically all my life," she said.

Another member of Brisbane Bhakti, Dhiraj Raniga (not related to Karuna or Prakash), described a similar experience of formalistic religious practice in Fiji, followed by an awakening of his spiritual interests after migrating to Australia. Born in India, Dhiraj migrated to Fiji as a child in 1957 and came to Australia in 1987. He described his spiritual journey as follows:

> In a place like Fiji, we should be a lot more spiritual, where there are a lot more Indians, but no, that wasn't the case. We became a lot more spiritual when we came here, because, I guess, we didn't relate back to home [i.e., to India]. We weren't being taught what's right or what our religion should be. We were being taught by my parents, simply, you wake up in the morning, you have a shower, you kneel down, and go to school [laughter]. We didn't even know why we were doing that. It's funny. But eventually, by coming over here, we began to mix around with a lot of people from our Indian

> background, and they were a lot more spiritual, and we began to meet up with them. I guess that's when spirituality arose.

As mentioned, not all members of the society were of Indian origin. Among a number of non-Indians was a fifty-two-year-old Anglo New Zealander living in Australia who had taken the Indian name Brajbala. She shared with the Indian members a diasporic experience, a search for a new identity, and a desire to reconnect with a tradition from her past. Coming from New Zealand, she expressed an affinity with the Indian-Fijian members "because of the Pacific thing—that was another thing that felt kind of nice." Brajbala came from what she described as a "spiritual culture" and as a teenager in the 1970s had worked in a Hare Krishna restaurant. She described herself as "getting a bit lost" in Australia and had felt a desire to reconnect with something in her youth that had fulfilled her spiritual needs. She was initially drawn to Brisbane Bhakti by her "love and respect of Indian tradition," and this led her to explore Indian spirituality more deeply. Brajbala described herself as "very involved," at first with ISKCON and then with Brisbane Bhakti, attending regular weekly practices for the last two years. She said that she had originally considered herself Hindu, but as she became more involved with this community, she now self-identified as Vaiṣṇava, the term preferred by many adherents to the Gauḍīya tradition.

Saptāhas provide a point of social contact and a framework for religious practice for the community. Participants and exponents also often expressed the belief that they are rare and auspicious events. This view was formulated originally by the text itself, especially in the Māhātmya, and is actively propagated by speakers. It was also routinely mentioned by audience members in interviews. As one informant put it:

> I would do anything to do this, because I see this as a lifetime opportunity, and I think it's a blessing. People who are fortunate, who Kṛṣṇa wants to hear, are the only ones who will hear. So I do make an effort, and I think people come from so far away, and all the time they travel and everything—and where do I live? It is so close for me, and I just think Lord Kṛṣṇa is helping me do things so closely.

This sense of predestination and divine election was echoed by Shulakshna Narayan, another leading member of the Brisbane Bhakti group:

> People are nominated to be here, nominated by him [the Lord], saying, "You have left your bhakti, so now is the time to get further,

> further, further." The same with us. When we met our Guru-ji, our Guru-ji looked at us and said, "In your [previous lives], you left your bhakti there, and now it is your turn to start again and see how far you can go." As Maharaj said the other day, we don't want mokṣa, we want *sevā-saukhya, sevā-saukhya, sevā-saukhya* ["the pleasure of service"] with Rādhā-Kṛṣṇa. We want to be there. So if we don't reach our goals and we miss something, then we have to come back again and continue from where we left off. So the people who come here are nominated people from the Lord who belong here. The invitation went to so many people, but no, it's just the people whose soul is searching for Rādhā-Kṛṣṇa, and they are the people we have here.

The concept that the saptāha is a rare event and that those who are attending are divinely chosen is one of several sets of ideas that seem to have the effect of elevating and empowering the discourse in the minds of attendees.

Hari, a young IT professional originally from Bangalore, attended the saptāha one evening. He had been to a dozen or so similar events in the past, so I asked him what drew him back to saptāhas time after time. He peppered his answers with rapid-fire quotations in Sanskrit (which I have translated here in italics), and the theme of thirst for spiritual knowledge also emerged in his response:

> *That which is of Bhagavān is the Bhāgavata.* The Lord himself manifested in that, and every single word of Bhāgavata when you keep listening to it, it is so *sweet,* it is so pleasant, that you want to sit down and hear it. Whatever very little knowledge that we can get, because Bhāgavata is *That which, even though old, is new, a purāṇa.* Every time I go there and sit down, I still feel that my thirst is not fulfilled. I want to go back again and learn more. I come here, and if someone else is doing a Bhāgavata again next week, I would definitely go there. Since it is classified as a purāṇa, every time I go there, I get new information. . . . So I've got that thirst for that knowledge. Going to places like this helps me.

In additional to providing a structure for religious practice and satisfying a spiritual thirst, saptāhas play an important social role. As the New Zealand expatriate Brajbala expressed it, "I come for two things: to engage with the community, because there are lots of people here I really like and respect and love, so to strengthen and deepen our relationship; and to strengthen and deepen my knowledge and relationship with Kṛṣṇa." Karuna also recognized the important social function of the saptāha in bringing the community together in a social context:

> And some of them would be here for entertainment, also because we have got a very good *kirtankar* [singer] here who is singing beautiful kirtans, and some people may be here for prasād, because the prasād is very nice here [laughs]. And some people are here to get to mingle with other people, for the social aspect. There could be many reasons why people are attending here. But surely I can say there is a serious group of people who are attending for the sake of attending Śrīmad-bhāgavata.

Vows and Restrictions

In addition to exploring an audience's motivations in attending saptāha events, I wanted to find out the extent to which the various vows and restrictions (saṁkalpa and niyama) prescribed in the instructions for the archetypal saptāha are observed in a contemporary context. The dictionary definition of *saṁkalpa* is "a conception, idea, or notion formed in the mind or heart, a desire, purpose, definite intention, or determination or decision or wish for." Attendees may take a vow to complete the seven days of the event, with or without an additional set of niyamas (restriction on diet, sleeping arrangements, etc.), in the expectation that a specific wish or intention will be fulfilled. This vow may be taken formally before the exponent or another figure of ritual authority such as an officiating priest. Alternatively, it may be taken silently by the individual.

Many attendees at the Brisbane saptāha adhered to what they termed "Vaiṣṇava culture." This involved adopting a sattvik vegetarian diet and fasting twice a month. The saptāha in Brisbane was described by several participants as "not very strict." Few, if any, attendees were observing niyama over and above their regular practices, nor was an individual or family group identified as the principal sponsor or yajmān. This was a niṣkāma event, having no specific purpose or goal other than "the pleasure of the Lord," as one attendee put it. Participants expressed general approval of the concept of niyama, but the pressures of daily life—work, family, community—made following even the simplest restrictions difficult. For example, one person acknowledged the importance of bathing before attending a saptāha but added that as she was coming straight from work, this was impractical. Another attendee commented, also with reference to the impracticality of bathing: "As long as you are clean at heart, the Lord accepts you [laughs]. A lot of them might be just clean from the outside, but they should be clean from the outside and inside, and that is the reason that we come here. It's for cleansing ourselves." Another attendee stated that she would prefer to eat only one meal a day, the prasād after the discourse, but this seemed to be more of an ideal than an achievable practice. The same individual spoke eloquently and at great length about how she tried not to talk too much when attending a saptāha. Yet another spoke about the advantages of restricting one's diet. He also expressed his aspiration to "eat less and think more" during these events but went on to admit that living in the West and going to the office every day made these restrictions difficult to follow.

At most saptāhas, the first day's discourse covers the Māhātmya, including the story of Gokarṇa and narratives describing the efficacy of listening to the Bhāgavatapurāṇa. These narratives are intended to excite the audience's resolve to listen devotedly for the entire week. Even in the absence of a formal saṁkalpa, exponents often use these prefatory narratives to encourage attendees to make their own informal saṁkalpa to attend for each of the seven days. The first and last days of most saptāhas are generally the best attended, and audience numbers tend to dip during the middle days. Saṁkalpa is a sensitive subject. As Shrivatsa Goswami said during an interview in Vrindavan:

> It is a common attitude in the religiosity of human beings. I say, "Religion, thy name is transaction"—and I mean it—but more so in Hinduism. I don't know about Christianity; I am not a Christian. It may be a pure religion without give and take, but Hindus, we always give and take: "I will get these virtues if I take a dip in the cold water, then only will I take a dip in the cold water. If you don't give me virtues, I will not take a dip in the cold water." "I will walk around fifty kilometers of road if you give me this."

The implication is that everyone expects a return on his or her spiritual investment. A disinterested informant, but one within the tradition, while watching a video of a vast tent crowded with devotees, wryly remarked that most of the women in the audience were attending for the sake of their husbands' health or their sons' careers. Understandably, no one I spoke to would admit to harboring such worldly motivations, nor would they admit that people in their circle of acquaintances would do so. A mundane, ambitious, or personal saṁkalpa would imply a lack of spiritual sophistication. Most participants claimed to believe that the Bhāgavata, like the wish-granting cow, would bestow anything one desired, but it would be wrong to ask for anything specific, as illustrated by the following quote from a woman attending the Brisbane saptāha. I asked her, "Did you come to this saptāha with a particular wish or desire?" Her response:

> I did once, but as I moved on, I learned that you don't have a desire. When I was very sick last year at the Bhāgavata, I didn't have a job. All of a sudden, I think because of more stress, I got more sick. But anyway, as soon as I went there, I got the job straight away. As soon as I finished the Bhāgavata-saptāha on Sunday, on Monday I was at work. But then I learned—I learned—and as I got closer to Lord Kṛṣṇa, I started feeling that you never go to Kṛṣṇa with something in your heart that you want, because he already knows.

Hari, the young IT consultant, also expressed a general disdain for the idea of worldly saṁkalpas. The only legitimate desire one should entertain while attending was to drink the nectar of the Bhāgavata in full:

> The only saṁkalpa should be, if at all, that you are there to enjoy the mellowness of Śrīmad-bhāgavata. As it says in the Bhāgavata, this is nothing but the essence. The sweet mellowness that comes out of the words of Śuka Maharaj-ji is so beautiful, especially the tenth skandha of Śrīmad-bhāgavata. I think if one has to take a saṁkalpa, that should be the saṁkalpa. That's my humble opinion.

The Audience Experience

For some audience members, saptāhas were primarily opportunities for learning, during which they added to their store of religious knowledge. Others experienced heightened religiosity and remarked on the atmosphere of spirituality generated by the saptāha.

Kamala Wood is the administrator of a yoga center in North Wales, United Kingdom, whom I met in Vrindavan. She had attended a saptāha conducted by Ramesh Oza, a well-known speaker with an international reputation, at Crawley, south of London, in 2007.[2] With a thousand or more people, she sat in a huge tent in a field: "It was almost like a festival, people handing out food from the food tent, a place for people to go and buy the recordings." As she did not understand Hindi, she could only listen with her heart; as she put it, "You can listen with your head or listen with your heart. Sometimes it is better to listen with your heart." She added:

> I thought it was really amazing to sit among hundreds of people with the same intention, trying to get a benefit from listening to Bhāgavata. It was a very communal thing, a community thing.... You sat down as a group, not just as an individual.... [I felt that I was part of that group], but I can't tell you exactly why [laughter].... It felt like a festival—very, very joyful. It was one of those things you will never forget. And I think even sitting in the presence of someone like Ramesh Oza, very established, well known, and famous for what he does ... just to go and see someone who is renowned and famous for what he does, that in itself is actually special.... So it is not just about going and sitting in a room and listening to the Bhāgavata. It is also about eating together. There is always food. There is always prasād. Everybody wants to feed you what they brought. There is always this feeling that it is a social event, the sort of thing that brings people together.

For Brajbala, the Brisbane saptāha's blend of narrative and philosophy was the most meaningful. Her initial interest was in hearing the stories of Vrindavan, of the Bhāgavata and the Bhagavadgītā, but she also expressed admiration for how exponents mobilized narrative to convey specific teachings:

> I like the narratives. I like the human condition. When I read, I am attracted to that. Every time you come, you learn. There is a foundation block, and then you add layer upon layer upon layer, and your practice every day and every week is like the concrete that sticks it all together. And I just keep coming and coming and coming and contributing what I can and sitting here.

Brajbala's strong response to the narrative as the key element in her experience may be understood, at least in part, in terms of her background. Raised outside the tradition, she had joined the community only a few years before. Although she was familiar with some of the fundamental narratives of the Bhāgavatapurāṇa through reading and movies, many of the stories were new to her, whereas those who grew up in this or similar Hindu traditions often possessed a deep cultural familiarity with narratives of this kind.

Shulakshna, who organized the saptāha in 2005 mentioned earlier, held a second event at her home in 2012. For her, the key feature was the experience of community and the sense of shared endeavor:

> Two years ago, the maharaj from our *saṅgha* [religious community], Bhaktivedanta Sridhar Maharaj, did Bhāgavata at my place. It was so beautiful. It was heart-warming. It was so relaxing. The good part was that my house was like Vrindavan, and we had both Eastern and Western people there, and they just enjoyed being there. We prepared them breakfast, lunch, and dinner, and we told them, "This is your house. Feel as if we are all in Vrindavan, because Maharaj-ji is here." Kirtan was going on, and two lectures in the morning and afternoon. We had the Maharaj's *pravacans* [expositions], so it was beautiful, wonderful. Every day, we might have had one hundred plus or one hundred and twenty plus people.... Then we also had donations of food, money—humongous!—people just came with their hearts open with food. Whenever I have programs like that, everyone is so generous, they give like that.

Shulakshna also commented on the challenges of emigrating from Fiji, where she left established networks of family and friends, and the importance of establishing new social contacts in an alien environment. Through the saptāha, she was able to recreate an imagined sacred place—not Fiji, not Brisbane, but Vrindavan itself. To foreshadow a topic I treat at more length in chapter 8, one of the factors that makes the Bhāgavata-saptāha popular is that it is rooted in a location but is not tied to that location. The practice is "of Vrindavan" but can be held anywhere. For devotees, saptāhas transform the venue into a sacred realm. The claimed experience of the joy generated by this focused, collective endeavor also shone through Shulakshna's narrative. Her descriptions of the event as beautiful, wonderful, and heart-warming and Kamala's references to the joy of shared experience in a festive atmosphere are all classic examples of *communitas*, another topic I return to later.

The woman I had identified as a good potential interviewee outside the venue on the first evening of the saptāha in Brisbane turned out to be a most interesting informant. She claimed to have witnessed "miracles" and to have experienced profound transformation during a previous saptāha in Brisbane:

> Yes, it was this hall, here, in Purushottam-mās [the thirteenth month of the lunar calendar] the year before last, and Pundrik Goswami was here. I came here, and that is when I started coming into this group a bit. The stage was there similarly, and from the day he came, something happened to me so that my heart was just attached to Kṛṣṇa. All these people had been in Bhakti Yoga for years, and that was my first Bhāgavata here, and Pundrik was so young, and he was admirable. There was a context which was upsetting me in my life which was so difficult that I could not talk to anybody about it, and it had been going on very harshly. So I came here, and I sat there . . . and one day, this thing was happening. I was sitting right up front there, and there were all marigold flowers that we had put there. I always sat right at the front, as there were lots of people for Purushottam-mās, and it was packed. This thing was upsetting me, and all of a sudden, he started talking about that, and a flower from him started dropping, and it came and fell in front of me. It was a white gardenia flower, and I am looking at it, and it's all marigolds. Where did this gardenia come from? Bhāgavata is there, I'm not lying. It came down, and whatever was upsetting me, he started talking about that, and I just picked up the flower, and he said, "If you take someone else's wealth . . . it will all go in hospitals, so you will never enjoy it." And I was thinking, "You are just answering my things!"
>
> So when I went home, Lord Kṛṣṇa came in my dream. Now that Lord Kṛṣṇa is my Lord Kṛṣṇa, meaning my photo, the one I have at home. He just came with the big bowl of the *makhan* [butter], you know. He had put his hand in there, and he was smiling and lights flashing, and I'm thinking, "How blessed is that!" Because if you dream Kṛṣṇa comes to you, it means that he is thinking of you, and you are just blessed.
>
> Last year, when I went to Bhāgavata, three times he came. You know how Lord Viṣṇu has an avatāra as a fish and a boar? And I had

> big fish in my dream, and the next day I had a big boar, like a pig, and I'm thinking, "Some people brought this pig," and I am thinking, "My God, you're putting a pig in your house! Do you think it's a pet?" This is in my dream. And they said, "Yeah," and all of a sudden, I am thinking, "Anyway, it's their way, I'll move on." As soon as I get out, this pig is beautiful. It turned around. I didn't know, so I went to Guru-ji Maharaj, and I said, "You tell me—this is what happened to me," and he said, "Oh, that's Lord Viṣṇu." And then Lord Kṛṣṇa came that very last day, and I told Shulakshna, and she said, "It [the previous saptāha] was at my house, and I never got any dreams!" She was joking.

In Vrindavan, I spoke about the saptāha experience with Mr. H, mentioned earlier, the retiree from Delhi who had a successful candy business. He presented himself as a devout disciple of Bhaktivedanta Madhusudan Maharaj and was actively involved in administering his guru's association. Mr. H stated that he got up at 3 a.m. to do chanting and that he studied the Hindi edition of the Bhāgavatapurāṇa for one to two hours, or one chapter a day, calling Madhusudan Maharaj on the phone if he had any problems in understanding it. Mr. H sponsored Madhusudan to give several saptāhas at his house in Delhi. These events were attended by as many as a hundred family members, friends, and neighbors. He did not have any particular saṁkalpa or desire that he wanted fulfilled: "We don't think of results. Hearing is most important. When we hear the nectar, it goes into our hearts." Nor did he follow any of the special restrictions or niyama, such as a restricted diet, sleeping on the floor, or avoiding contact with foreigners: "No problem. We are all servants of God." But he did try to have only "pure thoughts":

> Saptāha is light to the soul. If you are not in touch with Bhagavān, you are a dead person. Bhāgavata is food for the soul.... It is all transcendental. It is not of this world. It is all joy and bliss. Here it is all illusion. A fool's paradise.... The vibrations will really enter into you. You feel you are part of it. You are aspiring to it, and you get it. You are wanting that thing, that happiness, because the reservoir of bliss is nowhere else. It is the supreme reservoir of pleasure.... This is the real substance. You are tasting it. Something is coming into you. A real thing, the true nectar, is purifying your existence. It is taking away all the bad things in you and giving you the food, and

> that is sustaining you. We have to constantly hear, hear, hear. That is the real nectar. That gives you the real bliss. . . . I was a boozer and a chain smoker—all the bad habits. But when I came into this line, slowly and gradually, I left all the bad habits. Now I never think of them.

Two prominent and related themes arise from these comments and those of other audience members. The first centers on food and nourishment, the second on joy. Respondents spoke of the saptāha experience as being "sweet" or inducing a "sweet mellowness." One attendee mentioned his "thirst" for knowledge, while another called the events "food for the soul." One organizer spoke of "relishing" the stories. The Bhāgavatapurāṇa was described as "true nectar," which provides spiritual food and is "sustaining you" "This is the real substance. You are tasting it."

Related to the theme of food and consumption is the polysemy of the word *prasād*, meaning kindness or blessing but also the term used for the consecrated food often distributed at the close of a kathā session. At a saptāha, one may receive the prasād of the Divine through hearing the narratives. Similarly, one internalizes the blessing of the Divine by consuming the sacred foodstuffs after the event or taking a plate home to share with one's family.

Eating brings satiation. In addition to the theme of food is the concept of the saptāha as bliss and joy. Attendees spoke of a sense of "fulfillment," which suggests the filling and fullness that follow a meal. One respondent said that for her, a saptāha was like a joyous festival; another described it as "all joy and bliss." "Heart-warming" was another term used by an audience member that seems to unite the food and bliss metaphors. The ideas of saptāha as food and saptāha as bliss may arise spontaneously and independently in the minds of respondents. It is also true that these metaphors are frequently employed in the text itself and by exponents in their performances, but this does not detract from their validity as ways of describing the audience experience.

Accounts such as these and many others given by audience members tend to be overwhelmingly positive, even to the extent of sounding doctrinaire or sanctimonious. On occasion, I had the impression that respondents were saying what they thought a foreign researcher should hear and were perhaps repeating the "party line." Sometimes responses sounded more like the exhortations of exponents rather than the audience members' own experiences. These responses need to be placed in a critical context. It is unreasonable to expect that every attendee experiences every saptāha in such positive ways. Is no one ever bored, frustrated, irritable, or simply mystified? What about people who remain untouched by these events, such as the occasional Anglo-Australian who drifted in off the street in Brisbane, listened in bemusement for half an hour, then disappeared into the night? What about the young woman who described herself as a nāstik, an atheist? We can safely presume that saptāhas do not affect all people equally, that socialization and expectation play important roles in how the events are experienced, and that pride in one's culture and practices will color how they are reported.

Given the context of the interviews—insiders addressing an outsider—audience members have an understandable desire and perhaps a vested interest in presenting the tradition in the best possible light, as this serves to validate the tradition itself and their own participation. Positive accounts of the saptāha experience may also serve to cement audience members' relationship with their guru and consolidate their positions within the community. The same sort of critical distance may also be invoked with regard to audience members' descriptions of the transformative power of saptāhas, described in the following section. That said, it is equally unreasonable to deny the validity of all these accounts out of hand. This is how some attendees claim to experience saptāha, and for them, this may indeed constitute the reality of their experience.

Saptāhas as Transformation

It is frequently claimed by the Bhāgavatapurāṇa itself, and also by exponents and audience members, that saptāhas provide transformative, life-changing experiences. When discussing this claim with participants in the Brisbane event, three kinds of changes emerged: lifestyle, spiritual, and social. Karuna and Shulakshna both noted that many families who attended saptāhas subsequently modified their lifestyles. Some who had previously eaten meat became vegetarian and gave up certain foods, including alcohol, onions, and garlic. Some took up daily chanting, kirtan, and reading the Bhāgavata and the Bhagavadgītā. Dhiraj, for example, said:

> I feel myself being transformed from what I was to what I am now. Before, I used to have a few beers and things like that. That's while in Fiji, because we never knew that this is right or this is wrong, because no one explained to us. But when we came over here, the maharajs

> explained to us that you shouldn't drink. Luckily for us, we have been brought up in a vegetarian family, so we have never eaten meat in our life before, so we don't miss that for a start. The thing that was difficult was, we used to run businesses in Fiji as well—we used to go to parties, you have to mingle around and have a few beers, not that I enjoyed drinking but just to be with the crowd. But then, when I came over here, when I started to find out, I totally stopped.

In addition to these practical lifestyle changes, Karuna said, "I also notice the behavior, the enviousness, the jealousy, all that has also changed in the group that we are associating with and who are constantly attending the Śrīmad-bhāgavatas."

In addition to these changes in day-to-day habits, informants often claimed deeper spiritual changes in their lives, which they attributed to the saptāha experiences. Shulakshna, for example, likened the experience of saptāha to an electric shock:

> If you are doing something and you are not careful, you get this shock. "Wow! What's this? How did I get that?" The same thing is in the Bhāgavata-saptāha. If people come and listen to it from their soul, from their heart, and if it sinks into them, that's when they change. They say, "Wow! This is something I have never thought of or never heard of." When they first heard my Bhāgavata-saptāha at Wynnum [a suburb of Brisbane], people totally changed. Totally changed. They were so into Hinduism. Because we come from the culture, but we have forgotten that. When you remind them, they say, "Yeah, this is where we belong, and now we should start." But it is just one of those things in our culture; everything is there.

The woman who described the miracles and dreams she experienced during the saptāha in 2012 attributed a series of life changes to that event. She took up reading the Bhagavadgītā regularly, changed as a person, and was now taking part in regular charity work at a nursing home.

> So that's how, ever since I had Purushottam-mās here and all these miracles that happened to me, I started reading Bhagavadgītā, and since then—it's three times a week, at least in the morning on the train, on the bus, anywhere, I read my Gītā—and that helps me, and it has changed me as a person. Because of all the stress due to

> some family problems . . . I was sick, and I used to get angry within myself and everything. As soon as I started chanting and reading Gītā, I changed, and my husband said, "You are so changed." He noticed, and I have just changed, and all of a sudden, I don't care how the world is, nothing is mine, and I feel so light, and I just wanted to do service, so we started to do a lot of service work, and my girls are involved in a lot of service work.

In Brajbala's case, that same 2012 saptāha was transformative in two dimensions: first, as a spiritual experience in which she expressed a heightened degree of "closeness" to the Divine, and second, as a social transformation from being an outsider to being an insider when she became a fully fledged member of the community.

> My first [saptāha] certainly was [life-changing]. I met my *didi* [elder sister], as I call her . . . and she invited me. "Our maharaj-ji is coming for a week. Would you come to my house?" And I did, and it was really transformative. I am not learned enough to say "This line in the scripture says this," but I know that they certainly say that when you reach out to Kṛṣṇa, he will provide that opportunity for you. . . . And I had really kind of said, "I just want to be closer, Lord. I just want to be closer." And I then met this didi, and I came to this house, and I met this tradition. I had always been a very involved layperson in ISKCON. I was there every week. I contributed. I dressed the altar every week. I worked in the restaurant. But I always felt I would be a supportive layperson. I never felt that I would have my own guru-ji. I would never take those steps to make those promises. From that very first time, I realized maybe actually I will. So it was very transformative for me. From the outside, from the outer circle, to stepping right in.

I asked Brajbala what she took away from her saptāha experience, and she replied without hesitation:

> Deeper knowledge. I want to say "boldening" but I don't know if that is the right word. Deeper sustenance. I'm getting old; just sustenance for those cold mornings or the tired mornings, just something. Fertilizer, even, maybe! I feel I am getting this, and that's why I come back and come back. . . . Sustenance. Fertilizer. Just something to make my journey—because I see it as a journey, my

> faith. You need sustenance on the way. These are like the feasts, the feasting times of your journey. You get together, you feast, and then you do your own cooking, and then the feasts come around again.

Karuna, as one of the key members and organizers of the Brisbane Bhakti group, was also aware of how this and previous saptāhas had attracted and integrated new members into the society. She described how individuals had originally attended a saptāha, listened to the exponents from India speak, and then joined in the kirtans:

> So they would be feeling something, that something is there, and that would lead them to probe more, to get deeper into that. Then they would inquire, and they would give us their emails and get the newsletters. In the beginning, they would not be coming, but once they are reading the newsletters and listening from other people that they are doing something, then they start.

Many individuals who came to the early saptāhas subsequently joined the society, began attending regular weekly practices, and became more deeply socialized and integrated into the community as a result. Many families went on pilgrimage to India, which led to further deepening of their religious practice.

As mentioned, it would be more or less unthinkable for a devotee to deny the transformative power of the saptāha, as this is deeply embedded in the discourse surrounding the practice. To deny this potentiality would be tantamount to placing oneself outside the tradition. A further corrective to the one given by Shrivatsa Goswami in the previous section is an observation from Abhishek Goswami, another Vrindavan "insider" of impeccable lineage. He remarked that in a saptāha audience of two thousand, he would only expect "four or five" individuals to be truly transformed. Yet we may still assume that the experiences described here were at least in part significant and the reality for the participants who reported them.

Sources of Transformation

As we have just seen, many participants believed that saptāhas were potentially transformative, and some claimed that their own lives had indeed been changed as a result. What factors give saptāhas this power? There is no single answer to this question, and each respondent highlighted a different aspect. Karuna, for example, immediately identified the lineage and personal integrity of speaker as the key. An exponent coming from a bona fide spiritual lineage would have received his knowledge through his *paramparā* (guru lineage). It was also important to Karuna that the speakers adhered to the appropriate niyamas. For her, this included the facts that exponents were "chanting the Lord's names, they are renounced, they are realized, and their whole life is devoted to this Kṛṣṇa bhakti." Listening to an exponent with these qualities certainly would "change the hearts of the people":

> We say that this fire of love that we are yearning for, that love of God, is from *kṛpā*, from mercy. So if that is glowing in the heart to the full amount in the speaker, or in the guru paramparā, then it is certainly going to touch the hearts of the people who are listening.

For Brajbala, it was the intensity and depth of being immersed in the practices for many hours a day for an entire week. She likened immersion in saptāha to the experience of fasting or trekking in the mountains; the intensity of immersion lent it the power to transform. Hari, on the other hand, pointed to the important role of expectation and socialization. Most "insiders" who attended a saptāha, including individuals from an Indian cultural background and anyone familiar with the main themes of the Bhāgavatapurāṇa, would generally be familiar with the framing narrative: King Parīkṣit achieved liberation through hearing the Bhāgavatapurāṇa from the sage Śuka. Individuals were socialized into receiving Bhāgavata discourse, that is, into experiencing the narratives, in certain ways. They brought certain sets of preconceptions and expectations to the event. Hari suggested that, just as Śuka's original Bhāgavata-saptāha had transformed Parīkṣit,

> That is the kind of expectation people would have going forward to a Bhāgavata-saptāha: "It will transform me as well." . . . We can't cheat ourselves. We know what sort of personality we are and how we can transform and because people like Parīkṣit Maharaj and all the other great sādhus [have been transformed].

Are These Experiences Typical?

Many of the accounts included here were from audiences at saptāhas outside India, in either Australia or the United Kingdom. How typical are

FIGURE 7.2. Audience at the Naluna saptāha, November 2009.

FIGURE 7.3. Village women on the way to attend the saptāha at Naluna, November 2009.

their experiences in general, and how do they compare with saptāhas elsewhere? Some of the elements described here are shared by saptāha audiences irrespective of where the events are held. These include the pull factors that attract an audience, the role of saṁkalpa and niyama, and the dominant discourse of power and transformational potential. This is in large part because the same exponents who perform in India also perform for the diaspora abroad. Speakers such as Ramesh Oza, Chandan Goswami, and Siddhanti Maharaj travel frequently and conduct saptāhas all over the world. In this sense, the diasporic saptāha is little different from the event in India.

Two factors distinguish the diasporic saptāha from the Indian saptāha. The first includes the practical aspects of living in the West. Because of the pressures of employment, diasporic audiences are less likely to take a full week off work to attend a saptāha than are audiences in India. This results in truncated saptāha performances, such as the event in Brisbane, which was conducted for only two to three hours each evening, whereas saptāhas in India usually run for much longer each day. Other practical aspects, such as bathing beforehand and following dietary restrictions, were said to be more difficult to follow in the West. Second, among diasporic communities, saptāhas have an important role in forming group identity, especially "Indian-ness" and "Hindu-ness" in an otherwise non-Indian and non-Hindu environment. In Brisbane, for example, the saptāha was an important means by which the community expressed and consolidated itself and created and maintained its own identity within the broader Australian society. It should be noted that the role of saptāhas in forming group identity also applies in India. There the groups might be followers of a particular guru, members of a particular community, an extended family, or residents of a given neighborhood.

Is it reasonable to distinguish a diasporic saptāha from an Indian saptāha? To what extent is it possible to generalize? Consider the variety of saptāha audiences and the different ways in which they experience the events. Attendees in a tiny village hall in Andhra Pradesh and an audience at a "super-bowl" event in Mumbai will obviously have very different experiences. We must also assume that each individual will experience a saptāha differently, yet particular audiences do indeed share some features. For diasporic audiences, the experience of Hindu-ness and Indian-ness in an alien environment is salient. For educated middle-class audiences, such as that at Satchitananda Sai's saptāha, there may be a more cerebral engagement with narratives, but there is also plenty of evidence of deeper affective involvement. In a charged atmosphere such as the one that prevailed at Mridul Krishna's saptāha in Vrindavan, there is an emotional response of bhakti amid the dancing and singing. For the saptāha at Naluna, the village men in homespun jackets and the women in thick wool cardigans walked down from their villages in the surrounding hills and only on those days when they could take time off from planting. Having made a simple offering of some grain in a plastic bag, the women sat knitting, their children asleep in their laps. Talk of transformation and ecstasy seems remote from this setting. One village girl said she simply came to hear "stories about God." While all saptāha audiences share some features, each one is also unique.

The Audience "Makes" the Event

Narayana Rao (1993, 99) holds that devotional purāṇas, such as the Bhāgavatapurāṇa, "essentially create an atmosphere of participation in religious ecstasy. The emphasis is not on information but rather on a renewed opportunity to experience the divine. It is not communication but communion." This statement requires some qualification. It is clear from attendees' own accounts that hearing the narratives and adding to their store of religious knowledge are significant imperatives. Saptāhas are communication *plus* communion. As Desai (2013, 127) found, audiences at Kolapalli in Andhra Pradesh regarded attendance at a saptāha as bringing religious merit (puṇya) and "peace of mind" and that it was "a good thing to do." Even those who did not understand the discourse reported that they "enjoyed hearing the stories of Kṛṣṇa."

Audiences do much more than just listen passively; they sing and clap and take part in the invocations and bhajans. In Mridul Krishna's Vrindavan saptāha, sādhus rhythmically rattled their fire tongs, and women shook brass castanets. Audiences applaud, laugh, cry, and participate in call-and-response interchanges. They shout words of encouragement or approval and sometimes even provide a correction or clarification. Audiences dance or sway during bhajans, and in the more musically oriented performances, most attendees are on their feet, some dancing in trancelike states of ecstasy. Audiences are often called on to throw their hands in the air to receive darshan. They take part in āratī before and after the event, accept prasād, and make donations. All these forms of activity illustrate the fact that audiences are active participants, not merely passive listeners. They are essential to the creation of the saptāha performance. These activities are also part of the meta-communication that surrounds the event and are an important conditioning factor in the audiences' experience of it.

Attendance at saptāha events is an important way to adopt a devout identity, that of a "good Hindu," something most attendees desire to cultivate. People flock to saptāhas for more than the social capital, the free food, and the opportunity to show off their saris and jewelry. The religious learning, cultural values, social connectedness, and spiritual nourishment provided by saptāhas constitute real and meaningful experiences for many attendees. Having looked at these factors at the level of the individual, next I step back and explore the growth of the saptāha phenomenon in its broader context.

8

Results—Phala

THE SUCCESS OF Vedic worship is seen in its outcomes, known as its *phala*, or fruit. The sponsor of the ritual traditionally sought sun, rain, cattle, sons, and victory. The deities, if satisfied with the ritual, granted these boons to the petitioner and ensured the prosperity of the individual and the maintenance of the universe. In this chapter, I examine the growth of saptāha practice. My underlying assumption is that the tradition is growing because it is fulfilling some social or experiential needs and that the various participants—sponsors, exponents, and audiences—all derive some benefit from it. As a step toward explaining its growth and development, I briefly review the outcomes, the phala, of saptāha performance accruing to these three classes of participants. As these outcomes arise only if the event is experienced as authentic, I next look at the sources of this authenticity. Finally, I suggest some external social factors that are contributing to the growth of the practice in terms of its popularity and scale. This enables us to sketch out some answers to the questions posed at the beginning of this book: Why is the saptāha tradition growing? What makes these performances powerful and transformative for participants? What spiritual needs and social imperatives do they fulfill?

The Results of a Saptāha

The goswamis of Vrindavan agreed unanimously that while saptāha events are not a new phenomenon and are "an eternal thing, since the sages in the forest," they are certainly more common, larger, grander, and louder today than they were in the past. Shrivatsa Goswami gave this evocative illustration of the growth of the practice:

> In my childhood, Vrindavan used to be crowded only a little bit in March to May and a little bit in Shravan [July and August] or something, but today, every Saturday or Sunday, there is not one single parking space available in Vrindavan. Whether the temperature is fifty degrees Celsius or zero degrees, it doesn't matter. Whether there are school vacations or no vacations, it doesn't matter. It's a round-the-year phenomenon.

A middle-aged attendee at the Canberra saptāha looked around in wonder at the varied audience—young and old, men and woman—and compared this with saptāha events when she was growing up in India. In those days, she said, saptāha audiences consisted "mainly of grandmothers." The practice is growing in size, complexity, and appeal because some or all of the parties involved must be drawing some benefit from it. In the following sections, the benefits accruing to each group as a result of its members' experiences are explored.

Initially, of course, a sponsor may have the same spectrum of experiences as any member of the audience. These range from deeply transformative to socially expedient to moderately entertaining. One crucial difference is that while an individual might attend many saptāhas during his or her lifetime, in a traditional setting, sponsorship of a saptāha, especially of a sakāma event, is usually a once-in-a-lifetime experience. As the center of attention and the focus of much ritual activity, in addition to being the "primary listener," the sponsor usually has a more intense experience than most audience members. For some sponsors, the saptāha does indeed provide a significant religious experience, perhaps even a life-changing one. Sponsoring a saptāha may be the culmination of a lifelong desire for some families, such as the one described earlier by Siddhanti Maharaj. That couple, and other sponsors I spoke with, came to describe their lives in terms of "before and after the saptāha." For others, such as the sponsor of the event at Naluna, the successful saptāha conferred peace of mind as a result of ensuring the welfare of a deceased relative and reaffirming his own social position as a leading benefactor in the community. Underwriting even a small-scale, local event provides a sense of virtuous achievement for the sponsor, the satisfaction of having contributed to the religious life of friends, family, and neighbors.

In addition to these intangible spiritual "fruits," sponsors may derive certain worldly benefits. India has a long history of private patronage of religious practices. In earlier times, emperors, kings, and local potentates played the roles of pious benefactors, building temples, underwriting performances, and sponsoring worthy supplicants. In modern India, this function has been assumed by successful business dynasties and wealthy individuals. Leading families and enterprises are expected to sponsor religious events as part of their social duty. In doing so, they win public recognition as important community-minded devotees. For affluent sponsors, this is a way of expressing support for, and in turn gaining recognition from, high-profile gurus or organizations. It is also a proven means of expressing, consolidating, and enhancing their social standing. Sponsors' names, and indeed the names of their businesses, are often featured prominently on billboards, posters, and handbills. Sponsors are regularly called onto the stage as "primary listener," piously dressed in traditional dhoti and kurta, surrounded by family and friends, their piety and munificence on public display. A sponsor's generosity and devotion are frequently extolled by the exponent. As a result of all this exposure and praise, sponsors acquire social capital, in addition to personal, religious capital. Sponsoring a saptāha brings with it a certain status, like earning a certificate or a degree. Speaking from his perspective as sponsor, Yogendra Yadav identified three further areas in which he believed the saptāha had a positive impact: his health, the birth of a long-desired grandson, and the welfare of his estate.

> I had problems with my back. I could not sit. I gradually began to recover, and I am really feeling much better ever since. It is not part of saptāha, but you know, you never know what it is. . . . So saptāha overall did wonderful things to me.
>
> Back in my subconscious, I wanted to become a grandfather, and my son was married for the last ten years without any issue, and it was deep in my heart that he should have a child. . . . And I do say, I really want to say, that it was the power of saptāha, and I have no problem. Because the saptāha happened at the end of November, and we knew that [daughter-in-law] Bharti was pregnant in January. Not only pregnant. In the first week, [son] Sumedh said he's buying a house, and we were very happy, and the week after he said that Bharti is pregnant. So good things did happen. It could be coincidence or whatever, but it was.
>
> After the saptāha, there was a lot of flooding and chaos everywhere. I was the one who was saved. The whole neighborhood, whole villages, they know that I was saved because I did good things.

> So the whole society knew about this one. I did saptāha, and I am a pious person, and these are the results.

I asked him if the saptāha had changed his relationship with the village people in the community in any way. His response:

> It was like you have attained a certificate, like a degree, in a way, so people will say, "Oh, this is Yadav. He did saptāha." So I am known, because there are not many people who do saptāha. In the vicinity, people know who did saptāha. It has certain status. That is sort of a capital. Not sort of a capital, it *is* a capital. Other things come and go, but this really stays.

Turning now from sponsors to exponents, what benefits do they derive from saptāha performances? For some, it is a joyous vocation and part of their own deeply held spiritual practice. This is evident from the way many speak of the divine inspiration they experience when seated on the vyās-pīth, the speaker's throne. Some see themselves as fulfilling their divinely appointed destiny, such as the young Chandan Goswami, who received instructions in a dream from Kṛṣṇa to spread the word of the Bhāgavata. Others are responding to a personal mission, such as Shri Krishna Chandra Shastri "Thakurji," who had been on the road for thirty-five years and had just returned from his 1,031st consecutive saptāha when I interviewed him in 2013. Some exponents, such as the goswamis of Radha Raman, are following a family tradition.

No exponent will admit to conducting Bhāgavata-saptāhas primarily for money, but for many, donations and fees from these performances are an important means of support for themselves, their families, and their institutions. The whole Vedic Yatra college relies on the earnings of the young exponent Anurag Krishna Shastri. For young graduates from this and other Bhāgavata colleges in Vrindavan, giving saptāhas in their faraway hometowns in Nepal or Bihar may be their only way of making a living. Some exponents live little more than a hand-to-mouth existence in humble circumstances. On the other hand, some established performers have become very wealthy, earning millions of dollars per appearance. Some of the most opulent mansions in Vrindavan have been built with proceeds from saptāha performances. Exponents also use income from saptāhas to support a range of charitable ventures, including ashrams, schools, and temples. Mridul Krishna Shastri's mega-saptāha in Bombay in 2009, which attracted approximately twenty thousand attendees, was specifically held to raise funds for a shelter for abandoned cattle in Vrindavan. The acquisition of great wealth by exponents is not seen as a bad thing in itself; in fact, it is viewed as a sign of divine recognition of their devotion. More critical than wealth is motivation. "Professional" exponents are widely condemned (though never named) for having money as their motive. It is acceptable to make a fortune as a Bhāgavata exponent but not to have money as one's primary incentive. This is in accord with a famous line in the Bhagavadgītā: "Pitiable are those who have the outcome as their cause."

As noted, sponsorship of saptāha events is often a mutually beneficial arrangement for sponsor and exponent. Important business, social, or political figures gain status from backing prominent exponents. In addition to financial rewards, exponents also derive prestige and the potential for future engagements and further patronage from being sponsored by high-profile individuals and organizations.

For some exponents, an invitation to deliver a high-profile saptāha can be a significant boost to their careers. Ever since the saptāha at Naluna in 2009, the exponent Bhadri Prasad has been in high demand and has reportedly become the most prominent Bhāgavata-saptāha performer in the district. According to Yogendra Yadav, Bhadri Prasad "is so busy that now he is just changed, because the power comes, the wealth comes, and everything comes with it."

What are the results of saptāhas for the audiences? Their primary response to these events is perhaps a sense of heightened religiosity. Large numbers of devotees claim a spectrum of significant religious experiences arising from saptāhas. At one end of the spectrum, attendees report deeply moving, life-changing experiences of the Divine. Others speak of more transitory sensations of well-being, a warm afterglow, and an experience of collective joy or *communitas*, "a group's pleasure in sharing common experiences with one's fellows" (Turner 2012, 2). The successful completion of a saptāha creates a celebratory atmosphere comparable with that of a wedding party. There is an unspoken consensus among participants that together they have achieved something significant. As Ilona Wilczewska commented, attending a saptāha can be physically demanding and is not unlike undertaking a pilgrimage or ascetic practice. For many, simply sitting cross-legged on a concrete floor for seven days is no small achievement. For others, there is also the satisfaction of fulfilling a saṁkalpa, a vow, and of believing that they have done something beneficial for an ancestor's afterlife, a son's career, or a husband's health.

For some members of the audience, a saptāha marks the beginning of a significant spiritual relationship with a guru, as in the case of a young salesman from Sydney who became a close devotee of Satchitananda Sai after attending one of his saptāhas. It may also be the means by which a group of established devotees, such as members of the Australian Sai community, strengthen and deepen their relationship with their guru. The Brisbane Bhakti Yoga Centre continues to develop its relationship with its parent body in India by inviting speakers to conduct saptāhas. Saptāhas are occasions for individuals to reaffirm and perform their religious and social identities. Attendance at a saptāha instills a sense of belonging to a given language, regional, or devotional community. Saptāhas are also important sites for socialization into a religious identity and practice. Looking around at the children on the fringes of saptāha performances—listening to the stories, dancing to the music, dozing on their mothers'

FIGURE 8.1. Children in the audience at the saptāha in Naluna. Events like these are important sites of socialization.

laps—I was reminded that this was one place where they learned to be Hindu and learned to be Indian.

Audience members at saptāhas may establish, assert, or subtly contest positions within a social hierarchy. As Shrivatsa Goswami wryly observed, the saptāha is the perfect venue for attendees to show off their best clothes and finest jewelry. By seeing and being seen, attendees have a chance to ingratiate themselves with an important sponsor or express solidarity with a family member, friend, or neighbor.

On a more prosaic level, it is common to hear testimonials of audience members who have given up "bad habits" such as smoking or drinking after attending a saptāha. One exponent told the story of a sixty-five-cigarette-a-day smoker who attended a Bhāgavata. After listening for just half an hour, he vowed to quit the habit, and he now offers himself as a living testament to the power of the saptāha.

Internal Sources of Authenticity

Several potential sources of authenticity are found within the context of the saptāha performance. These factors contribute to the experience of the event as powerful and transformative and are among the elements that contribute to the growth of the practice.

Potency of Oral Transmission

In the Abrahamic traditions, there is an understanding that individuals can achieve direct access to the Divine through personal experience of the written text. Protestants, for example, might seek God through private reading of the Bible, Muslims through the Koran, and Jews through the Torah. Quite the opposite is generally the case in Indic traditions. The text was (and still is) the province of trained religious specialists and not generally accessible to the individual lay devotee. Buddhists do not seek truth by reading the sūtras; the text is mediated and interpreted orally by a qualified teacher. The situation is similar in Hindu faith communities. Texts are not necessarily self-accessible or self-explanatory; it is usually assumed that an expert in the form of a paṇḍit or a guru is necessary to convey and interpret the teachings to the faithful (Cenkner 1982).

Even those Hindus who have direct access to the text may not necessarily read it for their own spiritual enlightenment. The practice of pārāyaṇa, the private reading of the Bhāgavatapurāṇa, described earlier, is not usually undertaken for the spiritual enlightenment of the reader but rather as a ritual act for the benefit of the sponsor. For the text to be truly effective, it should be transmitted orally from a qualified expert who has received it through an authentic lineage. This lineage may stretch back to an inspired founding saint, a great sage of the past, or, better still, a form of the Divine.

It is important and indeed normal to receive the transmission of sacred knowledge orally, but even more important is the lineage of the person from whom it is received. The lineage of religious teachers in general, and of saptāha exponents in particular, is an important source of authenticity. Lineage has two components. The first, *sampradāya,* is defined as "a religious system" or "a cumulative tradition." It is "a body of precept, practice, and attitudes, which are transmitted to, and redefined by, each successive generation of followers" (Gupta 2005). Membership in a sampradāya lies at the heart of a given group's sense of identity and is one of the important ways in which religious bodies in India conceive, define, and represent themselves. The sampradāya also acts as an important source of authenticity, authority, and legitimacy for discourse created by its members (Adluri 2014). As mentioned, many exponents in Vrindavan trace their spiritual lineages back to one or another of the six goswamis dispatched to Vraja in the sixteenth century by the founding saint of the tradition, Caitanya, a fact that is frequently publicized.

The second concept, *paraṁparā,* is closely related to the first. Within each sampradāya, gurus confer initiation on their disciples and pass their religious knowledge directly to their own students. In this manner, the teachings are passed "from one to another," as implied by the Sanskrit term itself. Membership in a paraṁparā, in other words, confers on the student a quantum of the authority inherent in the lineage. This concept is also of great significance in other performance communities in India, such as classical dance, art, and music.

Saptāha audiences are generally aware of the exponent's sampradāya and paraṁparā, and exponents frequently remind audiences of both. The various forms of advertising for saptāha performances often include portraits of the exponent's guru and sometimes of the guru's gurus stretching back multiple generations, as in the advertisement for Radhikadas's saptāha shown earlier. Images of the exponents' gurus are often placed in prominent positions on the stage during performances, where they are garlanded and ritually honored with āratī. The prayers and invocations that open each daily session usually include homage to the exponents' gurus. During the spoken discourses, exponents often quote directly from their predecessors, recounting episodes from their lives and explicitly relating teachings learned from them.

Exponents' emphasis on their sampradāya and paraṁparā is an important element of the meta-communication in which the saptāha experience is embedded, and it colors the reception of the discourse. By implying membership in a sampradāya and close association with one or more respected gurus, exponents acquire in the minds of the audience a share of their predecessors' authority. In this manner, membership in a sampradāya and a paraṁparā establish the exponents' own legitimacy and, by implication, the authenticity of their discourse.

Exponents' Qualities

In every saptāha, the exponent is the source of oral transmission, and saptāha audiences therefore expect exponents to demonstrate membership in an authentic lineage and to have a high degree of spiritual attainment themselves. This is not just storytelling or recounting narratives from the Bhāgavatapurāṇa in an engaging or entertaining manner. Audiences expect exponents to speak from their own direct personal experience of the Divine. Exponents are unlikely to claim such experience explicitly, but audiences believe that they can discern such qualities from an exponent's performance. Attendees expect an exponent to speak joyously, as if enraptured or divinely inspired, and to maintain this for hours and days on end. They expect the exponent to be exhilarated or moved to tears during particularly intense points in the narration. A portion of exponents' authority and authenticity rests on the fact that audiences assume the speakers have undergone deep personal spiritual experiences in relation to the Bhāgavata. Abhishek Goswami links the exponent's experience directly to the efficacy and transformative power of the performance:

> A vaktā [exponent] should definitely speak from his own experience. You have to be touched deep inside. Only an experience can make you experienced. Just words, repetition of the same words, they would lose the substance. They would lose the power which is in them.

Siddhanti Maharaj's explanation of the power of saptāha also refers to the authenticity of the exponent's own experience. To be effective, the discourse must "come from the heart," as he put it:

> There are two ways [of performing the Bhāgavata]: Bhāgavata which is just coming from the mouth and Bhāgavata which is coming

> from the heart. When it comes from the heart—when we speak on the Bhāgavata with our heart full of things relating to the stories of past times, to Bhāgavata—it gives so much devotion to us and also is helping the masses. It gives a tremendous effect on the audience.

Siddhanti drew a parallel with an iron rod placed in a fire. Once the rod itself is heated, it radiates heat to other objects nearby. So, too, when one is imbued with bhakti through the Bhāgavata: "It becomes very easy for the masses to spread these things."

As a contrast to Siddhanti, who prioritizes the role of the exponent as the agent of transformation, Abhishek Goswami shifts the emphasis back to the individuals in the audience and their willingness to be transformed. He described what makes these events powerful for individuals:

> If a pot is empty, only then can it be filled. So it is very, very important that in those seven days a person empties his pot. "Empties his pot" means he should not keep desire, anger, greed, delusion, intoxication, and all these things in his mind, because mind is the only pot. Why do instances make such a transformation in human beings? Transformation is only possible when somebody is actually looking for a transformation. If you are there only to listen to the discourse—"Ah, good"—and you like the way the speaker plays with words, a good speaker for you can be someone who has used the words and the vocabulary and his mastery of good words. But in Bhāgavata, it is not about the mastery of the words. It is not just the words. It is what you travel, what you take with words, how you absorb it, how ready you are. And I think, in any Bhāgavata, there might be two thousand people hearing you. Out of them, only four or five can be transformed.

The Role of Sanskrit

What role do the verses of the Bhāgavatapurāṇa play in the saptāha audience's experience of authenticity? Among exponents, I found a full spectrum of views. At one end is the opinion that the Sanskrit verses lie at the heart of the event and are largely responsible for the saptāha's transformative potential. At the other extreme is the view that they are an unintelligible, irrelevant distraction.

Among those who hold the more traditional, orthodox view are exponents such as Abhishek Goswami, who said confidently, "A Sanskrit verse, just one verse, if you narrate it properly, you cannot imagine all you can get." Similarly, Satchitananda Sai saw great transformative power in the Sanskrit verses. He attributed this power to divine inspiration:

> The *ślokas* [verses] I pick up are those that jump out and demand to be explained. And each time I do a saptāha, there are different ones that clamor for attention, and I give them that. There is no human intelligence involved in selecting these ślokas. Which is perhaps why they have the impact they always do. I myself watch with a childlike awe and wonder at the transformation that is accomplished in those that listen to the saptāha. There is no trace of human in that; it is purely Divine, which is why it can have that effect. (Satchitananda Sai, email, June 23, 2013)

On the other hand, Chandan Goswami took a less sanguine approach. Like several other speakers, when I asked him how many Sanskrit verses he used, he replied, "Not really a lot." His justification was interesting:

> In Gauḍīya, we have two Kṛṣṇas. Our Kṛṣṇa never studied, and he only speaks Braj-bhāsā [the local Vrindavan dialect]. All the āchāryas, gurus, and saints who have had direct realizations of him in Vrindavan see this Kṛṣṇa speaking in Braj-bhāsā. It was only after Kṛṣṇa went to Mathura, where he studied in Sāndīpani-muni's school, that he learned Sanskrit. So that Kṛṣṇa is different for us. So I try from my side to speak and deliver the kathā in Braj-bhāsā, because I feel connected with it. And with the Sanskrit, I feel that there is more *aiśvarya* [grandeur, power, authority] there, so I try to keep myself a bit far from it, but obviously, as Bhāgavata is written in Sanskrit, we cannot really ignore it, so I do deliver it, but I try to keep myself a bit far from Sanskrit and emphasize Braj-bhāsā more.

Like a number of other speakers, Chandan is trying to bring the narratives within reach of his audiences by minimizing the use of Sanskrit verses, while he acknowledges the inherent authority and dignity that they infuse into the discourse.

I asked Shrivatsa Goswami how many verses he used in his saptāhas, and in the course of his answer, he revealed a fascinating and contrary attitude toward language, power, and authority:

> Actually, I have minimized it to very, very few. Very few. But what I will do—*sūtākhyāhi kathāsāram* ["O Sūta, narrate the essence of the story," BhP 0.1.4]—I will just literally translate a verse and give that. I will not give the Sanskrit, as I will take that as waste of time, because in the audience, not one person knows Sanskrit. Not even one person, so why waste their time? And I am not there to prove my scholarship, that I know Sanskrit and '"Look at the authenticity of me." The authenticity of an idea will not come because of Sanskrit. I will not do that. The idea should be logical; it should be intellectually viable and verifiable with your experience. If it is not that, then no amount of Sanskrit is going to help. It is useless. So since the audience does not know Sanskrit, why talk about it? Why waste their time with it? Their time is more precious than yours. So I will do that—I will present the ślokas in Hindi so that they will have the raw experience of the text, but in Hindi.

When I first heard Shrivatsa say this, it seemed to run counter to my whole thesis that the transformative power of saptāha was in some mystical and/or performative way tied up with the Sanskrit verses. But on closer reflection, it is even more revealing. First, it confirms my supposition that few, if any, in a general saptāha audience really understand Sanskrit. Second, Shrivatsa's comment clearly supports another basic contention: that speakers include Sanskrit verses to demonstrate their erudition and do indeed say, "Look at the authenticity of me," as Shrivatsa put it, by doing so. While distancing himself from the use of Sanskrit as a crutch for authenticity, he suggests that this function is widespread among other speakers. For him, there is no ineffable, mystical power, no śabdabrahman, in the Sanskrit utterances. If it is not in the Sanskrit, where is the transformative power in Bhāgavata? According to Shrivatsa, power lies in the logic of argument, which must be "intellectually viable and verifiable with your experience." As a result of this conversation, I came to realize that my basic contention about the relationship of power and Sanskrit was not inherently incorrect but that there are multiple sources of transformative potential. For some, the transformative power of saptāha is found in the Sanskrit verses; for others, it is found in logical, viable, and verifiable argument and experience. The exponents, too, are happy with this multiplicity. Shrivatsa disparaged the use of Sanskrit in performance, yet he cited a Sanskrit verse in his explanation for doing so. As we have seen, Satchitananda Sai expressed great faith in the transformative power of Sanskrit verses. At the same time, he held that it is the very nature of the Bhāgavata as a form of Kṛṣṇa that empowers the text irrespective of language. At the end of a saptāha in Melbourne, he remarked, "Every word that was spoken here, although spoken in English, was no less than the Vedas themselves. Śrīmad-bhāgavata is *Kṛṣṇa-svarūpam* [Kṛṣṇa's own form], whether it is said in Sanskrit or it is said in English" (Satchitananda Sai 2013, 4.49.2.5:20).

Śabda-Brahman: The Power of the Divine Word

In spite of Shrivatsa Goswami's dissenting voice, most participants, audience and exponents alike, maintain that the Sanskrit verses are central to a saptāha performance and that they lie at the heart of its capacity to transform. But how exactly do they effect this? What power do Sanskrit verses have to transform people's lives? I asked Siddhanti Maharaj about the role of Sanskrit in the discourse and its effect on the audience. His view, which is shared by many on both sides of the microphone, is that Sanskrit has a "transcendental effect" on account of its "transcendental sound vibration." This is a common English translation of the Sanskrit concept of śabda-brahman.

There is a widely held traditional belief that śabda can become brahman—that is, sound can become transcendental, transformative power—when the śabda, the sounds of the Sanskrit verses, are enunciated in the correct manner by a qualified individual in the right circumstances and with the appropriate motivation. Rao (2007, 98) has noted that while the Vedas are generally regarded as *śabda-pradhāna*, "important for their sound," the purāṇas are *artha-pradhāna*, "important for their meaning." In contemporary practice, while the meaning of the text—the narrative—is important, the actual sound or śabda of the Bhāgavata is also accorded great power, not unlike the mystical power of Vedic recitation. Siddhanti Maharaj described the experience of śabda-brahman by a member of a saptāha audience as follows:

> Something happened in his mind. He thought, "What am I doing?" and "What this person is saying, this saint is saying, is effective." This is called śabda-brahman. This is called transcendental sound vibration. It goes from the ears to the heart. It tries to move the heart. This is the most important thing.

In the Gauḍīya Vaiṣṇava tradition, it is held that the sound of Sanskrit in general and the verses of the Bhāgavatapurāṇa in particular possess this capacity to go "from the ears to the heart" because they originate from Lord Kṛṣṇa himself and have been faithfully preserved and passed down a divine lineage to contemporary audiences. Siddhanti further explained the role of Sanskrit in a saptāha:

> It gives a transcendental effect, because the ślokas in Bhāgavata are not written by an ordinary person. It is transcendental sound vibration. It was emitted from the mouth of Veda-Vyāsa for Śuka-deva Goswami. It came through the lineage. If you go deep into the understanding of Bhāgavata, the very first person who gave the light of Bhāgavata-kathā to Brahmā, it came from Kṛṣṇa. He put the light into the heart of Brahmā, and Brahmā imparted it to his disciple Nārada. Nārada gave it to Veda-Vyāsa. Veda-Vyāsa gave it to Śuka-deva Goswami. Śuka-deva Goswami gave it to Parīkṣit. There is a whole lineage.[1]

Siddhanti conceded that it would be possible to have a saptāha without Sanskrit ślokas and to conduct the whole event in Hindi, but he indicated that there are two reasons to include the verses: first, they demonstrate to the audience that the discourse is authentic and is rooted in the text, and second, the verses exert the śabda-brahman:

> Because the audience, the general masses, don't know Sanskrit, so we look at the audience. If there are some people who understand Sanskrit, if they have some knowledge, some background, then we utter more Sanskrit ślokas, so that they can understand that what we are speaking is evidenced from the scriptures. Also, we try to speak ślokas but not so much even for the general masses, so that even they can understand what we are saying is authentic. . . . It also has a transcendental effect, śabda-brahman.

Abhishek Goswami used the simile of a bell: just as the clapper causes a vibration when it strikes the rim, sound issuing from the mouth of the speaker creates a vibration within the devotee's body. It is the śabda-brahman, or "divinity in words," as he put it, that endows the performance of the Bhāgavata with the power to transform the lives of the faithful:

> When you ask where śabda-brahman happens, it is right from the first word you utter on the vyās-pīth, and that is how you are basically inviting the brahman [the Absolute], so that he should be

> sitting—brahman is not Brahmā but the divinity in words. Because if śabda-brahman is not present in the sharing of the words, then the Bhāgavata does not make any sense. Why would you come to do research on seven days of Bhāgavata, and why would millions of people like to listen to it? And why would individuals like to spend millions and millions of rupees organizing it? And then something has happened in these forty or fifty years; people have understood that by this process, people have achieved something, they have got something. I have seen families where the śabda-brahma has taken such an intense place in their household or in their entire families that they refer to their lives now as "before the kathā" and "after the kathā."

None of the exponents denied the power of śabda-brahman, but each had a slightly different interpretation. Chandan Goswami drew the parallel between śabda-brahman and mantra. In his understanding, the important effect of śabda-brahman is not so much that it has the capacity to transform the individual, but, like a mantra, it has the power to bring about a change in the world. Chandan gave the example of particular verses from the Bhāgavatapurāṇa that produce wealth and employment, stimulate devotion, or cause Kṛṣṇa himself to manifest:

> Obviously, śabda-brahman has its own power and has some mystery behind it, and Śrīmad-bhāgavata itself is a śabda-brahman, because it is nondifferent from Lord Śrī Kṛṣṇa, and there are many ślokas or verses which our āchāryas use as mantras. You can say that in the Gopī-gītā, every śloka or every verse is a specific mantra to achieve or to get something specifically. If one wants money, one can recite one verse. If one wants to attract work, one can recite one verse. If one wants the bhakti only, one can recite one verse. If one wants Kṛṣṇa to appear in front of him, he should recite one verse as a mantra. So obviously, many āchāryas in our lineages have given those sādhanas or those practices to us. And when we practice and when we recite those mantras or verses, then we find that Kṛṣṇa appears or Kṛṣṇa gives that. When we are seeing and realizing that, we cannot deny the fact that it is actually the śabda-brahman.

As we have seen, it is widely believed that śabda-brahman is linked to the Sanskrit language itself and that without Sanskrit, śabda-brahman cannot be generated or experienced in performance. Yet again, a contrasting view was expressed by Shrivatsa Goswami. I asked him whether śabda-brahman was inherent in the Sanskrit verses used in performance or if the effect and experience of śabda-brahman could be reproduced in other languages such as English. His response was characteristically cerebral and unconventional:

> I have never found anything in the *śāstras* [scriptures] or in other books that only Sanskrit is śabda-brahman. . . . The seers have access to Sanskrit language, so they produce that [śabda-brahman] in Sanskrit. Other saints have access in Bengali, in Braj-bhāsā, in Tamil, in Punjabi—it is śabda-brahman. To me, there is no difference between the śabda-brahman spoken by Kabir-das and Bhāgavata.[2] I am not trying to be derogatory to Bhāgavata, but theoretically speaking, who decides? This is the word of Śuka, or originally from Vyāsa. So if Vyāsa's word is śabda-brahman, Tulsī's word is also śabda-brahman, because it is an expression of that experience, and Vyāsa did that.[3] Vyāsa received the Bhāgavata in his *samādhi* [meditative state]. Vyāsa received or he experienced the text first, and then he wrote this book. So if Vyāsa's word is śabda-brahman, why not others' experience? Who sets up judgment that only Bhāgavata is at the moment *artha-samam* [śabda-brahman]? I don't like it.

The numinous, transformative power of sacred sound is widely acknowledged in Indic religions but must be regarded as a cultural rather than a physical phenomenon, in spite of the pseudo-scientific languages of "vibrations." As a further corrective, it should be noted that saptāha audiences have been socialized to experience Sanskrit utterances in a particular way. It is most unlikely that the sole *nāstika* (nonreligious) attendee in Brisbane or the bemused Anglo-Australians who drifted in and out of the venue would experience Sanskrit ślokas as "divinity in words."

Satsang and Darshan

The Hindi term *satsang* (Sanskrit *satsaṅga*) may be translated literally as "an assembly of the good." Traditionally, it refers to a congregation of pious individuals, and in common usage, it is more generally applied to any occasion on which a devout audience receives religious instruction from a recognized teacher (Frisk 2002, 67). There is a deeply held tradition in the Indic thought-world that simply being in the presence of a powerful religious figure, especially in the company of fellow adherents, is beneficial and meritorious (*puṇya,* auspicious).

Allied to this is another ancient, strongly held belief in the efficacy of *darshan* (Sanskrit *darśana*). The term means "showing" but more commonly "seeing" (Eck 1996; Grimes 2004), and it is used specifically in Indic traditions when devotees purposefully and reverently direct their gaze toward an object of veneration. That object may be the image of a deity, a revered religious teacher, or a holy place or even an artifact such as the text of the Bhāgavatapurāṇa. Darshan is an important form of pious action in the Hindu world and one of the primary experiences acknowledged by devotees when visiting teachers, temples, or places of pilgrimage. Religious figures may bestow darshan simply by allowing a devotee into their presence. The faithful seek to acquire blessings, merit, or auspiciousness through the simple act of beholding an object of veneration and may experience heightened religious consciousness as a result. Receiving darshan is a way of performing one's Hindu identity and acquiring and maintaining a position in the community of devotees.

Both satsang and darshan are important factors that contribute to the authenticity of the saptāha experience. Audience members are conscious of being in the presence of a host of like-minded seekers. Similarly, there is a strong sense of the efficacy of darshan. This applies to beholding the exponents, who are often highly revered teachers in their own right. It is even more significant, as the exponents are said to be the embodiment of the sage Vyāsa or even Kṛṣṇa himself while they are recounting the Bhāgavata. Audiences also experience darshan from any images of deities on display in the venue and from the text of the Bhāgavatapurāṇa, which, as we have seen, is usually placed on an altar in front of the exponent and is worshiped as a form of Kṛṣṇa.

The Experience of *Communitas*

In addition to the socially conditioned responses to satsang and darshan, the natural experience of *communitas* contributes to the authenticity and transformative power of saptāha events. *Communitas* is defined as an intense feeling of social togetherness and group cohesion induced by a shared activity (Turner 1969; Turner 2012). The experience of *communitas* serves to differentiate one particular group from the broader community and to strengthen bonds within that group. The term was coined by anthropologists Victor Turner and Edith Turner in the 1960s and was originally used to describe the experience of individuals who undergo "rites of passage" such as coming-of-age transitions or puberty rituals.

The concept of *communitas* during rites of passage also provides a useful perspective for understanding how saptāha events work. Rites of passage "accompany every change of place, state, social position and age" (van Gennep 1960 [1909]; Turner 1969, 94). These are said to consist of three phases. The first is separation, when individuals are detached from the larger group. The second is a marginal or liminal state during which the subject "passes through a cultural realm that has few or none of the attributes of the past or coming state." In the liminal state, beings are "betwixt and between the positions assigned and arrayed by law, custom, convention, and ceremonial." This liminal stage is characterized by "intense comradeship and egalitarianism," distinctions of rank and status disappear, and a "communion of equal individuals who submit together to the general authority of the ritual elders" (Turner 1969, p. 95, 96). The third phase is reaggregation or reincorporation. The subjects' passage is consummated, and they reemerge in society with their new status. More recent work has identified the experience of *communitas* in a broad set of social activities, ranging from festivals, music, sport, work, and even the human response to natural disasters (Turner 2012).

Coincidentally, one of Victor Turner's seminal case studies on *communitas* centered on the notion of bhakti in the relationship between Kṛṣṇa and the gopīs, as he understood it through the writings on Gauḍīya Vaiṣṇava traditions by Edward C. Dimock, Jr. (Turner 1969, 155–164). Turner was particularly interested in the intense emotion of separation shared by the cow-herding women, as represented ultimately in the Bhāgavatapurāṇa, which he recognized as a species of *communitas*. It seems doubly appropriate to turn the lens of *communitas* back to the oral performative aspects of this tradition.

Can we understand saptāha events as rites of passage? And what is the role of *communitas*? The first stage of a rite of passage, as defined earlier, is separation, when individuals are removed from society at large. On joining a saptāha, devotees depart from the world, cross a threshold, and enter sacred space. The physical setting of the saptāha itself often serves to cultivate a sense of distance from the mundane. This is achieved by stimulating a range of senses in ways distinct from everyday life. Rich decorations of garlands, bunting, lights, and sacred images meet the eye.

The atmosphere inside the venue is often thick with clouds of incense. Sacred music emanates from the PA system. Even less formal spaces where saptāhas are held, such as large open-air tents, are experienced as demarcated sacred spaces distinct from the everyday world.

Attendees may also seek to remove themselves from daily life by following various observances. Under stricter regimes, such as the one described for the archetypal saptāha in chapter 1, individuals are supposed to restrict themselves to a pure sattvik diet, to wear only white garments, to sleep on the floor, and to avoid all sources of pollution. These restrictions, when followed either to the letter or merely in spirit, all serve to detach the individual from day-to-day existence. In addition, exponents often exhort audiences to leave all their mundane thoughts and habits behind so that they can "imbibe the nectar" of Bhāgavata discourse with a clear mind and a pure heart.

After separation, the second stage of the rite of passage is the marginal or liminal stage, when, as Victor Turner famously observed, individuals are "betwixt and between" sets of normal social constraints. We see this to an extent during saptāha events. Unlike many social settings in India, strangers sit together and experience a general feeling of equality and bonhomie. Members of different social groups usually separated by class, community, or tradition mix somewhat more freely while sitting, singing, and sometimes eating together. While it is true that men and women sit separately and there is some self-selection in terms of class and caste, there is a general sense of equality among participants. This is reinforced by a long-held belief within the Kṛṣṇa-bhakti tradition, unlike in some other more orthodox Hindu traditions, that access to the Divine transcends social divisions and is, in theory, equally open to all.

It is during the liminal state that *communitas* is experienced. It is evident in the kindly exchanges among attendees queuing for meals, the feeling of camaraderie among volunteers washing dishes in the kitchen, and the shared emotion of exaltation at the "wedding" of Kṛṣṇa and Rukmiṇī. In my field notes, I described the atmosphere at the end of the Naluna saptāha as feeling like Christmas Day. One audience member at a saptāha in the United Kingdom said: "I thought it was really amazing to sit among hundreds of people with the same intention, trying to get a benefit from listening to Bhāgavata. It was a very communal thing, a community thing.... It felt like a festival, very, very joyful."

The third and final stage of the rite of passage is reintegration, when the individual rejoins mainstream society but in a new and altered state. At the conclusion of the saptāha, attendees scatter into the night and make their way home. Everything appears outwardly to return to normal. Yet for many, the saptāha is indeed a rite of passage, a major achievement, and a milestone in their lives. I am reminded again of the family of sponsors, mentioned by Siddhanti Maharaj, who came to conceive of their life as having two phases: before and after the saptāha. Yogendra Yadav, the sponsor of the saptāha at Naluna, spoke in similar terms. Many audience members report a sensation of spiritual enrichment and heightened religious consciousness. As exponents frequently remind their audiences, those who listen carefully to the Bhāgavata may experience long-lasting personal change.

Audiences as Agents

I do not want to infer that audiences are passive, uncritical "victims of circumstance," that they are all swept away on a tide of lineage, Sanskrit verses, and śabda-brahman. As in any group of individuals, members of saptāha audiences are, of course, fully capable of making their own decisions regarding the veracity of the things they see and hear during a performance. At the same time, saptāha audiences constitute a particular epistemic community within the broader Hindu thought-world, a world shaped and informed to an extent by specific criteria for evaluating knowledge. Within this world, for example, individuals are socially conditioned to accept the words of the guru as truth. Scriptural authority is accorded much weight as a pramāṇa, a basis for correct knowledge. Lineage and paraṁparā, the experience of satsang, the throne, the imagery, the incense and music—all these metacommunicative elements have an impact on attendees, and all serve to condition the acceptance of particular sorts of discourse. Of course, people still choose what they want to believe. For the great majority of saptāha audiences, the narratives of the Bhāgavatapurāṇa are true—either literally, theologically, or both—and as such are powerful and affective. What is more, many in the audience *want* them to be true; they *want* to be touched, moved, transformed; they *want* to weep and dance for joy. This is their critical, independent choice and the exercise of their own agency.

External Drivers of Growth

So far, I have described some features internal to the practice and tradition, including oral transmission, lineage, the use of Sanskrit, and so on, that may contribute to the experience of Bhāgavata-saptāhas as authentic events, and I have suggested that these, in turn, contribute to the growth of the practice. The development of Bhāgavata-saptāha practice over the last few decades has not taken place in a social vacuum. Some external, technological, and social factors also contribute to the growing popularity of saptāhas.

Some exponents in Vrindavan attributed the expansion of the tradition to the reach of the media. The instructions for the archetype described in chapter 1 stated that invitations should be written and distributed far and wide. It is obviously so much easier to advertise and promote saptāha events in an age of information technology. When I first visited Vrindavan in 2009, most saptāha events were promoted in newspapers and through comparatively modest posters displayed on walls. By 2013, there were dozens, if not hundreds, of giant multicolored billboards lining the main roads. In addition to roadside advertising, there has been a massive growth in the use of electronic and social media for promoting saptāha events. Many exponents and their organizations maintain mailing lists of devotees, so that events can be promoted instantaneously, across India and indeed around the world. The younger, more "connected" generation of exponents all use social media, especially Facebook, Twitter, Instagram, and YouTube, for communicating with devotees, many of whom then tweet and retweet news of events among themselves.

Perhaps the most "globalized" and "wired" saptāha I attended was conducted by Pujya Sri Pundrik Goswami ji Maharaj, another charismatic young scion of the Radha Raman lineage in Vrindavan, who enjoys something approaching rock-star status. The event was held at the foot of the important pilgrimage site of Mount Govardhan, about thirty kilometers from Vrindavan, in November 2013. In the driveway of the venue was a broadcasting van with a satellite dish on its roof. The entire saptāha was telecast live on the Sanskar Channel[4] and internationally on Aastha TV, a channel devoted to Hindu religious and cultural content. Aastha is said to be available in 160 countries and claims to reach twenty million households and more than one hundred million viewers.[5] Promoting saptāhas has obviously come a long way from the letters "sent out in all directions."

In addition to the revolution in communication technology that has spurred the growth of the saptāha tradition, the importance of improved transportation was also mentioned by several informants. Abhishek Goswami shared a romantic image of the search for knowledge. In the old days, he said, an individual, having left home, would wander through jungle and forest in search of a guru meditating under a tree. But these days, the forests have all vanished, and the gurus are concentrated in places such as Vrindavan, where they are accessible to all. Not only that, but those who possess this sacred knowledge are now able to travel the world to propagate the tradition. Abhishek also pointed to the fact that boys (and some girls) from Brahmin families and other communities come from all over North India and Nepal to study the Bhāgavata in Vrindavan, and when they graduate, they carry the tradition home with them. Bhadri Prasad, the exponent at the Naluna saptāha, is one of this cohort. The fact that professionally trained exponents can now earn their livelihood and support their families by teaching jñāna—sacred knowledge of the Bhāgavata—is, according to Abhishek, "not a very old phenomenon" but one that only dates back "these thirty, forty, fifty years."

In addition to media and communication, several exponents cited deeper social factors that contribute to the expansion of the practice. We are currently experiencing the Kali-yuga, the era of decadence and suffering. According to this view, the more the suffering in the world increases, the more people are drawn to search for happiness. Seekers fail to find true happiness in the material world, experience a spiritual thirst, and come to hear the Bhāgavata. An audience member at the saptāha in Canberra, an Indian in his early fifties, observed: "You work hard, then you and your team are made redundant. You start to ask yourself, what is beyond this world?" As Siddhanti Maharaj put it, "Saptāha brings them true happiness, peace, and a new direction in their life, and how we are to lead our life. This is the most important thing."

For many within the tradition, it is assumed that during the Kali-yuga, the Bhāgavata will become the dominant text. Shrivatsa Goswami cited "the word of the sages" to the effect that the Bhāgavata will naturally take precedence over other textual traditions at this time. The Bhāgavata has gradually pushed most other traditional texts off the stage, he said. In the past, learned speakers delivered public discourses on philosophical texts such as the Upaniṣads. "But now who is doing Upaniṣad?" Shrivatsa asked. A little of the tradition survives in South India, but it has disappeared from the north. Shrivatsa also noted that fifty years ago, during his childhood, there were public performances of stories from the Mahābhārata and similar texts, but these traditions have also largely vanished. The Bhāgavata has even displaced the Bhagavadgītā, which was very popular fifty or a hundred years ago: "That is left far, far behind. If there are ten events celebrating Bhāgavata, then maybe half [an event] of Gītā. . . . The Bhāgavata has really taken over."

Abhishek Goswami offered an alternative view of the connection of the Kali-yuga to the development of the saptāha tradition. In his eyes, it is not the suffering experienced during the present age but the comforts of modern life that permit religious inquiry and trigger a spiritual thirst. He suggested that as society prospers and the basic questions of survival are addressed, people's minds turn to more existential questions:

> In our life also, as we live generally, we have hundreds and hundreds of questions: what we are going to cook today in the afternoon or what are we having for dinner. If these questions have already been answered and taken care of, then you start some deeper questions, which can be life-related questions, self-changing, transformative questions, and then you are in search of someone who will be able to give you answers for those.

These deeper questions, according to Abhishek, draw devotees to saptāha events and are a factor contributing to the growth of the tradition in recent times.

A further reason suggested for the increasing number and scale of saptāha events is the steady expansion in the range of occasions for which they are deemed suitable. Until the middle of the twentieth century, saptāhas were held primarily after a death. Just as Śuka's narration of the Bhāgavata liberated the soul of King Parīkṣit, a week-long recitation was believed to liberate the soul of an individual nominated by the sponsor, which was the motive for the saptāha at Naluna. According to Shrivatsa Goswami, "Now it is for any occasion. It can be anything: a desire to listen to it—purely spiritual—to get some religious virtues, or to get some wealth, or even to get a child, to get prosperity in your business, anything! It is unbound."

The use of vernacular languages as the primary medium of saptāha performances may also be a factor in their growing popularity. As we have seen, it is not clear how these events were conducted in premodern times, but it is likely that exponents used some Sanskrit in their expositions, at least for verses drawn from the Bhāgavatapurāṇa and other scriptural sources. If the audience was highly educated, the exponents may also have given their oral discourses in Sanskrit. On the other hand, the instructions for the archetype make it clear that women and people from non-Brahmin communities were expected to attend. It is likely, therefore, especially taking current practice as a guide, that most expositions were historically in the vernacular. One attendee at the Naluna saptāha remarked, "What would be the point of telling stories in Sanskrit if no one can understand them?"

Evidence suggests that the use of the vernacular is growing and the amount of material in Sanskrit is diminishing. Abhishek Goswami observed that forty or fifty years ago, it was felt that the Sanskrit narration was very important and that everyone expected the exponent to be well versed in the language. While the use of Sanskrit is still important today, "the usage of the common man's language has changed a lot of things," Abhishek said. He also made the point that if one is conducting a saptāha for twenty thousand people, the use of the vernacular is imperative:

> Their local language means so much to them. Why will [saptāhas] become more acceptable and more common? Because of the way Bhāgavata has been shared, discussed, and transferred or given to people in the form of a saptāha, it becomes very, very easily accepted. It means you don't have to apply a lot of brains. You just have to listen.

Many from the younger generation of exponents have not had the rigorous traditional Sanskrit education their predecessors had and simply do not know as much Sanskrit as the older generation. This may also partly explain the decline in the use of Sanskrit in contemporary performances, with the concomitant increase in acceptance, accessibility, and popularity.

National and Global Contexts

The development of the contemporary saptāha is also rooted in the broader social and economic context of modern India. The economic liberalization of the early 1990s enabled the expansion of an affluent middle class. Simultaneously, there has been a rise in public expressions of Hindu religiosity and a general uptick in Indian nationalism. Reforms first introduced under Prime Minister P. V. Narasimha Rao constituted a transition from a centrally planned economy to a more market-oriented one. With the dismantling of the so-called License Raj, import tariffs were removed, markets were deregulated, taxes were reduced, and foreign investment was encouraged. The historical annual growth rate of about three percent rose to an average of seven to eight percent for many years. While economic reform left numerous problems unaddressed (income inequality, poverty, corruption, environmental degradation), it has permitted the emergence of an ever-expanding middle class with access to discretionary income. Much of this new surplus wealth has been invested in conspicuous religious consumption. In her book *The God Market: How Globalization Is Making India More Hindu*, Meera Nanda (2011, viii, xv) argues, "The state-temple-corporate complex is enabling the resurgence of popular religiosity that is brimming with majoritarian and nationalistic sentiments." She demonstrates how the emerging Hindu middle classes "are successfully blending their religiosity with growing appetites for wealth and profits."

Conspicuous religious consumption and expenditure are evident across a range of spheres. For example, the period since 1991 has seen a boom in the religious construction industry. The Swaminarayan Akshardham, a religious center and theme park that opened in Delhi in 2005, is one of the largest Hindu structures ever built. Plans have been released for the world's tallest temple, the 213-meter Chandrodaya Mandir, to be erected at Vrindavan. Colossal statues of deities including Śiva, Viṣṇu, Rāma, and Hanumān are popping up all over India. In addition to extravagant construction, billions of dollars are showered on leading gurus and religious institutions, with donations growing annually. One of the best-known religious establishments, the Shirdi Saibaba Temple Trust, reported that in 2012–2013, it had cash deposits of 860 crore rupees ($200 million US), plus 300 kilograms of gold and 3,000 kilograms of silver, representing an increase of ten percent over the previous year.[6]

Pilgrimage and religious tourism have also grown dramatically since the start of economic liberalization. Annual pilgrimage to the Sri Amarnath Shrine, a previously obscure temple in Jammu and Kashmir, rose from 12,000 in 1989 to 400,000 in 2007 (Nanda 2011, 119) and has doubtless continued to grow since then. Similarly, annual numbers of pilgrims at the Vaishno Devi Shrine, also in Jammu and Kashmir, soared from 1.3 million in 1986 to more than 9 million in 2013. Pilgrims who don't want to walk can now book a helicopter transfer directly to the temple online.[7] Great Hindu festivals honoring deities such as Dūrgā, Rāma, and Gaṇeśa have grown in size, complexity, and expense as devotees seek to gain merit and status through ever-greater expenditure (McDermott 2011). There is a wealth of anecdotal evidence for the expansion of festivals such as Gaṇeśa Chaturthi in Mumbai. As one blogger noted, "The celebrations get bigger and bigger with each year that passes."[8]

The rapid growth of Bhāgavata-saptāha performances is an aspect of an economic process, but it is also an aspect of a broader political process. In the decades since independence but especially with recent economic liberalization, Indian society has witnessed the growth of a self-conscious, "muscular" Hinduism. This includes the rise of Hindu nationalism, continuing tensions among religious communities, and a postcolonial urge to revalidate and reassert Indian traditions. Events such as the riots following the destruction of the Babri Masjid in 1992, the anti-Muslim pogroms in Gujarat in 2002, and the periodic rise of activist Hindu politics in the form of the Bharatiya Janata Party (BJP) are all causes and effects of an assertive or even aggressive public religiosity.

The election of a socially conservative BJP national government in India under Prime Minister Narendra Modi in 2014 has further spurred these trends. The BJP's ascent at the central level has been accompanied by a conspicuous reassertion of "Hindu values," a rise in the visibility of radical conservative organizations such as Rashtriya Swayamsevak Sangh (RSS), and attacks on secularism as the underpinning philosophy of the Indian state. Conservative religious leaders are taking an increasingly prominent part in public and political discourse. Sanskrit is back on the political agenda and is being actively promoted in school curricula. These changes are not restricted to the Indian polity but have also been rapidly picked up and assimilated by diasporic communities.

The surge in saptāha performances can be viewed not only in the context of growing conspicuous religious consumption and the rise of Hindu activism in India but also in a much broader international context of globalization and media-enabled interconnectedness. The phenomenon of increased religiosity in India, of which the saptāha "industry" is but one aspect, has parallels around the world. The rise in religiosity and public religious expression in much of the world across many traditions is a response to globalization and is indeed part of that process. This is evident in Islam throughout much of its range, in fundamentalist and New Age practices in the West, and in new religions such as Falun Gong in China. Shrivatsa Goswami witnessed what he described as "a boost in religious ritualism as such, and Bhāgavata is part of that canvas. So there is nothing unusual happening for the Bhāgavata-saptāha. It is happening everywhere. It is part of a wider phenomenon."

The development of media, the fact of the Kali-yuga, growing economic prosperity, greater mobility, and national and global factors may all be contributing to the growth of the saptāha tradition. No one would deny that saptāha events have increased in number and scale in recent times, but not everyone sees this as a positive development. Shrivatsa, for example, paints a bleak picture of current and future Bhāgavata-saptāha practice. He paraphrased a passage from the Bhāgavatapurāṇa that foretells that during the Kali-yuga, people who know nothing about the Bhāgavata will discourse on the dharma from raised platforms, and as a result, dharma will be destroyed (BhP 12.3.38). To elaborate, Shrivatsa recounted this narrative of the divine sage Nārada:

> Once Nārada was so dejected that he knocked on heaven's door. The Lord Viṣṇu invited him in and asked what had brought him to Paradise at this time. Nārada said, "I am very angry. I am not seeing anything auspicious. Rather, there is the decay of values every year." Viṣṇu expressed his surprise: "How is it that human welfare is not taken care of? I have given you Bhāgavatapurāṇa. If Bhāgavatapurāṇa is there, there can be no inauspiciousness for humanity. What has happened?" Nārada replied, "Sir, Bhāgavatapurāṇa kathās have become ineffective—*kriyate gehe gehe bhāgavatī vārtā*—Now every home has a Bhāgavata-saptāha."
>
> Fifty years back, I never used to hear them. Occasionally, once in a while, there was some Bhāgavata there. My father also would do, say, five Bhāgavatas in one year. But now? *gehe gehe bhāgavatī vārtā*. Every home practically has a Bhāgavata-saptāha. I counted in Jaipur during one Adhik-mās or Purushottam-mās seventeen hundred Bhāgavatas concurrently going on. Seventeen hundred in the city of Jaipur! But the value system is missing. The *ras* [essence] is missing. Bhakti is missing. So the Lord asked, "Why has it happened? Why has Bhāgavata become different?" And Nārada says, *kriyate karalobhena kathāsāras tato gataḥ*. The *sāra*—the effect—is lost because they are doing it for the sake of money.

Similar sentiments were expressed by Abhishek Goswami, who remarked on the paradox that "Bhāgavata is very old, but the way it has become common is very new." With increasing frequency, he and some other exponents felt that the significance of Bhāgavata was being diluted. Such an event was once "something which is very rare to get, and if you get it so easily, people will not understand the value." According to Abhishek, as Bhāgavata-saptāhas become more common, some people come merely to admire the decorations; others come to see who else is there. If one of the big business families is organizing the event, then people are very concerned to attend: "Oh, we have to be present there, because *he* is organizing it." For people of this sort, "Bhāgavata is of absolutely no importance." Abhishek expressed the "pain from a Bhāgavata-vaktā's heart" and made this plea:

> Let's not make it so common. . . . Previously, people would narrate the Bhāgavata stories as they are, then *ṛṣis* and *munis* [sages and seers], and everybody would leave their meditative periods and come down and listen to Bhāgavata when it used to happen. Today it can happen in some individual's house or home, and he gives more importance to his worldly matters. If this keeps continuing, one fine day, it will lose its essence, its charm, how it attracts people.

9

Conclusion—Pūrṇāhuti

THE *PŪRṆĀHUTI*, "The full oblation," is the final offering to Agni, the fire, and is the last act of the yajña. In this concluding chapter, my final offering consists of four elements: first, a reflection on the popularity of the Bhāgavatapurāṇa vis-à-vis other texts; second, a discussion of some future trajectories that the practice of Bhāgavata-saptāha might take; third, a reexamination of the mandala of basic questions posed at the start of the book; and finally, my personal experience of the affective power of saptāha performance.

Why This Text?

Why the Bhāgavatapurāṇa? Why has this particular text come to the fore at this time? In contrast to these stories about Kṛṣṇa, it is comparatively easy to suggest social and political factors that have contributed to the growing popularity of the Rāmāyaṇa. In all its various manifestations from Vālmīki to Rāmcaritmānas, from Rāmlīlā to B. R. Chopra's TV version, the story of Rāma has often been associated with the perfect nation-state. With the evolution of Indian nationalism, the epic has provided a useful set of tropes, especially the concept of a utopian Rāmrāj. Is there something about the Bhāgavatapurāṇa itself that has contributed to the remarkable growth of saptāha practice, in comparison with other major texts such as the Mahābhārata, the Upaniṣads, or even the Devī-māhātmya, which have a much lower public profile?

The narratives of the Bhāgavatapurāṇa have strong, broad appeal. The text is notable for the large number of youthful characters—infants, boys, and young men—including the Sanatkumāras, Prahrāda, Dhruva, Kṛṣṇa himself, and his brother Balarāma. Even Jñāna and Vairāgya, the hapless sons of Bhakti, fall within this demographic. These characters are all readily accessible to a wide range of audiences and evoke powerful emotional responses at an instinctive or visceral level. Narratives of young children in crisis (Prahrāda, Dhruva) stimulate a parental response to nurture and protect. The narratives of infant Kṛṣṇa generate emotions of parental, especially maternal, love. The erotic elements of the Vrindavan episodes are always central and, even when desexualized, add to the overall appeal of the text. Of course, there is also the all-pervading sentiment of bhakti. The impoverished Sudāmā evokes a strong sense of empathy and even moves audiences to tears. Audiences respond in a deeply emotional way to the songs of praise offered by Bhīṣma, Kuntī, Prahrāda, Dhruva, Sudāmā, and the Elephant-king. The range and intensity of emotional responses the Bhāgavatapurāṇa evokes render it more "human" and more accessible than many other texts. There is also something uncomplicated about the basic theology. As the narratives stress, union with God is possible for everyone. You don't have to resort to the Himalayas or even leave home or family: "You are already the Divine—you just don't realize it."

While the broad appeal and emotional intensity of the Bhāgavatapurāṇa's own narratives may contribute to the popularity of saptāha performances, several other factors are also at play. The Bhāgavatapurāṇa is of a place but is not tied to that place. Every episode of Kṛṣṇa's boyhood and youth can be identified with a specific site in Vraja. The pastoral imagery of the forests of Vrindavan, with cow-herding boys and girls disporting themselves in moonlit glades, evokes deep and sentimental yearnings in audiences otherwise beset by nationwide environmental catastrophe. The Bhāgavatapurāṇa provides a rural idyll that is especially attractive to people who know only modern India's concrete wastelands and poisoned waterways. No Hindu text is more closely tied to an idealized locality than the Bhāgavatapurāṇa, yet the narrative and its performance are also transportable and can be reenacted anywhere. The narratives effectively recreate the prefect Vraja wherever they are heard. Exponents often call on audiences to imagine that they are in the forests of Vrindavan. Audiences, too, create Vraja wherever a saptāha is conducted. As Shulakshna, the organizer of a saptāha in Brisbane, said to her guests, "This is your house. Feel as if we are all in Vrindavan, because Maharaj-ji is here."

In addition to transcending place, the Bhāgavata transcends time. Many other important texts are tied to particular festivals, rituals, and seasons. The Devī-māhātmya, for example, the foundational text of the Śākta tradition which glorifies the Great Goddess, is usually recited during Navaratri, a festival held over "nine nights" in October and November. Rāmcaritmānas is often linked to the festivals marking the hero's birth, Rāmanavami (March and April), and Dusshera (October), which celebrate Rāma's victory over Rāvaṇa. Although the instructions for the archetype suggest that particular months are ideal for saptāha events and there is evidence that saptāhas are indeed more common during these months, performances are by no means restricted to those times. More and more, they are held whenever and wherever sponsors and exponents are available.

The general availability of the text may also contribute to its popularity. Just as cheap editions from the Gita Press in Gorakhpur made a major contribution to the popularity of Rāmcaritmānas (Lutgendorf 1991, 61–62), inexpensive editions of the Bhāgavatapurāṇa in Sanskrit, with translations in Hindi or English, are available in bookshops and at railway stations all over India. The broad and multifaceted appeal of the narratives, the text's transcendence of both place and time, and its ready availability may all help to account for its popularity over others.

The Future of Saptāha

Where will Bhāgavata-saptāha performances be in one, two, or three decades' time? Globalization will continue to shape the saptāha of the future. Rather than being the medium of secularization and the cause of a retreat from religious traditions, globalization also provides a stimulus and a means for the development of faith communities. With the increased mobility of populations and ideas around the world, globalizing processes create diasporic communities that bring their religious practices with them. Globalization is underwritten by the technology that enables instant communication between gurus in the homeland and devotees abroad. Worldwide virtual communities form around online digital performances. Diasporic and metropolitan communities continually feed off one another and sustain one another.

Moving from the global to the national, India seems to be embarking on a long period of what we might call Hindu activism, as the concept of the secular state comes under increasing pressure. The ascent of the radical-conservative BJP central government has created a sociopolitical climate in which the public expression of Hindu religion and practices is actively encouraged, validated, and rewarded. As long as Indians seek to express their Indian-ness in terms of Hinduism, especially contra Muslim communities at home and the non-Hindu world outside, forms of Hindu religious expression, including the saptāha, will play a role.

Technological development and the economic power of sponsors have already enabled the expansion of saptāha performances from private homes, community halls, and temple spaces to huge outdoor venues, giant sports stadiums, and arenas. More large-scale events are the natural progression as long as the wealth of sponsors and the numbers of devotees continue to grow, and there is every indication that this will indeed be the case.

Sanjay Srivastava (2009, 342), in his study of the religious theme-park complex Aksharadham in Delhi, identified a new species of middle-class religiosity in which individuals are able to identify simultaneously as devout "traditional" Hindus and modern Indians. This "moral middle class" consumes not only the products of capitalism but also "spiritual goods," such as religion and nationalism, a process he terms "moral consumption." The moral middle class is able to identify itself as "truly" Indian because it is not defined by foreign modernity but identifies itself on the basis of "traditional" values and religious discourses. As long as the Hindu moral middle class continues to grow, we can expect commensurate growth in conspicuous public displays of piety, including saptāhas, and the continued evolution of a Hindu modernity, with the reaffirmation of religious and cultural identities at home and abroad, as these offer a legitimate means of being at once "traditional" and "modern."

We are likely to see growing commercialization and professionalization of the practice, with an elite class of exponents receiving astronomical remuneration. This is in spite of the ethical dilemma of "selling" the Bhāgavata and a general distaste for material motivation expressed by exponents and audiences. For many speakers, performing saptāhas will continue to be an important source of income. The number of international events will grow as diasporic communities expand, as their self-confidence and economic power increase, and as the cost of bringing exponents from their home bases in India falls in relative terms.

In the past, saptāhas and many other forms of religious observance and practice were generally seen as the preserve of older people. As mentioned, one adult attendee at the saptāha in Canberra recalled that when she was a girl, audiences were mostly grandmothers. It is still true that some saptāha audiences consist predominantly of older people, especially during working hours when most younger people would be otherwise engaged. On the other hand, there is a new generation of hip, attractive, and charismatic exponents, such as Pundrik Goswami, which appeals to younger, globalized, "wired" audiences. The indications are that as more "rock-star" exponents take the stage and as long as it is cool to be devout, there will be no shortage of young audiences, both on the ground and online.

At present, the number of female exponents is very small. I estimate that less than one percent of speakers are women. In Vrindavan, I saw a single advertisement for a saptāha given by a female exponent. Sangeeta Desai (2013) described a saptāha given in Hyderabad by the well-known and respected female exponent Prema Pandurang. While there have always been some female religious teachers and saints in Hindu traditions—from Gargi to Mirabai to Amma—their numbers are small. As the educational, economic, and social status of women in India improves and as women become more accepted in public spaces, we can expect to see a growing number of female exponents.

To date, practically all saptāha exponents have been of Indian descent. Will non-Indian performers take the stage in the future? One of the few organizations in which non-Indians have sufficient background in the Bhāgavata tradition to give saptāha performances is the Hare Krishna Movement, ISKCON. It is already common for speakers of non-Indian backgrounds in that organization to give single-session Bhāgavata-kathā teachings. ISKCON, on the other hand, generally disapproves of saptāhas, especially large-scale events as they are conducted today, on account of their perceived commercialization. According to this view, the contemporary saptāha is tantamount to "selling the words of Kṛṣṇa." It is said that the founder of ISKCON, A. C. Bhaktivedanta Prabhupada, specifically spoke out against this practice. In spite of this negative disposition, one non-Indian saptāha exponent, Radhanath Swami Maharaj, an ISKCON member originally from the United States, is said to be an accomplished performer.[1] It is likely that the number of non-Indian saptāha exponents will grow in the future, not necessarily within ISKCON but perhaps from among the followers of other gurus such as Madhusudan Maharaj who attract large numbers of foreign devotees.

Bhāgavata-saptāhas have rapidly appeared in each new medium as it has emerged, first on cassette tapes, then CDs and DVDs. They are now widely available online and will doubtless continue to flourish rapidly in whatever new media evolve in the future. The number of complete saptāha recordings available online is growing exponentially. What happens to authenticity as the audience's experiences of saptāha are mediated through these various forms of technology remains to be seen. There is a broadly shared perception that direct access to the exponent is always preferable, but judging from the brisk sales of CDs and DVDs at stalls outside saptāha venues and the number of hits logged for saptāha videos on YouTube, even these mediated events are meaningful and worthwhile for devotees. Recent research on "cyber-bhakti" and "e-darshan" suggests that there will be large-scale participation and acceptance of these new forms of religious experience (Herman 2010; Karapanagiotis 2010; Scheifinger 2010).

What will become of the more "traditional," small-scale, local events, such as the ongoing saptāha tradition in Kolapalli described by Desai (2013), which was in its ninetieth year? It will be a long time before modernity squeezes out the rasikas, the traditional connoisseurs of the Bhāgavata tradition who are the backbone of events such as these. In recent years, this series has been underwritten by expatriates living in the United States.

Will we see a decline in traditional scholarship? Most contemporary exponents still make extensive use of the Sanskrit text of the Bhāgavatapurāṇa in their performances, but many have access to the Sanskrit only through Hindi or in some cases through English translation. While they generally understand the meaning of the verses they recite, this is usually at a relatively coarse semantic level, without a deep understanding of the syntax. Knowledge of Sanskrit grammar and exponents' ability to analyze on a scale of less than the individual verse appear to be limited in many cases. Facility with Sanskrit seems likely to decrease further as fewer exponents undergo either the traditional twelve-year training in a guru-kula or the equivalent modern Sanskrit education at tertiary level. The days of the old-fashioned scholar-exponent appear to be numbered. While more and more modern exponents speak English and quote from Abraham Lincoln, fewer and fewer comprehend the Sanskrit text in a deep grammatical sense.

Mandala of Basic Questions

I began this book with the image of a mandala consisting of three concentric rings. In the center of the mandala lay the question of authenticity in oral performance of the Bhāgavatapurāṇa. The second ring questioned the relationship between power and knowledge in Sanskrit texts in general. The outer ring embodied the more universal problem of how texts shape societies. It is now time to move back out through the rings of the mandala, traversing from the center toward the periphery and from the specific to the more general issues raised here.

The fundamental contention that lay at the center of the mandala and the primary concern of this book was that for the practice of Bhāgavatasaptāha to be expanding as it undoubtedly is, each class of participant—sponsor, exponent, and audience—must be deriving some measurable benefit from it. As we have seen, sponsors gain personal satisfaction from providing an opportunity for religious instruction and socializing for their community. They value the growth of their own religious knowledge base, and they may also acquire considerable social capital in the process. As for the exponents, in addition to the personal fulfillment they experience during performance, they may be following a vocation stretching back generations. For many performers, it is also an important source of prestige and income. Audiences, like the sponsors, add to their store of religious knowledge in an atmosphere of *communitas*—joyous, shared human endeavor. Saptāha events are sites at which participants also form, perform, and contest social identities. The growth of the saptāha "industry" and other forms of religious performance is taking place in a contemporary sociopolitical context of increasing public religiosity and the emergence of more "muscular" forms of Hindu self-expression.

Moving outward to the second ring of the mandala, we can generalize about power and knowledge of texts in Hindu traditions more widely. Texts that we know or assume were performed orally become effective if the audiences experience the performance as authentic. The sources of authenticity include a belief in the importance of direct oral transmission from a qualified teacher. Thus, the lineage and personal attributes of the guru are deemed to be of central importance. Many participants attribute numinous, transformative power to the sound of Sanskrit utterances; merely hearing the sound of the Sanskrit language has the potential to touch the heart and induce beneficial change.

At the outermost level of the mandala is the broader question of the relationship between power and knowledge. It is through oral performance that Indic texts in general and the Bhāgavatapurāṇa in particular are brought to life. This is how discourses of the tradition are propagated and perpetuated. The authority of the speaker is supported by his or her control over the text, while the text is also mobilized to validate the discourse of the speaker. Thus, social power creates textual knowledge, and textual knowledge creates social power.

A Personal Note

On the fourth day of the saptāha in Canberra, I experienced something far removed from my expectations and expertise, something that lay outside and intruded on the carefully circumscribed realm of scholarly detachment and quiet objectivity that I had cultivated while documenting these performances.

Satchitananda Sai had proclaimed at the beginning of the week that no one in the audience would remain untouched by the discourse. I had blithely assumed that this applied only to others and that as a sympathetic but disinterested observer, I was exempt. Perhaps he was only half-joking when he described the process of Bhāgavata-saptāha as a form of "brainwashing."

I shared lunch with fellow attendees at the venue, and as the afternoon session did not begin until 4:30 p.m., I was driving home for a break. It was a perfect, clear, sunny autumn day, and there were few other cars on the road. I was a little weary after the morning's session and after recording some interviews, but I was otherwise calm, happy, and contented. Out of the blue, I experienced a flash of total awareness, an instant of nonintellectual, nonverbal cognition, a moment of numinous insight, an epiphany. At that instant, I became cognizant that "all this is Brahman—*sarvaṁ khalv idaṁ brahma*." I sensed the identity and unity of all things with the ineffable Absolute—the cars, the road, the trees and parks, this overpass, those buildings, those distant hills and forests.

The extraordinary sensation, while crystal clear, was momentary, fleeting. As suddenly as it arose, like an ebbing tide, it subsided again. It left me elated, enriched, but also confused and unsettled. Was this what Satchitananda Sai meant by his "solemn promise" that everyone would be "touched to the core of their being"? So alien was this transitory sensation that I unconsciously set it aside. It did not even rate a mention in my field notes, which otherwise recorded every aspect of the week, every gesture, every sneeze. Looking back, I now see this omission as evidence of my inability to categorize, interpret, and integrate the experience.

In the weeks and months that followed, I came to realize that the experience had not permanently altered my beliefs or my perception of reality, but I still treasured the memory of it. Sometimes I feel that this moment of numinous insight was wasted on an outsider like me; a true believer would perhaps have put it to better use.

The greater significance of the experience lies not in its nature, its cause or effect. Its value lies in the insight it offers into this project and the ways some devotees experience saptāhas. It has helped me understand and empathize with those people who described these events as deeply transformative and life-changing. Irrespective of its ultimate cause—brainwashing, subconscious auto-suggestion, coincidence, the touch of the Divine, or a glimpse of Vaikuṇṭha—I now better appreciate from my own experience the power often attributed to the performance of the Bhāgavatapurāṇa. Having had the smallest taste, I began to understand the experiences of those who, just as the text itself exhorts, time and again drink deeply of this nectar.

Notes

CHAPTER 1

1. It is worth noting that this is not the only approach to the theology of the Bhāgavatapurāṇa. Other schools of exegesis offer a more nuanced interpretation of nondualism, and some take a clearly dualistic stance that the individual soul and the Divine are clearly two, not one.
2. http://www.ochs.org.uk/research/bhagavata-purana-research-project (accessed December 10, 2014).
3. http://is1.mum.edu/vedicreserve/puran.htm (accessed December 10, 2014).
4. http://www.vedabase.com (accessed 3 February 2016).
5. http://vedabase.com/en/search/site (accessed December 10, 2014).
6. http://www.ochs.org.uk/research/bhagavata-purana-research-project (accessed December 15, 2014).
7. All translations from the Sanskrit are my own.
8. Wilczewska (2013, 219, n. 20) apparently saw the same advertisements.
9. http://www.sribhagwatgeeta.org/voyager/tour_program.htm (accessed December 10, 2014).
10. A thirty-minute video documentary on the saptāha at Naluna, "Mountain God and Sacred Text," is available online at http://tinyurl.com/mt-god.
11. Frits Staal (1979, 123) provocatively overstated the case when he said, "Strictly speaking, there are no books in Hinduism."
12. Mackenzie Brown 1986, 72–73. See Kane 1974, 348. *pustakapratyayādhītaṁ nādhītaṁ gurusaṁnidhau | bhrājate na sabhāmadhye jāragarbha iva striyāḥ ||* (Parāśara-mādhavīya 1.1.154).
13. Its cognate in Sanskrit is *darśana*, which also means "view," "doctrine," and, by extension, "philosophy."

CHAPTER 2

1. Further case studies are given by Desai (2013).
2. A detailed description of Mridul Krishna's saptāha at Vrindavan was originally published in an article entitled "'*Rādhe, Rādhe!*': Continuity and Change in the Contemporary Oral Performance of the Bhāgavatapurāṇa," *Religions in South Asia* 6, no. 1: 83–101. See also Taylor (2010).
3. The text of Rāmcaritmānas is often treated the same way in public recitations (Lutgendorf 1991, 178).
4. The repeated use of the cry "Śrī Rādhe!" is one of many similarities between saptāha performances and American "spiritual" preaching as described by Rosenberg (1970). He identified similar formulaic "stall lines" and rhetorical questions such as "God from Zion!" and "Am I right this evenin'?" (see Lutgendorf 1991, 235).
5. For the full report on the saptāha at Naluna, see Taylor (2010).
6. The best sources on Garhwali culture are Berreman (1962; 1972 [1963]; 1964), Sax (1990; 1991; 2002; 2009), and Alter (2008).
7. I have edited citations from performances and interviews as lightly as possible to ensure grammatical accuracy and consistency in the use of terms such as *Bhāgavata*.
8. Literally, "Cow Finder," Govinda is an epithet of Kṛṣṇa that has special resonances with his boyhood and youth in the pastoral community of Vraja.
9. Some issues in interpreting participants' responses, which some might describe as "gushy boosterism," are addressed in chapter 7.
10. For a similar event, see Desai (2013, 97).
11. For further examples of similar "wedding" rituals at saptāha events, see Desai (2013, 85–86, 98, 154–156).

CHAPTER 3

1. http://seksaria.org/.
2. The use of the term *Rādhā-Kṛṣṇa* indicates the belief in the Gauḍīya Vaiṣṇava tradition that Rādhā is also a form of the Divine and that the two deities form an indivisible unity.

CHAPTER 4

1. For an excellent description of daily life and the annual cycle of events and rituals in Jai Singh Ghera, see Case (2000).
2. For an eloquent biography of Shrivatsa's father, Jagadguru Purushottam Goswami Maharaj see Case (2000, 22–44).

3. Mahāprabhu Vallabhācārya (1479–1531), a famous scholar, philosopher, and Bhāgavata exponent.
4. Lutgendorf (1991, 428) noted a similar contempt for the commercialization of Rāmkathā in the 1980s.
5. www.chandangoswami.com.
6. https://www.facebook.com/oceanofdevotion, entry for January 1, 2014 (accessed January 16, 2014).
7. http://www.purebhakti.com/teachers/bhakti-yoga-teachers/1192-sripad-bv-siddhanti-maharaja.html (accessed December 11, 2014).
8. See the college's website, http://vedicyatra.org/ (accessed December 11, 2014). It is also known as Bhagavat Sewa Sanstha and is commonly referred to as Shrinathji's Bhagavat Guru-Kula.
9. http://vedicyatra.org/ (accessed December 11, 2014).
10. Email from Shri Satchitananda Sai, June 21, 2013.

CHAPTER 5

1. I acknowledge Meera Ashar for this insight.

CHAPTER 6

1. Satchitananda Sai (2013). References to the audio are given in this format: disk.track.part.minute:second–minute:second. I have edited the transcriptions lightly to eliminate some repetition and circumlocution.
2. The exponent took *kāla*, which I translate as "fate," to mean the Kali-yuga.

CHAPTER 7

1. Details of these narratives are given in chapter 5.
2. On Ramesh Oza, see also Desai (2013, 70–76).

CHAPTER 8

1. For more on the divine origin of the Bhāgavatapurāṇa, see Edelmann (2014, 73).
2. Kabirdas, or Kabir, poet-saint, c. 1440–c. 1518.
3. Tulsidas, author of Rāmcaritmānas, 1532–1623.
4. http://www.youtube.com/user/TheSanskarGroup.
5. http://www.indianetzone.com/4/aastha_tv_aastha_tv_international.htm.
6. http://www.bullionstreet.com/news/shirdi-saibaba-temple-trust-receives-rs-15.54-cr-worth-gold-silver-diamonds-from-devotees/4733 (accessed October 8, 2014).

7. https://www.maavaishnodevi.org/yatra_statistics.aspx (accessed October 15, 2014).
8. http://www.indiamarks.com/ganesh-chaturthi-in-pictures/ (accessed October 15, 2014).

CHAPTER 9

1. See http://www.radhanathswami.com/.

Glossary

Sanskrit forms of some Hindi terms are given in parentheses.

āchārya (ācārya) Teacher, especially a revered religious instructor.
ānanda Joy, transcendental bliss.
añjali Gesture of two palms held joined as if in prayer.
āratī Ritual offering of lights, incense, etc., on a salver, also spelled *aarti*.
ātman Self, soul.
avatāra Earthly manifestation of a deity.
āyojak (āyojaka) Organizer.
Bhagavān Lord; refers to Viṣṇu, Kṛṣṇa, or Nārāyana.
bhajan Song of praise.
bhakta Devotee.
bhakti Intense emotion of personal devotion to the Divine.
darshan (darśana) Meritorious act of focusing the gaze on a sacred being or object.
devtā (devatā) Deity.
dharma Tradition, correct conduct.
dhoti Lower garment consisting of a single length of material tied around the waist.
dīkṣā Consecration in preparation for a religious ceremony.
ḍolī Palanquin.
dupatta Long scarf of light material.
gopī Cow-herding woman or girl.
goswami Honorific title among Brahmin families.
grāmdevtā (grāma-devatā) Village deity.
guru-kula Guru family, a traditional Brahminical school.
havan (havana) See *yajña*.
kalaśa Pitcher, ritual vessel filled with auspicious substances.
Kali-yuga The current, decadent age.
kathā Story, especially an oral performance of a religious narrative.
kirtan (kīrtana) Song of praise.
kṣatriya Second class of idealized Brahminical society, warrior.
kurta Traditional knee-length shirt.

līlā Game, sport, especially the activities of Kṛṣṇa in Vraj.
mandir (mandira) Temple.
mokṣa Liberation from cyclical existence, state of union with the Divine.
mridanga (mṛdaṅga) Large drum with a hollow earthen body.
muni Sage, seer.
niṣkāma Without desire.
niyama Ritual restriction on diet, daily conduct, etc.
paraṁparā Guru lineage.
pārāyaṇa Private reading of sacred text as a meritorious act.
prasād (prasāda) Blessed food.
pūjā Ritual act of worship.
pūjārī Priest who presides over an act of worship.
purāṇa Ancient, ancient narratives, genre of texts to which the Bhāgavatapurāṇa belongs.
Raslīlā (Rasalīlā) Kṛṣṇa's dance with the gopīs of Vraj.
ṛṣi Seer, sage.
śabda-brahman The Supreme or Absolute in the form of the sound.
sādhana Efficacious religious practice.
sādhu Religious mendicant.
sakāma With desire.
salwar-kamiz Long tunic worn over loose pajama-style trousers.
saṁkalpa Purpose, intention, desired outcome.
sampradāya Religious tradition or system of teachings.
sannyāsa Renunciation of mundane existence.
saptāha Seven days, a week, a week-long oral performance based on the Bhāgavatapurāṇa.
śāstra Scripture.
satsang (satsaṅga) Assembly of the good, a session of religious instruction.
sattvik (sattvika) Pure, especially of a diet.
sevā Pious service.
shāstrī (śāstrī) Holder of the equivalent of a master's degree.
skandha Book or canto of the Bhāgavatapurāṇa.
śloka Verse, especially in Sanskrit.
śūdra Fourth class of idealized Brahminical society, servant.
tulsi Sacred basil plant.
vaiśya Third class of idealized Brahminical society, merchant.
vaktā Speaker, exponent.
varṇa One of four divisions of idealized Brahminical society, also caste.
vrata Religious vow.
vyās-pīth (vyāsa-pīṭha) Vyāsa's throne, seat for exponent.
yajmān (yajamāna) Sponsor of a yajña or a saptāha.
yajña Act of worship.

Bibliography

Adluri, S. 2014. "Śabdapramāṇa as a Theological Category in Vedānta Deśika's Tattvamuktākalāpa." *Journal of Hindu Studies* 7: 54–69.

Alper, H., ed. 1989. *Understanding Mantras.* Albany: State University of New York Press.

Alter, A. 2008. *Dancing with Devtās: Drums, Power and Possession in the Music of Garhwal, North India.* Aldershot: Ashgate.

Ananth Rao, C. 2011. "Oral Performance of Ancient Texts: Presenting Stories to Contemporary Audiences." *Journal of the Oriental Society of Australia* 43: 131–145.

Austin, C. 2014. "The Abduction of Śrī-Rukmiṇī: Politics, Genealogy and Theology in Harivaṁśa 87–90." *Religious Studies and Theology* 33, no. 1: 23–46.

Austin, J. 1980 [1962]. *How to Do Things with Words.* Oxford: Oxford University Press.

Bauman, R. 1984 [1977]. *Verbal Art as Performance.* Long Grove: Waveland.

Bauman, R. 1986. *Story, Performance, and Event: Contextual Studies of Oral Narrative.* Cambridge: Cambridge University Press.

Bauman, R., and C. Briggs. 1990. "Poetics and Performance as Critical Perspectives on Language and Social Life." *Annual Review of Anthropology* 19: 59–88.

Berreman, G. 1962. "Sib and Clan among the Pahari of North India." *Ethnology* 1, no. 4: 524–528.

Berreman, G. 1964. "Brahmins and Shamans in Pahari Religion." *Journal of Asian Studies* 23, no. 1: 53–69.

Berreman, G. 1972 [1963]. *Hindus of the Himalayas: Ethnography and Change.* Berkeley: University of California Press.

Black, B. 2007. "Eavesdropping on the Epic: Female Listeners in the Mahābhārata. In *Gender and Narrative in the Mahābhārata*, edited by S. Brodbeck and B. Black, 53–78. London and New York: Routledge.

Bonazzoli, G. 1983. "Composition, Transmission, and Recitation of the Purāṇas." *Purāṇa* 25: 254–280.

Brodbeck, S. 2007. "Gendered Soteriology: Marriage and the Karmayoga." In *Gender and Narrative in the Mahābhārata*, edited by S. Brodbeck and B. Black, 144–175. London and New York: Routledge.

Bryant, E. 2003. *Krishna: The Beautiful Legend of God; Śrīmad Bhāgavata Purāṇa, Book X; with Chapters 1, 6 and 29–31 from Book XI*. London: Penguin.

Burkhalter Flueckiger, J., and L. Sears eds. 1991. *Boundaries of the Text: Epic Performances in South and Southeast Asia*. Ann Arbor: Center for South and Southeast Asian Studies, University of Michigan.

Case, M. 2000. *Seeing Krishna: The Religious World of a Brahman Family in Vrindaban*. Oxford and New York: Oxford University Press.

Cenkner, W. 1982. "The Paṇḍit: The Embodiment of Oral Tradition." *Zeitschrift für Religions- und Geistesgeschichte* 34, no. 2: 118–129.

Coburn, T. 1984. "'Scripture' in India: Towards a Typology of the Word in Hindu Life." *Journal of the American Academy of Religion* 52: 435–459.

Coburn, T. 1991. *Encountering the Goddess: A Translation of the Devī-Māhātmya and a Study of Its Interpretation*. Albany: State University of New York Press.

Cort, J. 1993. "An Overview of the Jaina Purāṇas." In *Purāṇa Perennis*, edited by W. Doniger, 185–206. Albany: State University of New York Press.

Damle, Y. 1960. "Harikatha: A Study in Communication." *Bulletin of the Deccan College Research Institute* 20: 63–107.

Demmer, U., and M. Gaenszle, eds. 2007. *The Power of Discourse in Ritual Performance: Rhetoric, Poetics, Transformations*. Berlin: LIT Verlag.

Desai, S. 2013. *Performances of the Bhāgavata Purāṇa in Andhra Pradesh*. Unpublished Ph.D. thesis, University of Wisconsin–Madison.

Doniger, W. 2009. *The Hindus: An Alternative History*. New York: Penguin.

Drake-Brockman, D. 1984 [1911]. *Mathura: A Gazetteer*. Delhi: South Asia Books.

Dumont, L., and D. Pocock. 1957. "For a Sociology of India." *Contibutions to Indian Sociology* 1: 7–22.

Eck, D. 1996. *Darśan: Seeing the Divine Image in India*, 2nd ed. New York: Columbia University Press.

Edelmann, J., and S. Dasa. 2014. "When Stones Float and Mud Speaks: Scriptural Authority and Personal Experience in Jīvagosvāmin's Sarvasaṁvādinī." *Journal of Hindu Studies* 7, no. 1: 70–97.

Erndl, K. 1993. *Victory to the Mother: The Hindu Goddess of Northwest India in Myth, Ritual, and Symbol*. New York and Oxford: Oxford University Press.

Frisk, L. 2002. "The Satsang Network: A Growing Post-Osho Phenomenon." *Nova Religio* 6, no. 1: 64–85.

Gaenszle, M. 2007. "The Power of Texts: Uses of Contextualization and Entextualization in Mewahang Ritual Speech." In *The Power of Discourse in Ritual Performance: Rhetoric, Poetics, Transformations*, edited by U. Demmer and M. Gaenszle, 100–120. Berlin: LIT Verlag.

Goffman, E. 1974. *Frame Analysis: An Essay on the Organization of Experience*. New York: Harper Colophon.

Gonda, J. 1963. "The Indian Mantra." *Oriens* 16: 244–297.

Goswami, C. 2005. *Śrīmad Bhāgavata Mahāpurāṇa (with Sanskrit Text and English Translation)*. Gorakhpur: Gita Press (7th reprint).

Goswami, S., and R. Beeche. 2001. *Celebrating Krishna*. Vrindavan: Sri Caitanya Prema Samsthana.

Grimes, J. 2004. "Darśana." In *The Hindu World*, edited by S. Mittal and G. Thursby, 531–552. New York and London: Routledge.

Growse, F. 1880. *Mathura: A District Memoir.* Allahabad: North-Western Provinces and Oudh Government Press.

Gupta, R. 2005. "Walking a Theological Tightrope: Controversies of Sampradaya in Eighteenth Century Caitanya Vaisnavism." *ISKCON Communications Journal*, no. 11. http://content.iskcon.org/icj/11/04-gupta.html.

Gupta, R., and K. Valpey. 2013. *The Bhāgavata Purāṇa: Sacred Text and Living Tradition*. New York: Columbia University Press.

Hawley, J. 2009. "The Bhāgavata-māhātmya in Context." In *Patronage and Popularisation, Pilgrimage and Procession: Channels of Transcultural Translation and Transmission in Early Modern South Asia*, edited by H. Pawels, 81–100. Wiesbaden: Otto Harrassowitz.

Hawley, J., and S. Goswami. 1981. *At Play with Krishna: Pilgrimage Dramas from Brindavan*. Princeton: Princeton University Press.

Hegarty, J. 2012. *Religion, Narrative and Public Imagination in South Asia: Past and Place in the Sanskrit Mahābhārata*. Abingdon: Routledge.

Hein, N. 1972. *The Miracle Plays of Mathurā*. New Haven: Yale University Press.

Herman, P. 2010. "Seeing the Divine through Windows: Online Puja and Virtual Religious Experience." *Online: Heidelberg Journal of Religions of the Internet* 4, no. 1: 151–178.

Hiltebeitel, A. 1988. *The Cult of Draupadī*, 2 vols. Chicago and London: University of Chicago Press.

Hiltebeitel, A. 1999. *Rethinking India's Oral and Classical Epics: Draupadī among Rajputs, Muslims and Dalits*. Chicago and London: University of Chicago Press.

Kane, P. 1974. *History of Dharmaśāstra (Ancient and Mediaeval Religious and Civil Law), Vol. 2, Part 1*, 2nd ed. Poona: Bhandarkar Oriental Research Institute.

Karapanagiotis, N. 2010. "Vaishanava Cyber-Puja: Problems of Purity and Novel Ritual Solutions." *Online: Heidelberg Journal of Religions on the Internet* 4, no. 1: 179–195.

Kuipers, J. 1990. *Power in Performance: The Creation of Textual Authority in Weyewa Ritual Speech*. Philadelphia: University of Pennsylvania Press.

Luce, E. 2008. *In Spite of the Gods: The Strange Rise of Modern India*. London: Little, Brown.

Lutgendorf, P. 1991. *The Life of a Text: Performing the* Rāmcaritmānas *of Tulsidas*. Berkeley: University of California Press.

Mackenzie Brown, C. 1986. "Purāṇas as Scripture: From Sound to Image of the Holy Word in the Hindu Tradition." *History of Religions* 26, no. 1: 68–86.

Mahalingam, T. 1988. *Inscriptions of the Pallavas*. New Delhi: Indian Council of Historical Research.

Matilal, B. K. 1986. *Perception: An Essay on Classical Indian Theories of Knowledge*. Oxford: Oxford University Press.

McDermott, R. 2011. *Revelry, Rivalry and Longing for the Goddesses of Bengal: The Fortunes of Hindu Festivals*. New York: Columbia University Press.

Nanda, M. 2011. *The God Market: How Globalization Is Making India More Hindu*. New York: Monthly Review Press.

Narayan, K. 1989. *Storytellers, Saints, and Scoundrels: Folk Narrative in Hindu Religious Teaching*. Philadelphia: University of Pennsylvania Press.

Narayana Rao, V. 1993. "Purāṇa as Brahminic Ideology." In *Purāṇa Perennis: Reciprocity and Transformation in Hindu and Jaina Texts*, edited by W. Doniger, 85–100. Albany: State University of New York Press.

Obeyesekere, G. 1984. *The Cult of the Goddess Pattini*. Chicago and London: University of Chicago Press.

Paranjape, M. 2004. *The Penguin Swami Vivekananda Reader*. New Delhi: Penguin.

Pintchman, T. 2005. *Guests at God's Wedding: Celebrating Kartik among the Women of Benares*. Albany: State University of New York Press.

Rao, V. 2007. "Purāṇa." In *The Hindu World*, edited by S. Mittal and G. Thursby, 97–115. New York and London: Routledge.

Rocher, L. 1986. *The Purāṇas*. Wiesbaden: Otto Harrassowitz (A History of Indian Literature series).

Rohlman, E. 2005. "Textual Authority, Accretion, and Suspicion: The Legacy of Horace Hayman Wilson in Western Studies of the Puranas." *Journal of the Oriental Institute* 52: 55–70.

Rosenberg, B. 1970. *The Art of the American Folk Preacher*. New York: Oxford University Press.

Satchitananda Sai, Acharya Shri. 2013. *Srimad Bhagavatha Sapthaham Canberra 2013*. Four CDs. Melbourne: Jnana Vedanta Institute.

Sawyer, J. 1999. *Sacred Languages and Sacred Texts*. London and New York: Routledge.

Sax, W. 1990. "Village Daughter, Village Goddess: Residence, Gender, and Politics in a Himalayan Pilgrimage." *American Ethnologist* 17, no. 3: 491–512.

Sax, W. 1991. *Mountain Goddess: Gender and Politics in a Himalayan Pilgrimage*. New York: Oxford University Press.

Sax, W. 2002. *Dancing the Self: Personhood and Performance in the Pāṇḍav Līlā of Garhwal*. Oxford: Oxford University Press.

Sax, W. 2009. *God of Justice: Ritual Healing and Social Justice in the Central Himalayas*. Oxford: Oxford University Press.

Schechner, R. 1993. *The Future of Ritual: Writings on Culture and Performance*. London and New York: Routledge.

Scheifinger, H. 2010. "Hindu Embodiment and the Internet." *Online: Heidelberg Journal of Religions on the Internet* 4, no. 1: 196–291.

Sihlé, N. 2010. "Written Texts at the Juncture of the Local and the Global: Some Anthropological Considerations on a Local Corpus of Tantric Ritual Manuals (Lower Mustang, Nepal)." In *Tibetan Ritual*, edited by J. Cabezón, 35–52. Oxford and New York: Oxford University Press.

Singer, M. 1972. *When a Great Tradition Modernizes: An Anthropological Approach to Indian Civilization.* New York: Praeger.

Srivastava, S. 2009. "Urban Spaces, Disney-Divinity and Moral Middle-Classes in Delhi." *Economic and Political Weekly* 44, nos. 26–27: 338–345.

Staal, F. 1979. "The Concept of Scripture in the Indian Tradition." In *Sikh Studies: Comparative Perspectives on a Changing Tradition*, edited by M. Juergensmeyer and N. G. Barrier, 121–124. Berkeley: Graduate Theological Union.

Staal, F. 1989. *Rules without Meaning: Ritual, Mantras and the Human Sciences.* New York: Peter Lang.

Sundaram, K. 2001. *Harikatha: Its Origins and Development.* Bangalore: Vidwan R. K. Srikantan Trust.

Tagare, G. 1976–1978. *The Bhāgavata Purāṇa.* Delhi: Motilal Banarsidass (Ancient Indian Tradition and Mythology series, Vols. 7–11).

Tambiah, S. 1970. *Buddhism and Spirit Cults in Northeastern Thailand.* Cambridge: Cambridge University Press.

Taylor, M. 2010. *Indian Idol: Narrating the Story of Kṛṣṇa in Globalising Contexts.* Seoul: POSCO TJ Park Foundation.

Taylor, M. 2011. "Village Deity and Sacred Text: Power Relations and Cultural Synthesis in an Oral Performance of the Bhāgavatapurāṇa in a Garhwal Community." *Asian Ethnology* 70, no. 2: 197–221.

Taylor, M. 2012a. "Empowering the Sacred: How a Text Creates Discourse in a Contemporary Oral Performance of the Bhāgavatapurāṇa." In *Orality, Literacy and Performance in the Ancient World*, edited by E. Minchin, 127–149. Leiden: Brill.

Taylor, M. 2012b. "'Rādhe, Rādhe!' Continuity and Change in the Contemporary Oral Performance of the Bhāgavatapurāṇa." *Religions of South Asia* 6, no. 1: 83–101.

Taylor, M. 2015. "How to Do Things with Sanskrit: Speech Act Theory and the Oral Performance of Sacred Texts." *Numen* 62, nos. 5–6: 519–537.

Turner, E. 2012. *Communitas: The Anthropology of Collective Joy.* New York: Palgrave Macmillan.

Turner, V. 1969. *The Ritual Process: Structure and Anti-Structure.* Chicago: Aldine.

Van Gennep, A. 1960 [1909]. *The Rites of Passage.* London: Routledge and Kegan Paul.

Wilczewska, I. 2013. "'Live with the Text and Listen to Its Words': Bhāgavata Recitation in Changing Times." In *The Bhāgavata Purāṇa: Sacred Text and Living Tradition*, edited by R. Gupta and K. Valpey, 202–220. New York: Columbia University Press.

Index